The Self and the Political Order

Edited by Tracy B. Strong

NEW YORK UNIVERSITY PRESS
Washington Square, New York

First published in the U.S.A. in 1992 by
NEW YORK UNIVERSITY PRESS
Washington Square
New York, NY 10003

1005817087

Library of Congress Cataloging in Publication Data

The Self and the Political Order / edited by Tracy B. Strong.
p. cm. — (Readings in social and political theory)
Includes bibliographical references and index.
ISBN 0−8147−7925−5 — ISBN 0−8147−7926−3 (pbk.)
1. Political science−Philosophy.   2. Self (Philosophy)
I. Strong, Tracy B.   II. Series.
JA71.S35   1991b
320′.01−dc20   91−6839
                                          CIP

Manufactured in Great Britain

Contents

Contributors

A. W. H. Adkins is Professor of Classics, Languages and Literature at the University of Chicago.

Plato taught philosophy in Athens before almost anyone else.

David Hume inquired into, treated of, and essayed the human condition in England.

Michael Walzer is Professor of Social Science at the Institute for Advanced Study in Princeton, New Jersey.

Michael J. Sandel is Professor of Government at Harvard University.

John Rawls is Professor of Philosophy at Harvard University.

Amartya K. Sen is a Fellow of All Souls College and Lamont University Professor, Harvard.

William Connolly is Professor of Political Science at the Johns Hopkins University.

Tracy B. Strong (Contributor and Editor), is Professor of Political Science at the University of California, San Diego.

Bruno Bettelheim was for many years before his death, Director of the Sonia Shankman Institute in Chicago.

George Kateb is Professor of Politics at Princeton University.

Donna Haraway is Professor in the History of Consciousness program and Women's Studies at the University of California, Santa Cruz.

Introduction: The Self and the Political Order

TRACY B. STRONG

To breed a self with *the right to make promises* — is this not the paradoxical task that nature has set itself in respect to human? Is it not the real problem regarding humans?
> F. Nietzsche, *Genealogy of Morals*, II, 1

Parcequ'il n'y a plus de patrie, il ne peut plus y avoir de citoyens.
> J. J. Rousseau, *Emile* (Manuscript Favre)

What we need ... is a political philosophy that isn't erected around the problem of sovereignty.
> Michel Foucault, "Truth and Power"

Here is a story often told: finding life alone difficult and inefficient, a number of individuals, almost always men, decide to do something about it. They gather in the woods, under an oak tree, away from their houses. There they each solemnly swear to forego some of their individual desires in return for the greater rewards of that which can be attained collectively. Society is founded. It soon appears that an enforcement mechanism is needed, in part to keep those so tempted from forswearing their commitment and in part to protect those desirable human qualities that society makes possible which would be lost in a failure of the social endeavor. Politics is invented.

This tale is, in one form or another, a popular explanation of why we have political society. It is thought to be the model of social contract doctrine, appearing in Hobbes, Locke, Rousseau, and with some variations in modern contractarians such as John Rawls. It is the tale of human beings whose needs are known and whose rights are unproblematic: the question is how best to ensure their actualization. The "I" is prior to the "We."

Here is another story: from time immemorial humans have lived together in groups. What it means to be a human being has no other basis than the interactions that take place in these groups. Each group, as part of what it means to function as a group, has developed — slowly, to some degree by experiment — a set of practices that are particular to it. To be a member of a particular group means, in effect, to conduct one's life in the ways that are characteristic of one's own group. Society has always been. Politics is the shaping of the necessary fact of social interaction: it is the human determination to live in a particular, chosen, manner, an invention that teaches what it means to belong, to be involved with each other.

This story is another popular explanation of what it means to live in political society. It is thought to be the model of citizenship as a fulfillment of our human nature. It admits the centrality of what we have been for who I am, of the historicity of my self, even that of my desires. Such a teaching appears, it is said, in the thought of Aristotle, of Rousseau (who makes his second appearance in this introduction), and of Hegel; in modern writers such as Alasdair MacIntyre and Charles Taylor. "We" has priority over "I."

In the first story, politics is an instrument, the kind of policing, laws, regulations that make life together possible. Humans *have* to have something like it. In the second story, politics is not necessary, but is an expression of a particular human capacity to shape life. Tellers of the first story may very well admit the truth of the second, but will add to it that human beings have the capacity to rise above their own stories and stand outside their historical and contextual selves. Tellers of the second story retort that whatever the being might be that does this, he/she, no, *it* bears no important relation to the kinds of "encumbered" or "thick" beings that humans (really) are, nor to that which makes human beings morally interesting.

This opposition has become academically known as that between "liberals" and "communitarians." It is, as of this writing, the basis for a minor industry: during the period I have served as editor of the journal *Political Theory*, I have received approximately three submissions a month that attempt to find a new twist on this dichotomy. These categories bid well to become the dominant structure of discourse in English-language political and social thought.[1]

Both of these stories are, well, just stories, or, perhaps, part of the story. These categories reflect an understanding of a world in which the fundamental question is the negotiation of the relation between individual human beings and society. It is the burden of this book to show that this dichotomy, posed as a dichotomy, captures neither the quality of human political experience nor that of political theorists who have written about it. Indeed, that Rousseau might appear in both stories suggests that something else is going on.

Plato's *Republic* is the first book the West possesses that systematically addresses the multiplicity of political arrangements of which humans are capable. As such, it is noteworthy that it does *not* pose the question of justice in terms of the relation between the "individual" and the "state," as if the two were naturally separate from each other.[2] The question is posed in terms of the respective *constitution* of the individual (the "self") and the polity (the "order").

Plato's argument is two-fold. First, he argues that we will see the one in the other, a kind of fractal political science. In the large we find the small, and in the small we find the large. Second, each structure — the self and the political order — is said to be composed of several parts, the relations of which to each other form the subject matter of justice.

Plato's first argument about the political realm is that the order of the city will be structurally close to that of the selves that properly occupy that city. We might think of two similarly structured fields of action, with each having some particular qualities. There is, for instance, a competitive honor-oreiented timocratic city and a timocratic self that goes along with it, but it is important to remember that the self and the order are not identical. Size makes a difference and the fit is not perfect.[3] The timocratic individual finds confirmation of the justice of his or her actions in the political order in which he or she lives.

Such legitimation, however, was never hermetically self-reproducing. Plato was fully aware of the reality of change and thought it to have its source in the interaction between individuals and the order in which they existed; he does not simply identify the self with the order. The self and the order codify in different manners a similar pattern of relations.[4] Thus the courageous soul of the timocracy slowly turns his activity, especially in old age, to the making of money. And slowly the competitive man becomes the wealthy one, commercially rather than honorably oriented.

We are able to see these relations — and this is Plato's second argument — because the soul, like the city, is composed of several elements. These elements — knowledge, spirit and appetite, or, in

Greek, *logos, thymos* and *eros* — can stand in different possible relations to each other. The important point is that whatever unity the soul has, it iş itself a kind of political unity — a regime, — as is the city with which it is associated. The aim of Plato's investigation is to determine how the relations of the elements can and should be codified.

From this understanding, politics is an awe-ful enterprise. Politics is an activity that provides at the same time one single answer to the questions "who am I?" and "who are we?".[5] It is the power that makes souls and orders. As such, the power of the political must itself be an object of our understanding, a source of our anxiety, and possibly a chance for hope. A book on *The Self and the Political Order* is thus a book that seeks to explore in what manner and by what processes a particular understanding of the self (the person, the agent) is organized as, implicated in, and legitimates a particular vision of the political order. Such a book also, necessarily, investigates the manner in which a particular ordering of the world is implicated in and organized as a particular way of being in the world, as a self.

Plato was perhaps the first to have written theoretically about these matters;[6] as the story of Oedipus shows, however, he was certainly not the first to have raised the question; nor was he the last to have worried about the structuring of the spaces of the self and the political order. What I might call a "Proteus-anxiety" has pervaded much of modern experience — a sense that both the self and the order could be too easily and too voluntarily structured.[7] This concern has not been confined to the rarefied texts of political theory. Here is a third story.

Starting in 1962 Stanley Milgram, a research psychologist at Yale University, undertook a series of experiments designed to investigate the compliance of subjects to commands that he expected they might find morally unacceptable.[8] Two subjects drew lots, apparently at random, to determine who would be the "Learner" and who the "Teacher." They were told that the experiment had to do with an investigation of the relation between punishment and learning. In the presence of the "Teacher", the "Learner" was taken to a separate room and attached to what was described as a shock generator. The "Teacher" was then led back to the first room and told that he was to read four word pairs over the microphone to the now out-of-sight "Learner". After reading the word pairs, "Teacher" was then to read back the first word of each pair, providing four alternative second words, one of which was the correct pair from the first recitation. The "Learner" was to indicate through a system of buttons which was the correct answer. If s/he made a mistake, "Teacher" was to throw a toggle switch from an impressive row on the "shock generator." The switches were marked sequentially in terms of voltage: 15, 30, 45, etc... up to 450 volts.

There was, of course, no shocking actually going on. The "Learner" was an accomplice of the experiment; he gave pre-planned responses, emitted cries of supposed pain at pre-planned levels, at a certain level complained of chest pains, and finally broke off answering all together. "Teachers" evinced great stress and anxiety as they moved up the row of toggle switches, but in response to the Laboratory assistants' repeated insistence that "the experiment required that" they continue, they did move on up. In the basic experimental situation, sixty-two per cent of subjects went all the way to the 450 volt level; the median "shock" inflicted by all subjects was 360.[9]

Milgram subsequently performed the experiment with men and women from a large variety of social-economic, ethnic, educational, cultural and national backgrounds. Results were generally similar, no matter to what group it was administered. He concluded, among other things, that one "could not rely on human nature" to keep people from engaging in actions that were clearly offensive to their own moral conscience.

Yet this story is also only part of the story. Milgram conceived of his problem as the "conflict between conscience and authority" which he saw to "inhere in the very nature of society."[10] The Milgram experiments were originally designed to investigate the influence of "national character" on behavior, an investigation prompted directly and explicitly by the behavior of Nazi Germans during the Second World War. In response to the apparently non-socially based data on compliance, Milgram dropped this theory and tended to interpret his experiments as demonstrating the centrality of the effect of the structured context on behavior. He paid little or no attention to the *interaction* between the individuals coming into his laboratory and the environment that was set up, suggesting that the power resources at the disposal of those who ran the labs were centrally responsible for shaping the distressing outcome. Milgram tended to conclude that a powerfully structured context could make people do almost anything.

The matter seems to me more difficult than that. The subjects may be thought of as engaged in a complex judgement about what they are doing as "Teachers," a judgement that is itself made available by their understanding of what social and political order is. Milgram seems to have assumed that the subjects could be thought of as existing outside of a political order until they came into the laboratory. Milgram tended to think of his experimental situation as *the* political order in which his subjects existed. What he did not see was that the structure of his experiment might be thought of as parallel to part of the structure of the social order each agent carried as his or her own life. (It is worth asking what difference it would have made had the laboratory assistant been visibly a person from Mars.) It is not surprising that the subjects obeyed — obedience is one of the qualities of being a subject. The realm they were in was thus not as external to them as Milgram seemed to believe; and the same, may, I think, be thought to be true of the conditions that Germans confronted in the 1930s.[11]

If with Milgram we understand these experiment as showing us what a powerfully organized structure can lead people to do, we will pay less attention to the involvement of individuals in the experiment in ordering. If we construe the problem as does Milgram, the responsibility of a human being for his or her behavior becomes either improbable or requires a supererogatory heroism.

The conclusions drawn by Milgram exemplify the kind of concern with the relation of the self to the political and social order that concern a large number of thinkers. "Liberals" tend to think that a self that is not socially shaped is, or should be, available: a "thin" self. "Communitarians" tend to emphasize the predominance of social and historical factors in the construction of the self: here the self is "thick." (Milgram is thus a liberal forced to admit the power of the communitarian argument.) Both tacitly accept a division between the social and the individual; neither focuses on whatever it is that makes us want to apply both of these categories to the same being.

Part of the limits with the liberal-communitarian dichotomy can be investigated by looking at circumstances when we have trouble knowing what to say about thick and thin selves. Another story: after all efforts have been made, a couple remains childless, and physicians and other experts determine that the would-be mother will not be able to bear children. The childless couple contracts with another woman to receive the sperm of the father and carry the conceived fetus to term, at which point the child will become the child (only) of the parents who are paying for him or her.[12] A child is born and the "birth-mother" refuses the terms of the contract. Of whom is the infant the child?

It is very hard to know what to say here. Courts have searched "legitimate" experience for the "right" metaphor: slavery, contract law, divorce, adoption. Yet none seems to work. Part of our notion of what makes up a person is to have been a child whose birth-mother has not contracted in advance to give up her child. We know the relation between wanting and having when it comes to children.

Contrast our problems in the above case to the fairy tale of Rumplestiltskin. There a woman contracts to give up the child she will bear for a suitable reward. The miller's daughter, however, does not suffer the same disorientation as the surrogate mother. Once it is known who the "odd little man" is, it is clear that he cannot be the father and the "natural" realm is restored. It is lack of identity that permits the "odd little man" to make his contract for the claim on the future first-born of the miller's daughter. When the woman knows how and what to name him, order reappears. But in the world of Baby M, nothing that makes sense naturally (or magically) appears. The identity of the parents is known and still we have a problem with who and whose the child is.

Such (post-Oedipal?) examples give us a sense, I think, of why questions of the relation between the self and the political order are much discussed in our times. Our notion of what a self is has been rendered insecure by developments in what Michel Foucault calls the "outside," here the development of embryo implantation techniques. The "outside" are those developments that have consequences with which we do not naturally know how to deal.[13]

It is to the inter-relation of the self and the social order, to the complexity of the manner in which they are co-determined, that this book turns. It appears to be difficult to try and think of a self independently of how one thinks of a social/political order. When we do not know what to say about the self we do not know what to say about the order; not knowing what to say about a social order makes language about the self difficult.

The matter is problematic because we are looking for a way of talking that does not force us to make a clear-cut distinction between how we talk about individuals and social orders. This is not, I repeat, a "new" problem. Hume, for instance, in the section of *A Treatise of Human Nature* included below, already had an understanding of this in 1739. He suggests that "the mind was a kind of theatre" and that personal identity ("which has become so great a question in philosophy, especially in late years in England") is merely a fictitious creation of the mind from appearances. Hume searches for the "right" metaphor and finds the most natural parallel to be with the social order. He compares the (idea of a) person to a "commonwealth," the "identity" of which depends on no single factor.[14]

Why is the matter so complex? An approach to an answer comes to us from Rousseau and Freud. They show that precisely the qualities that make human beings capable of social life are also qualities that make human beings divided or multiple. In an early version of the *Emile*, Rousseau wrote "we are not precisely double but composite."[15] Indeed, it was the burden of his *Discourse on the Origins of Inequality* (in response to Hume) to argue that it was not simply that there was no true notion of the self, but that our notion that there was a self did not arise until relations between beings had acquired relative permanence over time. The important consequence of this recognition is that there is no self that is social that is not complex — several. Freud, similarly, teaches us that the self is formed out of the struggle between conflicting relations to each parent and that the resolutions of these relationships take their particular shape in the relations of three divisions of the person — the over-I, the I and the it. (I use these terms rather than the more familiar Superego, Ego and Id because they more adequately translate Freud's perfectly ordinary German usage.)[16] Freud also goes on to make the parallel with a commonwealth, or more accurately, "a modern state," for Freud, contrary to Plato, believed that in the end the relations between the components of the self/order were ones of control and violence.[17]

If what we call a self is conceived in the same way that we conceive of political relations, then political theory becomes an important way to approach both the self and the order of which it will be a part. When political questions are imperfectly or partially resolved, the security of our self is equally fragile. Political relations, the above authors all show us, make possible that there be what we call a self; as political relations assume different forms so also do selves and orders.

The writings collected in this book exemplify some of the various approaches to understanding the relation between the constitution of the self and that of the order. I must reiterate that although these seem fashionable topics, I do not conceive of this as (only) a modern concern. I have selected readings that suggest the permanent and on-going nature of these concerns — concern with the co-determination of the self and the order is not simply a fancy question imported as the latest Parisian fashion — it has been with us since the beginning of Western thought. Indeed, Parisian fashion — inter alia Jacques Derrida, Michel Foucault, Julia Kristeva — is, from the perspective of this book, an attempt at un- or re-covering the age-old tradition of political theory.

Theoretical reflection on the relation of the self and the order begins in the city-states of the Eastern Mediterranean some time after around 1000 BC. It corresponds to the human understanding that there is a choice to be made as to with whom and how one will live — that humans and human lives are and can be shaped by humans themselves.[18] It is the basis of the demand that what one does be noticed and remembered, be made part of the past, that one have an identity.

There does exist a pre-reflective mode of self and social order, one that we see at its best in the Homeric poems. In the first chapter, A. W. H. Adkins, a noted classicist, argues that "Homeric man . . . has a psychology and a physiology in which the parts are more in evidence than the whole. . . ." He relates this to the social order in which the Achaian Greeks found themselves, a world centered on "the status of competitive excellence, the paramount importance of success and failure, and the irrelevance or intentions in evaluating the success and failures" of the admirable human being (*agathos*). In this world, the intellect and the emotions are not sharply distinguished from each other.[19] There can be no conception of a social order than is "rationally chosen" by beings who are capable of standing outside themselves. Adkins continues his book with an investigation of the slow transformation of the idea of the self from that of the "many" to the Stoical notion of the "one".

The world of Homer was not capable of surviving. It rested on the ability to differentiate clearly between those of one's own tribe and others. With the establishment of commercial patterns across the Eastern Mediterranean and the regularization of human inter-actions in cities, different forms and patterns of human interaction grew up, forms that humans were quick to identify as the principles of political organization.[20] Aeschylus' trilogy, the *Oresteia*, is, among other things, about reconciling the laws governing blood relations and those governing human justice.

The second selection, from the eighth book of Plato's *Republic*, is the first lengthy investigation of the possible relations between the self and the order that can both logically and empirically be encountered. They are five in number: aristocracy, timocracy, oligarchy, democracy, tyranny. For Plato, each form has both a dominant principle of order and a kind of personality structure that corresponds to and exemplifies it. To this, there corresponds a set of characteristic activities (honor, war, gymnastics, hunting in the timocracy, for instance), a kind of *paideia* or education, and a principle of change. Each self, and each order, is, however, a more or less harmonic relation of various elements. Plato's concern is with the relation.

Plato sought a notion of justice that had a self and social order corresponding to it. The relation between the just man and the just society appeared to him to be the central problem, and the *Republic* is a long presentation of the political order that would be the most receptive to the just self. Plato's analysis clearly raises the question of human action in relation to the particular constitutions of selves and orders. The question of the constitution of the self, of the shaping and elaboration of the self has thus been a characteristic of human activity in the West for close to three millennia.[21]

With Christianity, however, the idea of constitution acquires a new dimension. It is perfectly true that humans must *make* themselves into Christians, but the material from which selves are made is now seen as ultimately intractable. So while the notion of a constituted or shaped self is central to Christian thought, so also is the idea that humans are naturally endowed with a constitutive element that cannot be shaped, which operates out of time and which, to be changed, must be redeemed from time. Alasdair MacIntyre, in his recent *Whose Justice? Whose Rationality?*, has argued that Augustine introduces the notion of the will into our conception of a person, as "the ultimate determinant of human action."[22] Henceforth, who and/or what a person is (a Christian, for instance) must be an act of choice, the result of volition. Choice, however, was problematized by Augustine's recognition of original sin. Augustine was struck that at times humans engaged in acts that they knew, in their own terms, to be morally wrong and which they knew would produce no conceivable benefit for them. This meant that simply identifying the good would not be enough. Contrary to what the classics had argued, people might know the good but not do it.[23] Augustine condensed this understanding into the story of the time when, as a youth, he broke into a garden to steal some pears, which he "cared not to enjoy, but joyed in the theft and sin itself."[24]

Original sin thus entails a vision of a self that is in some quality unaffected by the order that it is in. What is to be done about a substantively intractable element of human beings? The answer Christianity introduced was to focus no longer on what to choose, but on how to choose. Since the good was given by God, it was much less of a problem than it had been for the ancients. Conscious of the fact that not every small choice could be predicted and dictated in advance, thinkers focused their attention on models of choice. Choices that were made in a particular manner would produce correct results. The essay by Michael Walzer addresses itself to the conflict between two models of choice. In the seventeenth century in England, he suggests, individuals might think of their choices as modelled on the kinds of choices that individuals would make as members of families and choices that they might make as human bodies which knew their own interests. The first position, loosely identified by Walzer with James I and the Royalist position, argued that the stuff of the social and political order was structured in the way that relations in families were structured. To this metaphor was opposed the new one of the body, as exemplified most famously in Hobbes. Bodies apparently had clear-cut boundaries;[25] they had different wills and different concerns than did families — survival was a more prominent problem, for instance, to a single being than it was to the less destructible and more extensive complexity of the family.

Among subsequent writers, David Hume's monumental and extraordinary *Treatise on Human Nature* addresses itself to the problem of discovering a conception of justice appropriate to all human society, despite the fact that no form of society appears to be necessary or other than contingent. Indeed, as the selection itself makes clear, this is true of the self as well. As noted above, Hume thinks of the self as a "commonwealth," an entity the unity of which is conceptual and made rather than natural.

If the self is constituted and thereby at least to some degree contingent, as thinkers from Plato to Augustine to Hume have held, then focusing on permanent, substantive qualities of the self will not lead to any general conclusions. Modern theorists of the self and society argue that actions have to be chosen in a particular *manner* in order to possess the qualities of the moral. Thus Rousseau suggests that the central political and ethical problem is to "find a form of association," a form that responds to willing in a particular manner, that which Rousseau refers to as "general."[26] At about the same time as he was writing the *Social Contract*, Rousseau noted that as nature is no longer a guide, "perfected art" will be necessary to forge a self capable of living under the conditions of modernity.[27] A few years later, of course, Kant insisted that autonomy and freedom of choice was a necessary quality for an action counting as moral. Again, the self is to be shaped in terms that are conceived of as independent of any particular society.

The above selections constitute only an introduction to a problem that has been at the core of Western political and social thought since its beginning. From Plato through the Christians, the emphasis is on the capacity that human beings have to shape who they are. The presumption in all of them is that a self that is properly shaped will be able to live in or develop a social order that is itself well-ordered.

The essays in the next section are informed by a new but ironically still derivatively Christian idea: that the capacity that humans have substantively to shape the self and the corresponding order may prove impossible or dangerous. No one caught the reason behind this conclusion so well as Sir Isaiah Berlin in his classic essay on "Two Concepts of Liberty":

> The world we encounter in ordinary experience is one in which we are faced with choices between ends equally ulti- mate, and claims equally absolute, the realization of some of which must inevitably involve the sacrifice of others.[28]

Berlin has given up on the existence of a world other than that which we "ordinarily" encounter, an afterlife. But his stance still has its origins in Augustine. The abandonment of such a quest has in the twentieth century turned the attention of theorists away from substantive pursuits to more formal ones. Theorists seek procedures that all rational beings might agree upon no matter what the substantive outcome.

Since the publication in 1971 of his *A Theory of Justice*, the work of John Rawls has occupied a central place in Western discussions. In that book, Rawls sought to deal with and to overcome what he saw to be the central moral inheritance of the wars of religion – the sense that the most important moral questions were not substantively resolvable. Instead, he tried to imagine upon what set of purely formal institutional arrangemets a group of rational self-interested individuals might all agree.

It was necessary to make only a minimum number of assumptions. In his early work, Rawls attributed a number of characteristics to individuals: they were to be thought of and to think of themselves as roughly similar one to the other, both in interests and in abilities; they had some idea of how to judge the consequences of their actions; and they were not naturally envious. Rawls argued that if such beings were to choose from behind "a veil of ignorance" – that is, without knowing how the consequences of their choices would fall on them in particular – they would settle on two fundamental principles. They would first agree that each person participating in a practice would have equal right to the most extensive liberty possible that was compatible with like liberty for all. Secondly, he argued that inequalities would have to be considered arbitrary (that is, without standing in the realm of justice) unless they worked to everyone's benefit and the positions that they offered were available to all.

Rawls's argument was subject to immediate and provocative critique, mainly from the group known as the "communitarians."[29] Writers such as Michael Sandel, Charles Taylor and Alasdair MacIntyre suggested that the self behind Rawls's veil of ignorance was too "thin" – that he/she/it had none of the qualities that made persons persons. In the extract printed here, Michael Sandel suggests that Rawls's resistance to extended substantive moral judgements in relation to justice requires a vision of persons that is too thin to be acceptable.

The article by Rawls that is here reprinted is a clarification of his original position against the criticism of the communitarians. Rawls denies that one need approach the question of justice in terms of a vision of a self or of a moral good held to be ultimately true. For Rawls, it remains the case that one need not decide the *truth* of a claim to justice – the *political* problem is to find a formulation for justice that all (rational, roughly equal) beings will choose. But he does now suggest that the political understanding of justice he proposes is one that corresponds to the intuitions that human beings living in industrial democratic states will have. Beings who live in such modern constitutional democracies are, he argues, the kinds of beings that, without deciding the question of "truth," can be expected to select something like Rawls's principles of justice as the basis of an informed and willing political agreement between citizens understood as free and equal persons.[30] It is the conception of justice that can serve as the basis for a "modern constitutional democracy."[31]

Central to Rawls's move here is his original belief that – at least under conditions of modernity – "to subordinate our aims to one end ... strikes us as irrational, or more likely mad," even if it does not "strictly violate the principles of rational choice."[32] It is the core of Rawls's notion of justice that no natural difference between two persons can be a reason for one having power over the other. This is in itself both a notion of a political order and of the self that corresponds to it. Rawls, in effect, understands his conception of modernity (what Richard Rorty has called "postmodern bourgeois liberalism") as a form of life, as a (political) ordering of the world. He indicates that he does not face whether the understanding of justice he advances applies to others at other times. He has been taken to task for this, but he is clearly right not to do so. He has thought through (at least an important part of) what justice means for *us*, and has, in my reading, understood that an important part of what we mean by "us" is, paradoxically, that "we" is not a centrally important word in our vocabulary.

In recent years, much attention has been paid to the claim that once certain basic ground conditions are accepted, it is possible and useful to interpret behavior as the revealed expression of preferences. Rawls has found himself forced to investigate and elaborate those ground conditions as historical. The economist Amartya Sen addresses the question of the economically rational person in his article "Rational Fools." He is not concerned so much to investigate the grounding that makes the choice of preferences possible. Rather, he argues that human beings appear to make different kinds of choices, ones that not only are not commensurable with each other, but which, more importantly, human beings do not and need not weigh against each other. Sen accepts an essentially plural nature to human existence, at least at the level of kinds of choices. He does not push his analysis in the direction of asking why these kinds of choices exist and what world is legitimated by them. But that route is open.

Odd as it may seem, it might prove interesting to compare Martha Nussbaum's analysis of Greek ethics with the perspectives that Sen opens.[33] In *The Fragility of Goodness*, she suggests that tragedy consists in showing the awfulness of mixing modes of choice. Thus, Agamemnon is faced with the choice between sacrificing his daughter and aborting the war effort. What is wrong with what he does, Nussbaum argues, is not the sacrifice of Iphigenia, but his insistence that it was justified, that both actions could be brought under some common measure. Perhaps I stretch a point here, but both Sen and Nussbaum reject the notion that either the self or the moral order is unified. This perspective in modern times has perhaps its classic statement in Max Weber's "Science As a Vocation:"

> It is now as it was in ancient days, not yet disenchanted of their gods and daemons, but in a different sense. As the Hellenic man sacrificed to Aphrodite and then again to Apollo, and especially the gods of his city, so is it with us, but disenchanted and denuded of the mythical but inwardly true plasticity of this position. And over these gods and their conflicts fate rules, certainly no "science."[34]

The essays collected in the last section respond to the routes that I suggest the above essays open. For these writers, the insistence on a single construction of the self and another single one of the political order is a dangerous move into the realm not of power, but of domination. Exposing the structures and ideology of domination motivates them all. For them the co-examination of the self and the political order is not even a question, but a natural move.

The writings of the late Michel Foucault are important in different ways to all of the authors in this section.[35] Foucault distinguishes two past periods during which the self and the order were quite different from what he thinks the future will hold for us. In the first of these, which he calls the "classical" (loosely pre-French Revolution and post-Antiquity), that which was essential to a human being was in principle part of an infinite; our experiences and the forms of our lives (here on earth) made sense only as limitations in relation to this infinity. What determined what and how we are was thus that which we were not, was God. The human form is the form that is not, cannot be, the form of God. Thus "man" was not the epistemological basis of the world; indeed, Foucault notes in *Les mots et les choses* that the classical age sought to determine the "character" of a living being, the "root" of language, the "core" of wealth. One thinks of James I isolating two newborns on one of the Outer Hebrides with a deaf-mute nurse to discover what the "natural" language was. (The first recorded sound of the children was vaguely like "aleph" and God's language was determined to be Hebrew.)

As the nineteenth century develops, changes occur. The shift is marked by Hegel as well as by anyone in section 124 of the *Philosophy of Right*, where he asserts that "the pivot and center of the difference between antiquity and modernity is the right of the subject's particularity, his or her right to be satisfied." Hegel refers to this, "the right of subjective freedom," as "a new form of civilization" and argues that the self is now conceived of as a particular entity whose nature it is to enter into relations with other (outside) forces. It is now the forces of the finite that give us who we are — life work and language, and new sciences like biology, political economy and linguistics come to the front. It is the case, for Foucault, that under these circumstances humans not only become "conscious of [their] finiteness," but even more that in confronting and becoming conscious of finiteness, (what we call) "man" becomes a reality. If, says Foucault, the nineteenth century is the century of man, it is because the human being is now defined against finite external forces. The world, not the person, is the source of limitation.

Foucault's next move here is obvious, perhaps even easy. He asks if the self and the order that are characteristic of "man" might not be replaced by another. If there were such a change, nothing would strike us any longer as the expression and satisfaction of human desire or intention. One might think of the surrogate motherhood situation described above as a Foucauldian epistemic crisis. As Foucault recognizes, Nietzsche was the first to have seen this development.

Foucault thus wants to escape the questions that correspond to the vision of individuals as separate from the social order, questions like "what legitimates power?" and "what is the state?"[36] These questions turn us away, he suggests, from consideration and analysis of the constitution of the field(s) in which the self and the order are defined. This is what Foucault calls the "microphysics of power."[37]

For Rawls, Sen, even Sandel, it is clear that one has to take into account the structure of the fields of action (an example would be Rawls's "modern constitutional democracies"). But these writers did not have to examine *how* these fields had themselves been structured and continued to be so. The writers in the last section — whether or not they consciously follow Foucault — share his concern with the physics of power.

Bruno Bettelheim's classic article on concentration camps is an investigation not so much of the limits of the shape to which the self can be brought but of how the achievement of limits is itself a conscious human, political, even existential decision. He begins to provide a more complex way of talking about the kinds of problems raised by the Milgram experiments described above. His "solution" — a kind of volitional Lutheranism — reminds us that if it is true to say with e.e. cummings that "there is some s-t I will not eat," it is also true that unless one says that, one most likely will eat.

William Connolly applies to contemporary America an approach that owes much to Foucault. Disciplinary control, he suggests, is obscured in modern society. It is Connolly's concern to bring out the nature of the controls that lie under, as it were, the "post-modern bourgeois liberals" with whom other theorists like Rorty appear to sit comfortably. Connolly's enterprise is not to debunk modern industrial society, but to make it more complex, that is, more political, because it is a realm in which truth has been more detached from forms of hegemony.[38] Connolly's article thus parallels in a certain sense that of Walzer, in that both of them are concerned to set forth the consequences of the different ways in which a society legitimates its daily affairs, with what one might call the politics of metaphor.

My article on Nietzsche raises the question of the self in relation to epistemological problems. I suggest — or suggest that Nietzsche suggest — that the idea of a unified self is itself the consequence (and not the source) of claims to knowledge of the world and/or others, indeed, that it is the consequence of making claims to knowledge of the self itself. Multi-dimensionality — what Nietzsche sometimes calls "perspectivism" — is thus a "truer" — that is, closer to the world — way of dealing with the world than is the attempt to find an order in it. Truth consists, one might say at the risk of being facile, in finding the disorder in order; domination consists in asserting order. Human beings live in both realms. One can only be struck by the parallels between Hume's notion of the self as a commonwealth and Nietzsche's desire for justice.

Some of these same Nietzschean themes are taken up in the article by George Kateb and given a specifically political thrust. In his examination of the thought of Walt Whitman, Kateb discerns a self that is itself never fixed once and for all. This self is the foundation of what Kateb calls "democratic individuality," which he quietly opposes to "individualism." Individuality is the self that has no stabilized definition. It is thus the self that for Kateb is the most capable of living democratically. Kateb celebrates what Plato had deplored.

Lastly, Donna Haraway, in "A Manifesto for Cyborgs," attempts to bring together developments in modern technology and feminism to provide an understanding of an order and a self that would be very differently structured. Haraway takes seriously the joining of technology to everyday life, a life now understood as a "hybrid of machine and organism."

In what might appear as a paradox but is not, Haraway requires (as did Nietzsche[39] and Kateb) the explicit discarding of a notion of original unity as a relation with nature that had somehow become problematic. (Such a question has, we saw, made possible the dispute between the liberals and the communitarians). Haraway's rejection of dualisms and their concomitant insistence on clear boundaries makes it possible, she insists, to begin to deal with the changes in the "outside" to which the world is increasingly subject. Her world and her self are no more (if differently) separate than were those in Homer.

The reader will have noted that both by chance and by design the selections form a curious symmetry. The Homeric individual, unseparated from his world, can be found reborn in Donna Haraway's Cyborg. The democratic individual that was the object of Plato's disdain is gloriously reborn in Kateb's celebration of Whitman. Nietzsche and Hume, skeptics and believers both, find politics the major metaphor for understanding the self. I will leave elaboration and further pursuit of the significance of these and other symmetries to the reader and only note here that our problems have a history as much as our history may have problems. It strikes me as a central mistake to want to jettison the whole of the history of philosophy or of political theory on the grounds that "those problems" are no longer available to us. Making political theory available continues to be, as it has always been, the task of political theorists: seeing clearly is not innovation.

The concerns evidenced in these essays thus strike me as continuous to the discipline of political theory. They seem to me to be, ironically, the pursuit of the understanding of ways that we order the world and of the "we" that does it, even when we have not recognized that. As such, perhaps they are subject to their own critique of the world. Would arguments such as these make sense to a Buddhist such as Upagupta? . . . to a Han dynasty Confucian like Sima Qian? . . . an Abbasid Moslem thinker such as Abu Nasr Al-Farabi? What do we make of the sense (or lack of it) that they would make, especially in relation to the various political practices associated with them? Such questions can lead both to arrogance and to excessive humility: both are a source of caution.

<h4 style="text-align:center">NOTES</h4>

1 To my mind the most interesting recent contribution to this discussion is Michael Walzer, "The Communitarian Critique of Liberalism," *Political Theory* 18, no. 1 (February, 1990). It is worth noting that "communitarianism" has ousted Marxism from this debate, perhaps more by forgetfulness than by any argument.

2 To the objection that the *Apology* makes such an opposition, one must retort that Socrates explicitly asserts his Athenianness both in the *Apology* and the *Crito*. The standard "how do you reconcile the *Apology* with the *Crito*" question rests on premises that were neither Plato's nor Socrates'. Nor were they, as Stephen Holmes wants to argue ("Aristippus in and out of Athens," *American Political Science Review* 73 (March, 1979), pp. 113–28), premises that modernity has made obsolete. See the discussion in J. Peter Euben, *The Tragedy of Political Theory* (Princeton: Princeton University Press, 1990), pp. 5–11.

3 Much, perhaps too much, is made of this difference by Leo Strauss and his followers. See Leo Strauss, *The City and Man* (Chicago: University of Chicago Press, 1978) and Allan Bloom, "Interpretative Essay," *The Republic*, trans. and ed. Allan Bloom (Chicago: Basic Books, 1968).

4 "Codification" is Michel Foucault's term. See "Truth and Power" in Michel Foucault, *Power/Knowledge*, ed. Colin Gordon (New York: Pantheon, 1980), p. 122.

5 See the development of this notion in my *The Idea of Political Theory* (Notre Dame, Indiana: University of Notre Dame Press, 1990), chapter one.

6 He is certainly not the first to have worried about them. As Nietzsche recognized, a central concern of Greek drama was this relation. See my discussion in "The Authority of the Tradition: Nietzsche and the Greeks," in T. Darby et al. (eds), *Nietzsche and the Rhetoric of Nihilism* (Toronto: University of Toronto Press, 1989). For a very important wide-ranging investigation see J. Peter Euben, *The Tragedy of Political Theory*.

7 See the ideas put forth in Robert Jay Lifton, *The Future of Immortality* (New York: Basic Books 1987).

8 Stanley Milgram, *Obedience to Authority* (New York: Harper and Row, 1974).

9 Milgram, *Obedience to Authority*, p. 35. A considerable literature grew up around these experiments. Some of the controversy can be pursued by an examination of the bibliography of the 1974 editions of Milgram's book.

10 Milgram, *Obedience to Authority*, p. 179.

11 This is, I believe, the kind of idea that lies in Foucault's suggestion that Deleuze and Guatarri are investigating the "fascist in us all" in his preface to the English-language edition of *Anti-Oedipus*, trans. R. Hurley, Mark Seem and Helene R. Lane (New York, 1977), p. xiii.

12 See the discussion in my *The Idea of Political Theory*, pp. 25ff.

13 See *The Idea of Political Theory*, chapter three, for a discussion of normalcy.

14 Derek Parfit (*Reasons and Persons*, Oxford: Oxford University Press, 1986) has developed and extended Hume's notion brilliantly and fully, adding especially a temporal dimension. See also the issue of *Ethics*, 96, 4 (July 1986), especially the article by Bart Schultz.

15 "Manuscript Favre de l'Emile," *Oeuvres Complètes*, (Paris: Gallimard, 1964) IV, p. 57. See also Amelie Oksenberg Rorty, "Self-deception, Akrasia and Irrationality," in Jon Elster(ed.), *The Multiple Self* (Cambridge: Cambridge University Press, 1987), pp. 115–32.

16 See the discussion in my "Psychoanalysis as a Vocation: Freud, Politics and the Heroic," *Political Theory* 12, 1 (February, 1984).

17 S. Freud, "My Contact with Josef Popper-Lynkeus," *Collected Papers*, vol. 5 (London: Hogarth Press, 1953), p. 297.

18 This is not quite the same thing as happens in the Old Testament.

God makes a covenant with the Hebrews by imposing it upon them ("I shall be your God and you shall be my people").

19 See Jean Pierre Vernant, *Mythe et pensée chez les grecques* (Paris: Maspéro, 1971), II, pp. 85ff.

20 See Vernant, *Mythe et pensée chez les grecques*, I, esp. pp. 207–29.

21 I have left out consideration of non-Western cultures in this book. The question of the self and the order already presupposes the problem of something like what the West calls a self.

22 Alasdair MacIntyre, *Whose Justice? Whose Rationality?* (Notre Dame, Indiana: University of Notre Dame Press, 1988), p. 157.

23 See the discussion in Sheldon S. Wolin, *Politics and Vision* (Boston: Little Brown, 1961), chapter three.

24 Saint Augustine, *Confessions* (New York: Dutton, 1951), Book II, 9 (p. 28). It is noteworthy that Augustine is probably the first person to think his self so important that he writes and entire book about it. Who is his audience?

25 See the discussion of bodies and boundaries in "Law, Boundaries and the Bounded Self," by Jennifer Nedelsky, in a special issue of *Representations* 30 (Spring, 1990) on "Law and the Order of Culture."

26 Jean Jacques Rousseau, "Social Contract," *Oeuvres complètes*, III pp. 360ff (Book I, chapter 6). A will is general for Rousseau not so much because of the number of people who hold it, but because of its object. It deals with, and only with, that which affects everyone in the same manner.

27 Jean Jacques Rousseau, "Premier Contrat" *Oeuvres Complètes* III, p. 288.

28 Isaiah Berlin, "Two Concepts of Liberty," *Four Essays on Liberty* (Oxford: Oxford University Press, 1984), p. 168.

29 Much of this criticism is collected in Norman Daniels (ed.), *Reading Rawls* (Stanford: stanford University Press, 1989). See also Robert Paul Wolff, *Understanding Rawls* (Princeton: Princeton University Press, 1977) and Ian Shapiro, *The Evolution of Rights in Liberal Theory* (Cambridge: Cambridge University Press, 1987), pp. 204–72.

30 See the critique by Patrick Neal in *Political Theory* 18, no. 1 (February, 1990).

31 This has led Richard Rorty to claim Rawls as a fellow anti-foundationalist. See Richard Rorty, *Contingency, Irony and Solidarity* (Cambridge: Cambridge University Press, 1989), p. 57.

32 J. Rawls, *A Theory of Justice* (Cambridge: Harvard University Press, 1971), p. 554.

33 Martha Nussbaum, *The Fragility of Goodness. Luck and ethics in Greek tragedy and philosophy* (Cambridge: Cambridge University Press, 1986).

34 Max Weber, "Wissenschaft als Beruf," *Gesammelte Aufsaetze zur Wissenschaftslehre* (Mohr: Tübingen, 1973), p. 604. (My translation; alternative translation in H. Gerth and C.W. Mills (eds), *From Max*

Weber (Oxford: New York, 1969), p. 148.

35 The following section draws heavily on my *The Idea of Political Theory*, pp. 23ff.

36 Michel Foucault, "The Subject and Power," in the "Afterword" to Hubert L. Dreyfus and Paul Rabinow, *Michel Foucault. Beyond Structuralism and Hermeneutics* (Chicago: University of Chicago Press, 1982), p. 209.

37 Dreyfus and Rainbow, p. 221.

38 See Foucault, *Power/Knowledge*, p. 133.

39 It can even be argued that Nietzsche thinks some of the same thoughts about women as does Haraway. See Sarah Kofman, "Baubo: Theological Perversion and Fetishism," in M. Gillespie and T. B. Strong (eds), *Nietzsche's New Seas* (Chicago: University of Chicago Press, 1989).

Part I
In the Tradition

1

The Homeric World

A. W. H. ADKINS

INTRODUCTORY

The Homeric poems are the product of a long oral tradition of bardic poetry. Their sources are saga and folk-tale; and neither from these, nor from oral epic itself, is a sustained analysis of their authors' view of human nature to be expected. Such bards have different concerns. Their compositions, however, bear witness none the less to a view of human nature whose several aspects are remarkably coherent, as will appear.

In these discussions "Homeric man" and "Homeric society" refer to the human beings and society portrayed in the Homeric poems. It is unnecessary to discuss here the extent to which these poems mirror any actual society of ancient Greeks. For later Greeks they portrayed the values and behaviour of the Heroic Age of Greece, and thus undoubtedly represent one of the Greek views of human nature and its possibilities. In the opinion of the present writer, the coherence of the phenomena discussed in this chapter argues powerfully that they, at least, are rooted in historical reality, even if no event described in the poems ever took place.

HOMERIC PSYCHOLOGY AND PHYSIOLOGY

Our clue to Homeric psychology and physiology must be the manner in which the poems use certain words. There must be studied without importing preconceptions from other cultures; for, if we suppose that our own everyday presuppositions and use of psychological words are "common sense," and that the phenomena must always have presented themselves in this manner

Reprinted by permission of Constable Publishers from A. W. H. Adkins, *From the Many to the One* (Ithaca: Cornell University Press, 1970), pp. 13–48.

to the man in the street, we may not take Homeric psychological language seriously. We may insist that the language is merely poetic, particularly as similar expressions occur in a fossil state in certain kinds of English poetry; and we may forget that the reason why a phrase is coined in the first place is likely to be that it expresses better than anything else that has occurred to its author what he is trying to say. All fossils were once alive; and Homeric psychological language finds a suitable habitat in the Homeric world as a whole.

The most important words are *psuche*, *thumos*, *kradiē*, *ētor*, *kēr*, *phrenes* and *nŏŏs*. I begin with *psuche*, since it becomes the most important word in later chapters, and "psychology" is derived from it. In Homer, however, it is less important. It has been said that its *esse* is *superesse*, that its role is simply to survive death, that it has no function in the living human being; and indeed it is the *psuche* which leaves the body at death, through the mouth (*Iliad* IX, 409), through a wound (*Iliad* XIV, 518), or simply from the limbs (*Iliad* XXII, 362). To say that the *psuche* left the body is to say that the human being (*Iliad* V, 696) or the animal (*Odyssey* XIV, 426) died; and no return of the *psuche* is possible (*Iliad* IX, 408).[1] Having left the body, the *psuche* passes, when the appropriate rites have been performed, down to Hades. However, though it is inactive in the living individual, the Homeric Greeks are conscious of its presence: Agenor reflects (*Iliad* XXI, 569) that Achilles has only one *psuche*, and that he might be killed; Achilles complains (*Iliad* IX, 322) that he is forever staking his *psuche* in war; and (*Iliad* XXII, 161) Achilles and Hector as they ran round Troy were contending for Hector's *psuche*. Homeric man is aware that he possesses a *psuche* while he is alive.

His *psuche* is not his self, or his personality. (It is, as will appear, in many ways almost devoid of personality.) Achilles says (*Iliad* IX, 401) that all the treasures of Troy are not worth his *psuche* to him; he and his *psuche* are separable in his mind.

We may of course render some of these uses of *psuche* by "life," others by "ghost;" but in thus using different words we misrepresent the position, for Homeric man used the same word in all the instances, and the presumption is that all appeared alike to him; whereas the range, and consequently the overtones, of "life" and "ghost" are very different in English, and break up in translation what in Homeric Greek is one. The *psuche*, then, is an individual while he lives, and departs at death to continue an existence (to be discussed later) in Hades. Patroclus' *psuche*, before his body is buried, comes to Achilles in a dream:

There came to him the *psuche* of wretched Patroclus, like him in every respect, in size and beautiful eyes and voice, dressed in just such clothes as he used to wear. (*Iliad* XXIII, 65)

The *psuche* of Patroclus looks and sounds just like Patroclus in life. The differences are expounded by Odysseus' mother when Odysseus calls her *psuche* up from the dead:

My son, most hapless of all mankind, Persephone, daughter of Zeus, is not cheating you. No, this is the way of it for mortals when they are dead: the sinews no longer hold together the flesh and bones. The mighty fire subdues them, when once the *thumos* has left the white bones, while the *psuche* has flown away like a dream. (*Odyssey* XI, 216ff.)

Since the *psuche* looks and sounds like the living person, Odysseus had expected other characteristics to persist, and had attempted to embrace his mother; but the *psuche* flew off "like a shadow or a dream;" and Odysseus lamented that Persephone had cheated him with a mere image of his mother.

Neither Homer nor any other early writer has a concept of "spiritual" as opposed to "material": the *psuche* is composed of a very tenuous stuff, which resides in the body while the individual is alive, flies away through some orifice at death and goes down to Hades.

From there it may be summoned and, if given blood to drink, may address the living (*Odyssey* XI, 98). Already we may see that the distinction between physiological and psychological is difficult to draw in these poems.

The Homeric *psuche* has no specific mental or emotional functions in life: it is simply that whose presence ensures that the individual is alive. To observe the mental and emotional activity of Homeric man, we must turn to the other words listed above, whose conventional renderings, all of which are somewhat misleading, are: *thumos*, "spirit," *kradie, etor, ker*, "heart;" *phrenes*, "mind" or (physiologically) "diaphragm" or "lungs;" *noos*, "mind." The manner in which these words are used, if we take it seriously, reveals a psychological landscape quite different from our own. We are accustomed to emphasize the "I" which "takes decisions," and ideas such as "will" or "intention." In Homer, there is much less emphasis on the "I" or decisions: the Greek words just mentioned take the foreground, and enjoy a remarkable amount of democratic freedom. Men frequently act "as their *kradie* and *thumos* bids them": Odysseus (*Odyssey* IX, 302) was wondering whether to attack the Cyclops when "another *thumos* restrained him;" Athena tells Telemachus to give her on some future occasion (*Odyssey* I, 316) "whatever gift his *etor* bids him give," and "grief came upon Achilles, and his *etor* debated between two alternatives in his shaggy chest" (*Iliad* I, 188). Examples could be multiplied: this is "ordinary language" in Homer.

The words require separate discussion. *Thumos* differs somewhat from *kradie*, *etor* and *ker*, since the latter are *prima facie* more physical and "organic," while *thumos*, as we have seen (*Odyssey* XI, 216ff.), may be said to leave the white bones at death. The difference, however, should not be overemphasised. True, food and drink cause men to receive *thumos* in their chests once again (*Odyssey* X, 461); and a stirring speech may stimulate a man's might and *thumos* (*Iliad* XV, 500). But a man's might may be not co-ordinate with his *thumos*, but in it: Achilles filled his *thumos* with might (*Iliad* XXII, 312, cf. *Odyssey* I, 320); and this raises the question whether *thumos* is a psychological function, an organ with a physical location in the body, or something physical, but not an organ. That is to say, it raises the question for the modern reader; but it is doubtful whether it is a relevant one. Philologists link *thumos* with Latin *fūmus* and Sanskrit *dhūmas*, both of which mean "smoke." Even if the link were treated as certain, it would not follow that *thumos* necessarily conveyed any idea of "smoke" to a Homeric Greek, for it is usage, not etymology, that "gives words their meaning." However, since Homer has no non-material language, it is worth exploring the possibility that, though the word never "means" "smoke" in Greek, some notion connected with smoke is conveyed by *thumos*. Some scholars seem to find a link in the idea of breath as it comes visibly from the nostrils in cold weather. I find this not fully convincing.[2] If we think of smoke in everyday life as neatly encased in fireplace and chimney, and in literary terms as the blue smoke from the distant shieling, such a link may appear reasonable; but we have still to account for the usage of *thumos* in Homer and in later writers. The examples already quoted suggest that *thumos* is impulsive; but there seems little reason to correlate impulse with breath emerging from the nostrils. However, early man's fire was not enclosed in fireplace and chimney; he must sometimes have found himself close to it; and in these circumstances the smoke and air immediately warmed by the fire are hot, swirling, choking and apparently very active. If we suppose that the remote Indo-European chose to denote this aspect of fire with the common ancestor of *thumos*, *dhumas* and *fumus*, and that the *thumos* (in the Homeric usage) which one notices first is most likely to be one's own, then what is denoted by *thumos* seems clear: the hot, swirling, surging – and sometimes choking – sensations produced by feelings of anger and other violent impulses, Plato (*Cratylus* 419E) derives *thumos* from "the raging (*thusis*) and boiling of the *psuche*." *Thumos* had a more restricted (and *psuche* a wider) usage in Plato's day; but his words convey a similar impression.

Thumos, in fact – and the same is true of *kradie*, *ker* and *etor* – records Homeric man's experiences in the manner in which he experienced them. He had not the conceptual framework with which to distinguish between a psychological function and an organ with a physical location; and though he could doubtless have distinguished between the latter and, for example, a vital fluid in the body, his interests gave him no reason to do so.

He felt a surge within, a hot sensation within the chest, and that was *thumos*. If he felt a backward impulse he might say, with Odysseus (*Odyssey* IX, 302), "but another *thumos* restrained me." If he did something without external constraint, but reluctantly, he might say, as Zeus says (*Iliad* IV, 43), that he acted "willingly, but with unwilling *thumos*;" and he supposed, as we have already seen, that food and drink increased the *thumos*, and that it departed at death, and – unlike the *psuche* – vanished altogether. An insistence on classification and treating English equivalents as real entities might induce us to suppose that in the first case we are concerned with an impulse (since presumably, even if *thumos* is sometimes a psychological function, Odysseus only has one), in the second with a psychological function, in the third with a generalized vital force; but the classification would be ours, not Homer's. In different circumstances, his experience of the inner surge induced him to use language in these ways as the most accurate method of recording it: he has no answer to the question whether *thumos* is a function or an expression of a function, for he has never asked the question.

Since the Homeric poems do not distinguish the material and the spiritual, it follows that *thumos*, *kradie* and all the rest are, like *psuche*, conceived of as possessing confusedly together qualities which we should distinguish in this manner. It is not, of course, that Homer reduces mental and spiritual qualities to material ones: by not distinguishing, he just as much ascribes mental and spiritual qualities to aspects of the individual to which we should not ascribe them. In the case of *kradie*, *ker* and *etor*, which are translatable as "heart" in most contexts (though *etor* may be part of the heart), it has sometimes been argued that the usage must have originally been psychological, since the internal sensations must have been felt long before man was familiar with his anatomy; and it has been argued in reply that wounds as well as dissection may furnish anatomical knowledge. Both arguments are unnecessary: the sensations within would be felt unanalysedly, the distinction between physiological and psychological not being present to the mind at all; and the physical organ, once discovered, would not be distinguished from its function and sensations. *Thumos, kradie, ker* and *etor* are all confusedly physical locations or organs to which certain emotions are ascribed, and the psychological functions whereby these emotions find expression. It may not be possible to find an exact location in the chest for the *thumos*; but when an author whose psychological language is not markedly metaphorical exhorts his heroes to put shame in their *thumos*, it seems reasonable to suppose that he is thinking of some definite location in space.

Again, these aspects of the personality are not merely emotional: they partake of consciousness. One may feel emotions in them, but they may themselves feel, and be conscious of, the emotions. I confine my examples to grief and joy: Aeneas' *thumos* rejoiced in his chest (*Iliad* XIII, 494); Hera rejoiced in her *thumos* (*Iliad* XIV, 156); Menelaus' *kradie* and *thumos* was gladdened (*Odyssey* IV, 548); Telemachus nursed mighty grief in his *kradie* (*Odyssey* XVII, 489); the suitors try to placate Odysseus with gifts until his *ker* is gladdened (*Odyssey* XXII, 58); Telemachus wished Mentes to be gladdened in respect of his *ker* (*Odyssey* I, 310); Zeus' *etor* laughed for joy when the other gods were embroiled in strife with one another (*Iliad* XXI, 389); and Aphrodite was grieved in respect of her *etor* (*Iliad* V, 364) when wounded by Diomedes. Illustrations could be given for the other emotions: there seems to be no emotion which the *thumos, kradie, ker* and *etor* cannot feel, and be conscious of feeling, nor which one cannot feel in them.

Consciousness being present, it is not surprising to find them thinking, or people thinking with them: Penelope rebukes her maidservants (*Odyssey* IV, 730) for not rousing her when her son Telemachus departed, though they knew well in their *thumos* when he went on board his ship; Odysseus' *kradie* had many forebodings of destruction (*Odyssey* V, 389) when Odysseus was wrecked and thrown into a rough sea; we have already seen Achilles' *etor* debating; Odysseus' *ker* was making plans for the suitors' downfall (*Odyssey* XVIII, 344); and it is very frequently indeed the *thumos* in which internal debate takes place: examples will be given below.

Accordingly, their functions overlap those of *phrenes* and *noos*, though these are the words usually rendered by "mind." The *phrenes* have a physical location – they "hold the liver" (*Odyssey* IX, 301) – understood by ancient Greek, and most subsequent, scholars to be the diaphragm, though R. B. Onians[3] makes a powerful case for the orignial location having been the lungs. The *noos* is sited in the chest, as will be shown below. The intellectual usages of these words require little illustration. Hector realised in his *phrenes* that Deiphobus was not near him (*Iliad* XXII, 296); Athena persuaded Pandarus' *phrenes* (*Iliad* IV, 104); Achilles was prudent in his *noos* (*Iliad* XXIV, 377); and Dolon (*Iliad* X, 391) complains that Hector has misled his *noos*. It is unusual for *phrenes* or *noos* to be said to instigate action; though (*Iliad* IX, 119) Agamemnon says that he acted foolishly through having obeyed his baneful *phrenes*.

The use of *phrenes* in contexts concerned with conduct ethically judged is similar. At first Aegisthus was unable to seduce Clytemnestra; for she had "good" (*agathai*) *phrenes* (Odyssey III, 266); and a similar reason is given for Eumaeus' remembering to make an offering to the gods (*Odyssey* XIV, 421), and for Penelope's chastity and loyalty to the absent Odysseus (*Odyssey* XXIV, 194). Ethical behaviour is described in intellectual, or apparently intellectual, terms in Homer and later Greek: a situation which will be discussed more fully below. It should be noted that the Homeric *noos* is not, though the word is the same, the pure intellect of later philosophy: Homeric man does not engage in abstract speculation, and is only concerned with practical reason.

Just as *thumos*, *kradie*, *ker* and *etor* are capable of thought, so are *noos* and *phrenes* capable of emotion: the shepherd rejoices in his *phrēn* (the singular is used as well as the plural) as the flock follows him (*Iliad* XIII, 493); while Paris says to Hector:

> Your *kradie* is always as unwearied as an axe which goes through a log, wielded by the hands of a man who is cutting out a ship timber by his skill, and it assists his own strength. Just so is your *noos* fearless in your chest. (*Iliad* III, 60ff.)

Here we pass readily from *kradie* in 60 to *noos* in 63. The functions of the two are clearly the same here, though to ask whether *kradie* and *noos* are considered to be identical by the poet in this context would be pushing the question too far. Certainly *noos* and *phrenes* are as capable of emotion as *thumos*, *kradie*, *ker* and *etor* are of thought. Furthermore, both the *phrenes* (whether in lungs or diaphragm) and, as we see from the last quotation, the *noos* are sited in the chest, as are *thumos, kradie, ker* and *etor*. This too suggests that in the experience of Homeric man thought usually has a high emotive charge.

Noos and *phrenes* are much more intellectual than emotional, however, and differ from each other in that *noos* is more concerned with noticing present facts or picturing future ones, *phrenes* with reasoning about them. *Thumos* is highly emotional, as we have seen; yet it is in the *thumos* that anxious deliberation — and in an epic poem most deliberation is anxious — characteristically takes place. *Ker, kradie* and *etor* are more emotional than intellectual, and seem not to differ significantly from one another. The reason for the existence of the three words may in part be metrical convenience; but to grant this is not to concede the type of idiom as a whole to be mere poetising: the representation of separate springs capable of impulse, emotion and thought, the existence of, so to speak, separate "little people" within the individual, seems natural in the light of Homeric psychology and, as we shall see, physiology in general.

For Homeric physiology — as we should distinguish it, though the line between physiology and psychology is blurred in Homer — must appear strange to the modern reader. Snell, in the penetrating first chapter of *Die Entdeckung des Geistes*,[4] starts from the ancient critic Aristarchus' observation that in Homer the word *sōma* does not mean "living body," but always "corpse," in opposition to the *psuche* which leaves it at death. Aristarchus held that *demas* was the Homeric Greek for "living body," but Snell points out that the word only occurs in the accusative of respect: e.g. "he was small in respect of his *demas*," and that where we would say "his whole body trembled," Homer would use *guia*, and for our "sweat poured from his whole body" *melea*. Both words are neuter plural, and mean "limbs": *guia* being the limbs as moved by the joints, *melea* the limbs in their muscular strength. In such phrases as "he washed his body," or "the sword pierced his body," Homer uses *chrōs*, which means "the skin." There is no word for the body as a whole: *chros* is the bounding limit of the body, *demas* its structure, and the plurals *guia* and *melea* refer to it as an aggregate of units. Snell points out that the drawings of the human figure found in geometric art — on Greek pottery, that is to say, of the eighth century BC — have precisely this property; and concludes that there is convincing evidence from Homeric language — and language both mirrors thought and helps to mould it — and from the visual arts that the early Greeks perceived the body as an aggregate, not as a unit.

Physiological and psychological phenomena, then, closely parallel one another in Homer. Another passage will serve to illustrate the completeness of the resemblance. Ajax says:

> And my *thumos* in my chest is zealous to fight ... and my feet below and my hands above are eager. (*Iliad* XIII, 73ff.)

Here *thumos*, feet and hands instigate the action, and in precisely the same manner. All are felt as springs of action: the blurring of what we should distinguish as psychological and physiological is complete.

It remains to enquire how far Homeric man feels himself to exist as a whole, and what relationship he experiences between himself and his parts. In the first place, a man may yield to his *thumos*, as in *Iliad* IX, 109, where this is given as the reason or cause of Agamemnon's slighting Achilles. Agamemnon might presumably have restrained his *thumos* or any other part of himself; as Achilles, when his wrath comes to an end, proposes that both should do:

> But let us allow these things to be over and done with, having subdued our *thumos* in our chests. (*Iliad* XIX, 65)

In such usages it is the whole personality, even if this can be expressed only by the personal pronoun, that inhibits impulses. This, as we have seen, is not the most usual picture in Homer: the parts appear more frequently than the whole, the relation to the whole is not clear, and there is no word for the whole, apart from the implications of the personal pronouns. Nevertheless, where there is to be restraint, the personality as a whole must restrain. In *Iliad* I, 188ff., Achilles'

> *etor* debated in his shaggy chest whether he (and here the pronoun is masculine, referring to Achilles: *etor* is neuter) should draw his sharp sword ... and slay Agamemnon, or check his anger and restrain his *thumos*.

The *etor* may have debated, but Achilles himself, not his *etor* or any other part of him, must control his *thumos*.

On the basis of the previous discussion, it seems clear that all these forms of speech constitute a direct record of the manner in which his experience presented itself to Homeric man — or had presented itself during the time when the formulaic epic vocabulary was being formed. The last is a necessary qualification in any

Homeric discussion; but in this case the general picture of Homeric psychology and physiology is so homogeneous as to suggest that these expressions to the end of the oral tradition still recorded experiences in the manner in which they were experienced. Indeed, it is as true to say that the psychological vocabulary a society uses moulds the manner in which it experiences as that its experiences mould its psychological vocabulary. The initial usage records the experiences; later generations learn it, and interpret their experiences in its terms. Homeric language, then, would have tended to encourage the fragmentation of Homeric man's psychological experience in any case. . . .

Homeric man, then, not only has a psychology and a physiology in which the parts are more in evidence than the whole: he believes that the gods may act directly upon him or some aspect of him to affect his actions for good or ill. If we are to understand the function of this belief for Homeric man, we must consider the manner in which he evaluates such ascriptions of causation.

They clearly do not, and are not intended to, absolve him from responsibility for his bad actions or failures, or deny him credit for his good actions and successes. In *Iliad* XII, 290ff. we are told that the Trojans would not have got the upper hand at this stage in the battle, had not Zeus stirred on his son (by a mortal woman) Sarpedon against the Greeks. This is followed by a simile comparing him with a lion whose *thumos* urges him against his prey; and in 307 we return to Sarpedon with

So then did his *thumos* urge Sarpedon to rush upon the wall.

The chain of causation is no longer pursued beyond Sarpedon's *thumos*; and for the acts which his *thumos* prompts him to perform Sarpedon is certainly responsible. This kind of instance is a particular case of a general tendency found in Greece and in other societies: a course of action said to be planned, caused, or instigated by a god, or prophesied by an oracle is nonetheless, when the actions are described in detail, and evaluated, attributed to the human beings who perform it; and certainly no warrior society could afford to allow the excuse for cowardice that a god had caused it, or would wish to diminish the credit for successes on these grounds.

The case of Agamemnon, however, is more complex.[5] He says that he is not the cause of his action, but that Zeus, *moira* and the Fury are; and he uses very emphatic language. Nevertheless, he is not attempting to avoid recompensing Achilles. He cannot: he treats the action as a disastrous mistake, but this does not absolve him from the necessity of remedying its consequences and bringing Achilles back into the battle, so that Agamemnon himself may avoid *elencheie*, shame (a term which will be discussed below). This is a necessity even if Agamemnon regards the action, as being the result of *ate*, as "not his action" at all. But does he? He may indeed say that Zeus, *moira* and the Fury are the cause; but in the very next line he says not merely "I took away" but "I myself took away," adding a very strong word for "myself." Agamemnon is able to ascribe an action to external causes and to himself in adjacent lines, despite the fact that he has said that he is not responsible in so many words immediately before. This may be illogical, but seems explicable. Agamemnon has committed an error which has led to disaster. Now no-one intends − or, in a calculative psychology, plans − to fail. Agamemnon cannot understand how he came to do such a thing, and feels there was some element in the situation not under his control. Since his society ascribes a wide range of unexpected psychological phenomena to divine instigation, Agamemnon naturally speaks in these terms. Nevertheless, at the same time Agamemnon is aware that he − the unity represented by the personal pronoun − harmed Achilles. The statement that he was not the cause may serve to relieve Agamemnon's internal stresses, but it does nothing else. Agamemnon's different statements are not harmonised with one another.

All these aspects of the Homeric situation reveal Homeric man as a being whose parts are more in evidence than the whole, and one very conscious of sudden unexpected accesses of energy. A study of Homeric man vis-à-vis his fellows and the gods, to which we shall now turn, will necessarily show him functioning more as a unit, but will also furnish the context in which his fragmented psychological condition can be understood.

HOMERIC MAN AND HIS FELLOWS

Here we shall consider the values of Homeric man in the social context in which they are found, and discuss the standard at which Homeric man had to aim in order to satisfy the demands of society, and the pressures on Homeric man which result from the attempt to behave in the required manner.

Homeric man[6] lived in a society of virtually autonomous small social units termed *oikoi*, noble households under the leadership of a local chieftain, or *agathos*. The *oikos* was the largest effective social, political and economic unit. Its head was responsible for defending its members in war and in what in Homeric society passed for peace — for such a society can never be securely at peace — and for ensuring his own prosperity and theirs, which derived from his own. He had also to defend the interests of any wanderer from outside the *oikos* whom he took under his protection: a defence which might require actual fighting. There was no larger effective group to which he could turn for help in discharging these functions.[7] An assembly of heads of *oikoi* could indeed be held to discuss questions which affected more than one of them; but, as Homer tells the story, no assembly was held in Ithaca between the departure of Odysseus and the occasion, some twenty years later, when Telemachus called one in *Odyssey* II; and that assembly achieved nothing. The head of *oikos* could rely on no-one else; and the other members of the *oikos* needed him to secure their very existence; so that the demand that he should succeed was categoric. The most powerful words of denigration used of actions in Homer are *aischron* — a neuter adjective whose range spans what we distinguish as "ugly" and "shameful" — and *elencheie*, the state of mind, or the condition vis-à-vis his fellows, of the hero conscious of having done something *aischron*. We may perhaps not be surprised to discover (*Iliad* II, 298) that Odysseus holds that, for the Greek army besieging Troy, it is *aischron* to remain for a long time and then return empty-handed; for our own values in wartime are not dissimilar. However, when Odysseus disguised as a beggar blunders into Eumaeus' farmyard, and is attacked by his dogs, Eumaeus says:

> Old man, the dogs came near to destroying you suddenly; and then you would have caused me *elencheie*. (*Odyssey* XIV, 37f.)

Again, Penelope thus rebukes Telemachus for allowing the disguised Odysseus to be maltreated by the suitors:

> How would it be, if our guest while sitting thus in our house should perish as a result of his grievous mishandling? For you there would be *aischos* (a noun closely linked with *aischron* in usage) and shame among mankind. (Odyssey XVIII 223f.)

Eumaeus did not know that Odysseus was coming; while Telemachus wished to protect his guest, but was heavily out-numbered by the suitors. In some societies Eumaeus could plead ignorance, Telemachus *force majeure*; but not in Homeric society. Here the most powerful terms of denigration are applied quite simply to failure to ensure the safety and well-being of the members of the group of which one is the head. It makes no difference to the evaluation of the situation whether the failure results from cowardice, or from mistake or *force majeure*: only the result is taken into account. Homeric society is a "results-culture."

Society's highest commendation is naturally reserved for those who can produce the desired results, and for those qualities in them which appear most relevant to their production. *Agathos* is not a title of the head of *oikos*, but the most powerful adjective available to commend a man in Homeric society; for the head of *oikos*, as a warrior-chieftain, is expected to unite in himself all the qualities which this society needs most and values most highly. He must be strong, brave and successful; for no quality has any value unless it leads to success. He has a great advantage over his followers, for he is wealthy and can purchase full armour and a chariot, and the leisure to become proficient in their use. He is, as they can see, a much more effective fighter than they are; and provided that he actually succeeds in preserving the group in war and in what passes for peace in Homeric society, they have every inducement to commend him as *agathos* and his admired qualities as *arete*, together with the success which in such a situation cannot be distinguished from the qualities which are conducive to it. The admired qualities are in fact best characterised as "strength-and-bravery-and-wealth-leading-to-or-preserving-success," the hyphens indicating the unitary and unanalysed nature of *arete* for Homeric man. High birth is included in *arete*, since in Homeric society, a society without coined money, wealth consists of land, flocks, house and slaves; and these are possessed by the *agathoi* and inherited.

Other qualities, such as justice and self-control, are less highly valued by this society. A wronged individual sets a high value on obtaining redress for himself; but society in general sees so much more need for the success-producing qualities of the *agathos* than for his justice and self-control that the latter are no part of his *arete*. It follows that so long as the *agathos* is successful in protecting the group he remains *agathos*, no matter how unjust he may be, and cannot be effectively censured, since he retains his *arete*, on which he sets most store. Both Agamemnon in the *Iliad* and the suitors in the *Odyssey* retain their *arete* no matter how much wrong they do to Achilles and to Odysseus: it is the latter whose position is *aischron*, and who are showing themselves *kakoi* (the opposite of *agathoi*), in so far as they are failing to protect their own interests. As a result, when (*Iliad* XIX, 85ff.) Agamemnon acknowledges that he was in some sense "wrong" to deprive Achilles of his prize, the slave-girl Briseis – the action which occasioned the whole Wrath – he does not mean that he has now realised that it was morally wrong to take Briseis. He concludes that he was "wrong" from the fact that Hector has carried his victorious attack right up to the Greek ships, as – it is implied – he would have been unable to do had Achilles not been sulking in his tent. Now though it was not *aischron* for Agamemnon to deprive Achilles of his prize, it is certainly *aischron* for Agamemnon, as leader of the expedition, if the Greeks fail to capture Troy. Agamemnon thought he could take Briseis from Achilles and capture Troy; and had he done so his *arete* would have been unsmirched. Discovering this to be not the case, he relinquishes Briseis to Achilles, and acknowledges that he has made a mistake. It is in this sense that he holds that he was wrong.

The behaviour of *agathos*, *kakos* and the other words which commend or decry most powerfully in Homer indicates quite clearly the kind of qualities expected of a man, the characteristics of – male – human nature at its highest. (Woman have their own *arete*: they are expected to be chaste and skilled in household tasks.) Qualities of character, physical attributes, intellect, social position and "external goods" – as we should distinguish them – are all confusedly commended together. All distinguish the *agathos* from the *kakos*, who is ineffective in war (since, whatever other characteristics he may have, he is inadequately armed) and of low social position. Since *agathos* and *kakos* serve in all their usages to commend and decry what is good and bad of its kind, the *agathos* represents the human being at his most admired, the *kakos* the reverse. In such a society, the *kakos* has little chance of becoming *agathos* – for he cannot save in exceptional circumstances[8] acquire land, the foundation of wealth – but, in a society of small and insecure units, the *agathos* may well fail and become *kakos*. There is little temptation to regard the *agathoi* and the *kakoi* as distinct species in these circumstances; though there are some signs of this in later writers.

The status of the competitive excellences, the paramount importance of success and failure, and the irrelevance of intentions in evaluating the successes and failures of the *agathos*, must be at least in part responsible for the characteristic Greek psychological "model," which is intellectual and calculative, not volitional; but this will require further discussion later.

Not only is the Homeric *agathos* always capable of falling from his *arete* by failure or mistake; he is also subject to the sanction of his society, which equally disregards intentions. In *Iliad* VIII, 139 ff., Nestor advises Diomedes to retreat before Hector, since Zeus is clearly favouring Hector. Diomedes acknowledges that Nestor's advice is reasonable, but adds, 147ff.:

> Yet this terrible grief comes upon my *kradie* and *thumos*:
> Hector one day will say as he speaks among the Trojans
> "The son of Tydeus (Diomedes) fled before me and went to
> the ships":

On that day, says Diomedes, may the earth swallow me up. Nestor replies, 153ff.:

> If Hector calls you *kakos* and lacking in valour, the Trojans
> ... and their wives ... whose sturdy husbands you have
> slain, will never believe it.

Nestor cannot say "Don't worry. It isn't true." If the Trojans believed, and spread it abroad, that Diomedes was *kakos* and lacking in valour, this would cause terrible *elencheie* for him. And naturally so: he lives in a society without writing, without permanent records which can be consulted later. What matters is what is said of him by his contemporaries, and remembered by future generations; and if that is false, there is no alternative source of information from which he could be rehabilitated. This is both a results-culture and a shame-culture: even where the result is not disastrous to the individual and his group, if the behaviour can be represented as being unworthy of an *agathos* by common report, this is *aischron* and entails *elencheie*. (We shall see below the effect this has on the psychology of Homeric man.) One's self, in the last resort, only has the value that others put on it: one cannot fall back, in Homer or for long afterwards, either on one's own opinion of oneself, or on the knowledge that one has done one's best. ...

[*After a consideration of the relation of Homeric man to his Gods, Adkins turns to the emotions. He argues that the emotions expressed in the Iliad cannot adequately be rendered by the terms that we use for emotions in our social and psychological make-up. Homeric persons, for Adkins, had one word for feelings that we would separate into many parts. Adkins sums up:]*

The reason for the existence of this vocabulary lies in the total situation of Homeric man. His most important terms of value evaluate not his intentions nor his efforts, but their results. He is always "up against it," judged in terms of his successes and failures; further the sanction is overtly "what people will say," and over this he has no control, and he cannot set his own consciousness of his self and its value against the estimation of his fellows, since his self has only the value which they put upon it. In these circumstances he can and does have intentions, form plans, make choices, but these are not the most important aspect of the situation in his eyes (or anyone else's). Externally, what is important is the result: internally, what is important to him is his psychological response to the situations in which he finds himself, partly because these are directly relevant to his success or failure, partly because, his choices and plans being less important, his psychological conditions gain added importance for him. These linguistic usages, in fact, give an accurate report of the psychological pressures of living in a shame- or (a phrase which expresses a more fundamental fact about Homeric society) a results-culture.

Apeilein and *neikeiein* are similarly affected by the nature of Homeric society and its values. *Apeilein* occurs in situations which we should distinguish as threatening, giving one's lineage, speaking magniloquently, or vowing, situations which may be considered both from the point of view of the person who *apeilein* and from that of the person affected, both of whom are living in the highly competitive Homeric world, in an environment indifferent and actively or potentially hostile, in the precarious condition I have already described. The pull of *arete* leads the person who *apeilein* to try to "make his presence felt," and all his efforts to do so are likely to be classified together by him, since this resemblance is more important to him than the differences emphasised by our translations. *Apeilein* fulfils this function in Homer. When Laomedon threatened Poseidon and Apollo, when Pelegonus narrated his lineage, both were asserting themselves; and if Hector were to have told of the flight of Diomedes, or Teucer had vowed a sacrifice to Apollo, they would have been manifesting themselves. The other *agathoi* in this competitive society are as precariously situated as those who are "making their presence felt;" and in such circumstances to hear another speaking magniloquently, magnifying himself, is to hear oneself by implication depreciated, at least relatively. The depreciation may be direct and intentional, as in the case of Hector and Diomedes; if Hector is believed, Diomedes' reputation will fall and he will incur *elencheie*. Hector is not threatening to do something to Diomedes; but he is threatening his status and reputation. However, in such a society it is unnecessary for another man to be mentioned by name, or even for the man who *apeilein* to have any particular person in mind. If he magnifies himself, or someone with whom he is associated, he is claiming a larger share of the attention of men for himself or the other person; and since it is on the attention of men that one's fame depends – and fame is of paramount importance – anyone who hears such magniloquent words may feel himself "threatened" to some extent. In so far as a man, or a society, can only pay attention to the deeds of a certain number of persons (and on that attention, in a non-literate society, depends any knowledge of oneself in future generations), if one person receives more of the attention there is less for the others. Similarly Apollo, who, like the rest of the Greek gods, has to be induced to cause himself trouble on a mortal's behalf, would feel himself impinged upon by Teucer's vow of a hecatomb, though he would welcome the sacrifice in itself.

Neikeiein too is closely linked to the situation of Homeric man: if only results count, it is not worthwhile to distinguish a moral error from a mistake, where both lead to disaster, whether one is reprehending or being reprehended: a disastrous result is *aischron*, and will meet with disapproval, the same kind of disapproval, whatever the cause; and the man disapproved of will feel the same kind of shame, whatever the cause of the disaster. On two occasions (*Iliad* VI, 442ff., XXII, 104ff.) Hector says "I feel shame, *aideomai*, before the Trojans, both men and women": on one occasion the shame would be caused if he skulked away from the war like a coward, on the other it is caused by a mistake in strategy which has led to a disaster. To reprove either a moral error or a mistake is *neikeiein*, as is Euryalus' terming Odysseus a merchant, and hence deficient in *arete*: all the situations are *aischron*, and show the person reprehended to be *kakos*.

All five words, then, classify psychological experiences and overt behaviour in a manner significant to Homeric society, a manner which is unfamiliar to us. The man who *ochthein*, *choesthai* or *meneainein*, and both the man who *apeilein* or *neikeiein* and the man who is affected by his doing so, are responding in a manner systematically different from ourselves. Once the barrier interposed by the lexicographers' 'equivalents' is removed, we can appreciate the subtlety and sensitivity of the Homeric poems as literature of action, emotion and response, and realise that we have in them documents of great anthropological and psychological interest; for here we have a language which records clearly and with precision what it is like to live in a shame- or results-culture.

CONCLUSION

In a sense, it is not the fragmentation of the Homeric personality, but the development in other cultures of the ego-centred personality, that requires explanation. However, it is desirable to recapitulate the several aspects of the Homeric personality, and to endeavour to indicate the extent to which Homeric society favours this personality pattern, and discourages others.

We have seen that success is of paramount importance, good intentions of no importance, in this society: a situation which renders it impossible to distinguish between moral error and mistake, where the success and failure of the *agathos* are in the balance. Further, the sanction of the society is overtly "what people will say of one's actions," over which one has oneself no control. If one's good intentions have no value unless crowned with success — which is not the agent's to command, and depends on more than good intentions — and one only has the value that other people put upon one, then one's actions are evaluated in terms of matters external to one's self; and there seems little likelihood of the development of a unitary self or of those aspects of "will" which are manifested in deciding. (Bearing up bravely against adversity, being self-controlled or strong-willed in this sense, is demanded of Homeric man: this is *tolmān* or *tlēnai*, an adjective formed from the root of the latter word being used to describe the storm-tossed Odysseus.) And, as we have seen, a unitary self is little in evidence in the Homeric poems. The Homeric hero's *thumos*, his *kradie* or some other aspect of him suggests or prompts action, though he acts. His *thumos*, *kradie* or some other aspect of him feels an emotion, or he feels an emotion in it. There is no automatism, for his consciousness is diffused through all the "parts" as well as residing in the unity represented by the personal pronoun. Even if, as in *Iliad* XI, 403ff. (where 403, "He addressed his great-hearted *thumos*" becomes at 407, with reference to the same speech "But why did my *thumos* say this to me?") we find formal contradictions in the language, we should not simply reflect that these are formulaic[9] utterances (as they are) and dismiss them from consideration. Formulae are metrically convenient units; but they do not, in a system so flexible and artistic as that found in Homeric epic, control in the first instance the *content* of what is said, though they may demand that when the content is the same the form should not vary. Here we can discern a reason for the existence of both forms of expression in the same context. Neither the *thumos* nor any other individual "part" is ever said to speak as a means of introducing direct speech in Homer: though one's *thumos* may bid one to do something, as we have seen, it is not credited with quoted sequences of words, whether the dialogue is internal, as here, or external; and this presumably reflects Homeric psychological experience. Accordingly, Odysseus addresses his *thumos* in 403. Having done so, however, he rejects what he has said, and accordingly distances it from himself by ascribing it to his *thumos*. The unitary self may not be important, but the unity represented by the personal pronoun exists: it can check the *thumos* and the other "parts" or, as here, distance itself from one of them.

Where there is no conflict, however, this unity is so lightly experienced that, as we have seen, not merely *thumos*, *kradie* and similar aspects of the individual, but also hands and feet, may be felt as springs of action. The great overlapping of function displayed by *thumos*, *kradie* and the rest may be thus explained: when the *thumos*, *kradie* or any other aspect is felt as prompting action or supplying ideas, it is, where there is no conflict, the whole active aspect of the personality that is manifesting itself in this particular "organ," the whole having, so to speak, flowed into whatever organ is mentioned. Similarly, when the "I" represented by the unity of the personal pronoun is addressing some "organ," that "organ" is for the moment imbued with the receptive aspects of the whole personality. Even when allowance has been made for metrical convenience, the number of words available indicates the low degree of unity and cohesion felt by Homeric man in his psychological experience: one "little man" (so to speak) within him after another addresses and prompts him, or is addressed and prompted by him. Experience furnishes all the "little men" with consciousness and emotions; and there is as yet no analysis to furnish a *conceptual* distinction between thought and emotion in general, which in practice occur together: Homeric language records the experience of Homeric man. A further indication that we have here not a mere use of language, but the experience of the active personality for the moment behaving in the manner suggested, may perhaps be sought in the language itself: even when Homeric language ascribes the prompting to *two* sources, the *thumos* and *kradie* together standing as subject, the verb remains singular even where the plural would be metrically possible.

Where such a structure, or absence of structure, prevails, it seems not unreasonable to suppose that sudden psychological surges, or equally sudden cessations of drive, will occur; and that these will be both more prevalent, and also more noticeable, features of a psychological landscape of this nature, as will the "given" nature of a suddenly occurring idea. We may suppose that the Homeric Greek misascribed these in attributing their source to Apollo, Athena and the rest, and yet acknowledge that the phenomena for which he was attempting to account were real and present to his experience. The language may, of course, overstate the case. Any psychological model may overemphasize some aspects of experience at the expense of others. More recent "ordinary language" psychological models have sometimes underestimated the "given" and spontaneous elements in our own psychological and physical behaviour and experience. However, it is so appropriate that the Homeric situation should have encouraged the formation of precisely the type of personality structure that we find in the poems that it seems difficult to deny that the language furnishes a broadly accurate record of the psychological experience of Homeric man. This impression is confirmed by the vocabulary of emotion to be found in the poems which, as we have seen, does not correspond to our own, but well expresses fitting responses to the stresses and strains of living in a results-culture.

The Homeric situation also favours, as a model for what we characterize as "deciding," the picture of a psychological balance inclined by the relative weight of the advantages poured into the scale-pans. Since the goal of action is to maximise one's own *agatha* ("advantages"), a desirable end, a positive drive towards that end, once discovered, will be present. The agent may feel the utmost doubt and anxiety over the identity of the more advantageous course of action in a crisis; but so soon as an answer to the problem presents itself, the identification of the course of action as the most *agathon* available in the circumstances carries with it a desire for its fulfilment, and bridges the gap between thought and action. For a variety of reasons, as we have seen, the personality has little core: it is not surprising that the emphasis should be on the "balance" during the period before action; and the nature of the goal, in addition to the psychological structure, does not encourage the idea of decision at the moment of action.

Lastly, we may consider one manner in which Homeric society describes the behaviour of others from without. We have already seen that the possession of good (*agathai*) *phrenes* is the basis of sound behaviour in tune with the values of society. Similarly, *eidenai*, a Greek word usually rendered "to know," is used in many phrases where we should use expressions to denote character. For example, Achilles (*Iliad* XXIV, 41) "*eidenai* fierce things," while Eumaeus (*Odyssey* XIV, 433) "*eidenai in* his *phrenes* things that were right." We should say that Achilles had a fierce disposition, Eumaeus a righteous one. There is here a great distinction between the Greek manner of experiencing and representing this type of situation and our own, a distinction which, in one form or another, is present throughout the whole period discussed in this chapter. The Greeks emphasize intellect and calculation in their accounts of behaviour. However, in each period discussed we must attempt to evaluate this situation in its wider context. Here Apollo says of Achilles that

His *phrenes* are not righteous, nor his *nŏēma* (similar to *noos* here) bendable in his chest, but he *eidenai* fierce things, like a lion which, yielding to its great might and proud *thumos*, goes against men's herds to find its food. (*Iliad* XXIV, 40ff.)

If we render *eidenai* here as "know," and then mentally transfer it to contexts in which we use the word "know," we shall regard the phrase as extremely intellectual; for we use "knowledge" of what we regard as certain, opposed to the subjective, the doubtful and the emotional. But Homeric man has no such concept or experience of knowledge. We have seen that his *phrenes* and *noos* may feel emotion; and he has no knowledge which is not practical, capable of leading to action, and none which he has divorced from emotion: Homer can pass with no difficulty from "*eidenai* fierce things" to a simile of a raging lion. We should consider the whole range of *eidenai*, which is used in "emotional" contexts, and so is linked with emotion, desire and impulse; and in using the word "calculative" to describe the Homeric model — and it is difficult to find a less unsatisfactory term — we should beware of correlating this with dispassionate calculation. The situations are instinct with emotion: all the resources of personality, not merely the intellect (which is not sharply distinguished in Homer), are involved.

The picture presented by the description and evaluation of Homeric man and his behaviour is remarkably coherent: the elements of which it is composed discharge functions entirely appropriate to the situation as a whole. Many of these elements persist into later Greek society, and affect the descriptions, analyses and solutions of later periods. We may not, however, assume that their functions remain entirely unaltered: this must be considered on each occasion the light of the evidence as a whole.

NOTES

1 Andromache "breathes out her *psuche*" in a swoon, *Iliad* XXII, 467, and this is clearly remediable. But this is an unusual usage.

2 Nor does E. L. Harrison, "Notes on Homeric Psychology," *Phoenix* XIV (1960), pp. 63ff.

3 *The Origins of European Thought* (Cambridge, 1951), pp. 23ff.

4 There is much more in Snell's account than can be mentioned here. The reader may consult T. G. Rosenmeyer's translation of Snell's work, *The Discovery of the Mind* (Blackwell, 1953); and, for other discussions of Homeric psychology, J. Böhme, *Die Seele und das Ich im homerischen Epos* (Leipzig and Berlin, 1929); Harrison, "Notes on Homeric Psychology," and the earlier writers there cited.

5 On Agamemnon's apology, see the brilliant and illuminating discussion in E. R. Dodds, *The Greeks and the Irrational* (Berkeley and Los Angeles: University of California Press, 1951), chap. I.

6 This is a condensed version of my discussion in *Merit and Responsibility* (Oxford: Clarendon Press, 1960), chap. III. Proof is there offered of a number of statements whose truth is assumed here.

7 The *Iliad* (e.g. I, 277ff.; IX, 37ff.) and the *Odyssey* (e.g. I, 391ff.) speak of kingship over larger groups than the *oikos*, so that this is in a sense an overstatement; but neither poem shows us kingly power being effectively exercised over a larger group, and the society's values seem to reflect the situation described in the text.

8 As Phoenix acquired land from Peleus (*Iliad* IX, 480ff.), where the language seems to show the exceptional nature of the favour. (Phoenix was, furthermore, an *agathos* by birth, driven away from his own *oikos* for offending his father.)

9 The Homeric epics, being oral poetry, contain many "formulae," expressions of convenient metrical form and length to suit the dactylic hexameter in which they are composed, which appear repeatedly in the course of the poems.

2

Republic: Five Types of City and Soul

PLATO

... "One hears of many strange types," said Glaucon.

"And you know that the human character must have the same number of forms as the regime. Or do you think regimes come from 'sticks or stones' or something, rather than from their citizens' dispositions, which sink like the scale of a balance and drag everything else along with them?" [said Socrates.]

"No, that's where they come from."

"Then if there are five types of city, there must also be five arrangements of soul. We've already described the best man, who resembles aristocracy, and rightly called him just and good. Shall we now go through the others — the honor and victory-loving man who corresponds to the Spartan regime, the oligarchic man, the democratic, and the tyrannical — to see the most unjust man and contrast him with the most just?[1] That would complete our examination of how pure justice and injustice compare in the happiness or misery of their possessors. Then we can either believe Thrasymachus and pursue injustice or follow our emerging argument and practice justice."

"That's exactly what we should do."

"We began before by first examining the dispositions of regimes, as being more distinct, and then of individuals. Shall we do the same thing now and first examine the honor-loving regime? It doesn't have a common name; we could call it 'timocracy' or 'timarchy,' I suppose. Then shall we examine the same type of man against it, go on to oligarchy and the oligarchic man, look next at democracy and the democratic man, and fourth go to tyranny and the tyrannical soul and so try to become competent judges of this issue we've proposed for ourselves?"

Reprinted by permission of Harlan Davidson, Inc from Plato, *Republic* Book 8, 544d–562c, pp. 202–28. Translation and notes by Raymond Larson.

"If we do, we'll be looking and judging in a logical way."

"Come on," I said, "let's try to say how timocracy, rule by honor, might arise from aristocracy, the rule of the best. Or is it simply a fact that every revolution comes from the ruling class, when civil war arises in it? As long as that class remains single-minded, no matter how small it may be, the city cannot be disturbed."

"Yes, that's a fact."

"Then how will disturbance come to our city, Glaucon, to make our auxiliaries and rulers fight in civil war with themselves and each other? Shall we, like Homer, invoke the Muses to tell 'how Faction first fell among men,' and make them rant in a high-flown, tragical style, as if they were serious and not teasing and playing with us as though we were little boys?"

"How?"

"Something like this: 'A city so constituted will be hard to disturb. But since all that becomes must fall to decay, even such a constitution endures not for all time but dissolves. Its dissolution is this: bearing and barrenness of bodies and soul come to all animals and plants of the earth whenever the turning circle for each species joins its circumference, winding close for the short-lived, wide for the long.[2] As for your race, the leaders you have educated, wise as they are, will nevertheless fail at some time to achieve either good offspring or none by combining perception and calculation, and they will beget children when they ought not to. . . .'"

"When in ignorance of it your guardians bed brides with grooms out of season their children will not be well formed or fortuned. The best of them will be installed by their elders, and when, though unworthy, they have succeeded in turn to their fathers' power, they will as guardians be the first to begin to neglect us, holding first poetry, then gymnastics in lower esteem than they ought, and so your young will grow Museless. Thence will issue rulers unequal to guarding and scrutinizing Hesiod's[3] races and yours: gold, silver, bronze, and iron. When iron mixes with silver, bronze with gold, they will deliver inequality and disjointed imbalance, which whenever and wherever engendered, always breed hatred and war. That, you must say, is Faction's lineage, wherever she may be born.'"

"We'll also say it's a very good answer," he said.

"It must be," I said, " − they're Muses."

"What do the Muses say after that?"

"That after Faction was born two groups of guardians began pulling apart, the ones polluted with iron and bronze toward making money and possessing land and houses and silver and gold, while the others, of silver and gold, being not impoverished but rich in their natures, tried to draw their souls back to excellence and the ancient arrangement. And so from opposing each other by violence they compromised in the middle and distributed houses and land as private possessions; and those they formerly guarded as free friends and providers they then enslaved as lackeys and serfs, giving themselves over to warfare and to guarding against them."

"It seems to me that that's where the change begins."

"Won't this regime be somewhere in the middle between aristocracy and oligarchy?" I asked.

"Certainly."

"Thus it will change, but how will it be governed? Being in the middle, won't timarchy – rule by honor – imitate the former regime in some things, oligarchy in others, and have some features of its own?"

"Correct."

"Won't it imitate aristocracy in honoring its rulers and exempting its defender class from farming, crafts, and other ways of making money, in maintaining public messes and in practicing gymnastics and the contest of war?"

"Yes."

"Won't it also have many distinctive features, such as being afraid to take wise men into public offices – because in this regime such men are no longer simple and intense but mixed – inclining instead to spirited men who are simpler and by nature more suited to war than to peace, honoring military stratagems and tricks, and spending all its time on war?"

"Yes."

"Men like that," I said, "will desire possessions, as in an oligarchy. They'll fiercely honor silver and gold and squirrel it away in treasuries of their own, making their homes into enclosures, private nests where they can spend lavishly on women and whomever else they may wish. They'll be sparing of their own money because they honor it and don't possess it openly, but squander other people's money because they desire. Such men will sneak their pleasures and run away from the law like boys from their father, having been educated not by persuasion but by force because they neglect the true Muse of philosophy and discussion and honor gymnastics higher than poetry."

"You're describing a completely mixed regime of good and evil," said Glaucon.

"It is mixed," I said. "But one feature stands out sharply because the spirited part prevails: love of honor and victory."

"Very sharply," he said.

"That's how timocracy comes about and what it would be like — drawn in outline, not in detail, because all we need is a sketch to see the most just and unjust man. It would be a hopeless task to describe every regime and disposition without leaving anything out."

"You're right," said Glaucon.

"Now how about the man who corresponds to it? How did he come about and what would he be like?"

"I think his love of victory would make him a lot like Glaucon here," said Adeimantus.

"Perhaps in that way," I said. "But it seems to me he'd have other traits that wouldn't correspond."

"Like what?"

"He must be rather self-willed and unmusical, though still fond of the Muses; fond also of listening, but in no way a speaker. Such a man will be harsh toward slaves and not disdain them like a well-educated person, but he'll be gentle toward free men, subservient to rulers, and fond of rule and honor. He'll expect to rule not from speech or anything like that, but from warlike deeds and the things of war, and he'll love gymnastics and hunting."

"That's the timocratic disposition, all right."

"And won't he despise money while young, but welcome it more and more as he grows older, because he partakes of the avaricious nature and no longer devotes himself purely to excellence after the best guardian has deserted him?"

"What guardian is that?" Adeimantus asked.

"The power of reasoned, educated speech," I said, "the sole preserver of excellence for its possessor all through life."

"Well put," he said.

"Such is the timocratic youth, similar to his city. He comes about something like this: sometimes he's the young son of a good father who lives in a poorly governed city and shuns offices, honors, lawsuits, and all such meddling, who purposely lets himself be bested so as not to have trouble — "

"But how does the timocratic man come about?"

"When he hears his mother first complaining that her husband isn't one of the rulers and that the other women slight her for this; then, when she sees that he has little interest in money or in brawling and fighting in courts or the assembly, that he's always occupied with his own thoughts and neither particularly honors nor dishonors her, she grows resentful and tells the boy that his father is unmanly and too easygoing, and harps on all the other things women love to say about men like that."

"Yes," said Adeimantus, " — nasty things, like themselves."

"And you know that seemingly well-intentioned servants also take the sons aside sometimes and talk to them secretly, and if the father doesn't prosecute someone who owes him money or has done him some other injustice, they tell the boy to punish all such men when he grows up and to be more of a man than his father. When he goes out he sees and hears more of the same: that men in the city who tend their own business are called foolish and held in low esteem while busybodies are honored and admired. When the young man has seen and heard all that, and also heard his father's words and seen his pursuits close up and against those of the others, he's pulled in both directions: his father waters and grows his soul's rational part, the others its desiring and spirited parts. And since he didn't have the nature of a bad man but kept bad company, he was pulled from both sides and came out in the middle as a compromise: he turned the rule of his soul over to its victory-loving, middle, spirited part and became a highminded lover of honor."

"It seems you've completely described the origin of the honor-loving, timocratic man."

"Then we have our second regime and man," I said...

[Plato now turns to an examination of the oligarchic man and the oligarchic city. With the slow triumph of the rule of the rich, the "rational and spirited parts" of humans are allowed only to calculate how to make money and how to admire it.]

"Next, it seems, we must examine democracy — how rule of the people comes about and what it's like — so we can recognize the democratic man's character and set him up for judgement along with the others."

"At least that will be consistent."

"Doesn't oligarchy somehow change to democracy because of insatiable greed for what it established as the good: the need to get as rich as possible?"

"How?"

"Since the rulers rule by possessing wealth, I imagine they're reluctant to prohibit self-indulgent young men from squandering and losing their property; they buy it up or lend them money against it in order to increase even more in wealth and honor. Doesn't this show that a city can't honor wealth and still have enough temperance in her citizens? It must neglect the one or the other."

"Very clearly."

"So when an oligarchy neglects temperance and encourages self-indulgence, it sometimes forces uncommon men into poverty."

"Absolutely."

"Who sit in the city armed with stings and weapons, I suppose, in debt, disfranchised, or both, filled with hate and plotting against the ones who took their property and against the others too, in love with revolution."

"True."

"But the moneymakers, stooped and pretending not to see them, sting any unresisting victim that remains and inject him with money, whose offspring, many times increased, they withdraw as 'interest' and swell the city's beggarly drone."

"They'll hardly shrink it."

"And when this evil bursts into flame they refuse to put it out by prohibiting people from disposing of their property or by stopping it with a different law."

"What law?"

"The second-best one for forcing citizens to be concerned for excellence: there'd be less shameless moneymaking in the city and fewer evils such as we've described if they decreed that most voluntary contracts be made at the contractor's own risk."

"Much less," he said.

"But as things are, the rulers put their subjects in the position we described. As for themselves and their families — don't they spoil their children and make them unfit for either physical or mental labor and too soft to hold up against pleasures, pains, and loafers, while they themselves neglect everything but making money and care no more about excellence than do the poor?"

"Indeed."

"In this state of affairs, whenever rulers and ruled come alongside and observe each other in the streets or at a communal gathering — at public spectacles or out on campaigns as fellow soldiers and sailors, or especially in the actual combat — there the rich can no longer despise the poor: when a tough, sun-baked pauper finds himself next to a shadow-bleached rich man hung with superfluous fat and sees him panting in helpless confusion, don't you suppose he'll think that such men are rich because of his own cowardice and say to his friends when they get by themselves, 'The gentlemen are ours — they're nothing'?"

"I know he will," he said.

"And just as a sick body needs only a tiny push from without to make it collapse, and sometimes falls into strife even without an external impulse, so a city in this condition falls sick and fights with itself on the slightest pretext: externally, when one faction calls in allies from an oligarchic city or the other from a democracy, and sometimes even without an external cause. And I think democracy arises when the poor conquer, kill off some of their enemies and exile the rest, and then give everyone an equal share in government and in offices, which they determine mostly by lot."[4]

"Yes, that's how democracy is instituted, whether in battle or because the others slip away out of terror."

"Next we must see how they live, Adeimantus, and what their regime is like. Obviously the man who resembles that will turn out to be the democratic one."

"Obviously."

"Aren't they above all free? The city is bursting with liberty and freedom of speech, and permits everyone to do whatever he wants."

"So they say, certainly."

"And where this is permitted, each citizen will arrange his own life privately, however he pleases."

"Clearly."

"So this regime, I think, will produce a multifarious variety of people. Like a variegated cloak splashed with every color, democracy is embellished with every personality and may appear the most gorgeous; and many, gaping like women and children at its colors, perhaps will judge it the most beautiful."

"They certainly will."

"And, you know, it's just the place to go shopping for a regime."

"How come?"

"Because it's permissive and has every kind, so that anyone who wants to construct a city, as we just did, ought to shop in a democracy as in a regime bazaar, select the style he likes, and found his city accordingly."

"At least I don't think he'd be embarrassed for models."

"And its total lack of compulsion," I said, "so that even if competent you don't have to rule, or be ruled if you don't feel like it, or fight when the rest are at war or keep peace when they do if you don't want to, nor yet, if some law prohibits you from holding office or being a juror — why, you can do both if it comes into your head — isn't that way of life divinely sweet in the short run?"

"In the short run, perhaps," he said.

"And isn't it exquisite how mild some of them are when convicted? Or haven't you noticed how in a democracy criminals condemned to death or to exile remain at large and haunt the streets like spirits, as though people would see right through them and not pay any attention?"

"Yes, many," he said.

"How about its indulgence and total lack of pettiness, its lofty contempt for the pretentious nonsense we discussed earlier when we were founding our city and said that no one, unless he has a transcendent nature, will ever become a good man without having played in and practiced beautiful pursuits from childhood — how magnificently they trample all that underfoot and don't care what pursuits a man has gone through to get into politics — they'll honor him if only he says he's a friend of the people."

"Oh yes, it's a noble regime."

"These," I said, "and other kindred traits characterize democracy, a delightful, anarchic, colorful regime, it seems, that dispenses 'equality' equally to equals and unequals alike."

"Yes, that's all common knowledge."

"Next observe what the corresponding man is like. As with the regime, let's first examine how he comes about. Isn't it something like this? — that stingy oligarch has a son and raises him, I suppose, in his own habits. Therefore, since the son too restrains by force those pleasures in himself that are not moneymaking but spendthrift, which are called unnecessary — "

"Obviously," he said.

" — Maybe we should first define necessary and unnecessary desires so we don't talk in the dark, Adeimantus."

"Yes, we should."

"Well, can't we justly call desires that we're unable to divert necessary, and also ones that benefit us if they're satisfied? Isn't it necessary for our nature to strive for both of these kinds?"

"Absolutely."

"So we'll be right in calling them necessary."

"Right."

"What about desires a person can get rid of by disciplining himself from childhood, some of which, moreover, do him no good, while others actually harm him? Can't we rightly call all those unnecessary?"

"Of course."

"Now let's give an example of each so we can grasp them as types. Wouldn't we class as necessary the desire for bread and other food and for eating to the point of well-being and health?"

"I think so."

"Isn't the desire for bread necessary in both ways — it's beneficial and without it we die?"

"Yes."

"And for other foods if it somehow promotes well-being?"

"Certainly."

"But desire that goes beyond that and craves entirely different kinds of food harms the body and impairs the soul for knowledge and temperance, though most people can get rid of it by training and restraining it from childhood. Shouldn't this desire be termed unnecessary?"

"Absolutely."

"Shall we call such desires spendthrift, the others productive because they're useful for production?"

"Yes."

"The same with desire for sex and other pleasures?"

"Of course."

"And didn't we just call one man a drone because he's full of those unnecessary pleasures and desires and is ruled by them, just as the man ruled by the necessary ones is oligarchic and stingy?"

"Certainly."

"Now let's go back and tell how the democratic man comes from the oligarchic. I think it's usually like this."

"How?"

"When a young man raised in the stingy, uneducated way we just described gets a taste of drone's honey[5] and associates with cunning, fiery creatures who can provide multifarious, colorful pleasures that go in every direction, there, you may assume, begins the change in him from an oligarchic to a democratic regime."

"An absolute necessity," he said.

"And just as the city changed when outside allies helped one of its parties, like with like, doesn't our youth change when a class of similar, related desires enters from outside to help his democratic faction?"

"Absolutely."

"If his father or some other relations now call up a counteralliance to aid his oligarchic faction by admonishing and berating him, then, I think, strife and counterstrife arise in him and plunge him into civil war with himself. Sometimes, I imagine, the democratic party retreated from the oligarchic, some desires were wiped out and others exiled, and a kind of shame was engendered in the young man's soul and brought him back to order."

"That does happen."

"But owing to his father's ignorance of childrearing, relatives of those exiled desires were again secretly nurtured and grew to be numerous and strong."

"There is that tendency."

"— And dragged him back to the same old companions, copulated furtively, and bred a new mob of desires. Finally, I suppose, they seized the citadel of the young man's soul, seeing it abandoned by learning, beautiful pursuits, and true argument, the best guardians and sentinels in the minds of god-beloved men. Boastful arguments and lying opinions charged up and occupied the territory in their place."

"Undoubtedly."

"So back he moves to the Lotus eaters[6] and lives with them openly, and should reinforcements arrive from his family for his soul's thrifty part, those boastful arguments slam his palace gates on them and refuse to let them pass or to receive ambassador arguments from older citizens; they subdue him in battle, denounce his shame as foolishness and push it out in shameful exile, define temperance as cowardice and banish it with foul abuse, and persuade him that moderation and reasonable spending are slavish peasant virtues which, with the help of a mob of useless desires, they drive beyond the borders of his soul."

"Absolutely."

"And when they've emptied their victim of all that and purified his soul for initiation into their Great Mysteries,[7] they bring back insolence, anarchy, extravagance, and shamelessness, crowned and radiant amidst their attendant choir, and adulate them with fair-sounding names, calling insolence 'good breeding,' anarchy 'freedom,' extravagance 'generosity,' and shamelessness 'courage.' Isn't that somehow the way, Adeimantus, that a young man raised among necessary desires changes into one who grants liberty and license to his useless unnecessary pleasures?"

"Yes," he said, " – you've made it rather vivid."

"After that, I think, he spends as much time money, and effort on his unnecessary pleasures as on his necessary ones. If he's lucky and not too frenzied – and also as he grows older his excessive agitation may pass – if he recalls some of the exiles and doesn't surrender all of himself to the invaders, then he grants a kind of 'equality' to his pleasures and submits the rule of himself to whichever one turns up – as if chosen by lot – until he's sated, then to another, and so on: he dishonors none but treats them all as equals. And he refuses to accept a true argument and allow it to pass into the fortress of his soul – if told that some pleasures come from good and beautiful desires, others from ones that are base, and that those should be pursued and honored, the others chastened and enslaved, he shakes his head and says they're all alike and should all be honored equally."

"That's just what a man in such a state would do."

"So," I said, "he lives from day to day, gratifying whatever desire happens to turn up — now drinking to the sound of flutes, now wasting away and drinking only water; now exercising, now loafing around indifferent to everything; and sometimes pretending to dabble in philosophy. Often he gets involved in politics and jumps up and says and does whatever comes into his head. If he admires some military men he drifts into that; if businessmen, into that. There's no order or necessity in his life, but he calls it blissful, free, and pleasant, and clings to it to the end."

"A perfect description of the man who grants equal rights to everything."

"I think this is the multifarious man of many personalities, colorful and gorgeous like his city. He contains countless models of dispositions and regimes, and many men and women might envy him his life."

"Yes, he's the one."

"Then isn't he the one to set up against democracy as the man properly called democratic?"

"Indeed," he said.

"Then we still have the most beautiful pair to describe, Adeimantus: tyranny and the tyrant."

"We surely do."

"Come, my friend, what is tyranny's character? That it comes from democracy seems pretty clear."

"Pretty clear."

"Much as democracy came from oligarchy?"

"How?"

"What it set up for itself as the good, the reason that oligarchy was instituted — wasn't that wealth?"

"Yes."

"And it was destroyed by its insatiable greed for that and by its neglect of everything else to make money."

"True."

"Doesn't democracy also define a good, for which it has an insatiable greed that also destroys it?"

"What?"

"Freedom," I said. "In a democracy you'll hear that freedom is its most beautiful possession, which makes it the only place for a naturally free man to live."

"One hears that slogan frequently."

"This is what I was just going to say: doesn't insatiable greed — for freedom — and neglect of everything else transform this regime too and prepare it to need a tyrant?" . . .

[Plato concludes his chapter with an examination of how the democratic configuration moves to tyranny. The "cloak of excessive, ill considered freedom" is exchanged "for the rags of the bitterest most oppressive bondage: thraldom to slaves."]

NOTES

1 Aristocracy in Greek means "the rule of the best," timocracy "rule by honor," oligarchy "the rule of the few," democracy "the rule of the people," and tyranny "dictatorship." These definitions have sometimes been added in the translation.

2 The period of gestation is compared to drawing a circle. Its beginning is conception. Birth or miscarriage occurs when the circle is completed and "joins its circumference." The circle is "close" for short-lived species because their gestation period is short, and vice versa. Note above that there are many bodies but only one soul.

3 Hesiod had divided men historically into races named after these four metals in *Works and Days*, pp. 109–201.

4 All officials at Athens were chosen by lot, except the generals, who were elected.

5 I.e. unnecessary, spendthrift pleasures. The "fiery creatures," below, are the stinging drones, filled with criminal desires.

6 The "drones" again. The lotus was a drug (perhaps opium) that produced a sensual stupor and made men forget the world around them. The reference is to Odysseus's visit to the Lotus eaters in *Odyssey* 9.82–104. The "citadel," "palace" or "fortress" of the soul is intelligence, the rational part.

7 A reference to the Eleusinian mystery religion, into which members were initiated by secret rites.

3

Of Personal Identity

DAVID HUME

There are some philosophers, who imagine we are every moment intimately conscious of what we call our *Self*; that we feel its existence and its continuance in existence; and are certain, beyond the evidence of a demonstration, both of its perfect identity and simplicity. The strongest sensation, the most violent passion, say they, instead of distracting us from this view, only fix it the more intensely, and make us consider their influence on *self* either by their pain or pleasure. To attempt a farther proof of this were to weaken its evidence; since no proof can be deriv'd from any fact, of which we are so intimately conscious; nor is there any thing, of which we can be certain, if we doubt of this.

Unluckily all these positive assertions are contrary to that very experience, which is pleaded for them, nor have we any idea of *self*, after the manner it is here explain'd. For from what impression cou'd this idea be deriv'd? This question 'tis impossible to answer without a manifest contradiction and absurdity; and yet 'tis a question, which must necessarily be answer'd, if we wou'd have the idea of self pass for clear and intelligible. It must be some one impression, that gives rise to every real idea. But self or person is not any one impression, but that to which our several impressions and ideas are suppos'd to have a reference. If any impression gives rise to the idea of self, that impression must continue invariably the same, thro' the whole course of our lives; since self is suppos'd to exist after that manner. But there is no impression constant and invariable. Pain and pleasure, grief and joy, passions and sensations succeed each other, and never all exist at the same time. It cannot, therefore, be from any of these impressions, or from any other, that the idea of self is deriv'd; and consequently there is no such idea.

Extract from Section VI of Book I of *A Treatise of Human Nature*, edited and with an Introduction by Ernest C. Mossner (New York: Viking Penguin, 1985); originally published 1739 and 1749.

But farther, what must become of all our particular perceptions upon this hypothesis? All these are different, and distinguishable, and separable from each other, and may be separately consider'd, and may exist separately, and have no need of any thing to support their existence. After what manner, therefore, do they belong to self; and how are they connected with it? For my part, when I enter most intimately into what I call *myself*, I always stumble on some particular perception or other, of heat or cold, light or shade, love or hatred, pain or pleasure. I never can catch *myself* at any time without a perception, and never can observe any thing but the perception. When my perceptions are remov'd for any time, as by sound-sleep; so long am I insensible of *myself*, and may truly be said not to exist. And were all my perceptions remov'd by death, and cou'd I neither think, nor feel, nor see, nor love, nor hate after the dissolution of my body, I shou'd be entirely annihilated, nor do I conceive what is farther requisite to make me a perfect non-entity. If any one upon serious and unprejudic'd reflection, thinks he has a different notion of *himself*, I must confess I can reason no longer with him. All I can allow him is, that he may be in the right as well as I, and that we are essentially different in this particular. He may perhaps, perceive something simple and continu'd, which he calls *himself*; tho' I am certain there is no such principle in me.

But setting aside some metaphysicians of this kind, I may venture to affirm of the rest of mankind, that they are nothing but a bundle or collection of different perceptions, which succeed each other with an inconceivable rapidity, and are in a perpetual flux and movement. Our eyes cannot turn in their sockets without varying our perceptions. Our thought is still more variable than our sight, and all our other senses and faculties contribute to this change; nor is there any single power of the soul, which remains unalterably the same, perhaps for one moment. The mind is a kind of theatre, where several perceptions successively make their appearance; pass, re-pass, glide away, and mingle in an infinite variety of postures and situations. There is properly no *simplicity* in it at one time, nor *identity* in different; whatever natural propension we may have to imagine that simplicity and identity. The comparison of the theatre must not mislead us. They are the successive perceptions only, that constitute the mind; nor have we the most distant notion of the place, where these scenes are represented, or of the materials, of which it is compos'd.

What then gives us so great a propension to ascribe an identity to these successive perceptions, and to suppose ourselves possest of an invariable and uninterrupted existence thro' the whole course of our lives? In order to answer this question, we must distinguish betwixt personal identity, as it regards our thought or imagination, and as it regards our passions or the concern we take in ourselves. The first is our present subject; and to explain it perfectly we must take the matter pretty deep, and account for that identity, which we attribute to plants and animals; there being a great analogy betwixt it, and the identity of a self or person.

We have a distinct idea of an object, that remains invariable and uninterrupted thro' a suppos'd variation of time; and this idea we call that of *identity* or *sameness*. We have also a distinct idea of several different objects existing in succession, and connected together by a close relation; and this to an accurate view affords as perfect a notion of *diversity*, as if there was no manner of relation among the objects. But tho' these two ideas of identity, and a succession of related objects be in themselves perfectly distinct, and even contrary, yet 'tis certain, that in our common way of thinking they are generally confounded with each other. . . .

[*Hume now argues that we often do not perceive the changes that apparently stable entities undergo because the change is either very small in proportion to the object, or else is so gradual as to be imperceptible. He then suggests that we may also think something the same, such as an oak, because we confuse "sympathy of parts to a common end" with identity. "Identity" is a matter of what we are used to.*]

What is natural and essential to any thing is, in a manner, expected; and what is expected makes less impression, and appears of less moment, than what is unusual and extraordinary. A considerable change of the former kind seems really less to the imagination, than the most trivial alteration of the latter; and by breaking less the continuity of the thought, has less influence in destroying the identity.

We now proceed to explain the nature of *personal identity*, which has become so great a question in philosophy, especially of late years in *England*, where all the abstruser sciences are study'd with a peculiar ardour and application. And here 'tis evident, the same method of reasoning must be continu'd, which has so successfully explain'd the identity of plants, and animals, and ships, and houses, and of all the compounded and changeable productions either of art or nature. The identity, which we ascribe to the mind of man, is only a fictitious one, and of a like kind with that which we ascribe to vegetables and animal bodies. It cannot, therefore, have a different origin, but must proceed from a like operation of the imagination upon like objects.

But lest this argument shou'd not convince the reader; tho' in my opinion perfectly decisive; let him weigh the following reasoning, which is still closer and more immediate. 'Tis evident, that the identity, which we attribute to the human mind, however perfect we may imagine it to be, is not able to run the several different perceptions into one, and make them lose their characters of distinction and difference, which are essential to them. 'Tis still true, that every distinct perception, which enters into the composition of the mind, is a distinct existence, and is different, and distinguishable, and separable from every other perception, either contemporary or successive. But, as, notwithstanding this distinction and separability, we suppose the whole train of perceptions to be united by identity, a question naturally arises concerning this relation of identity; whether it be something that really binds our several perceptions together, or only associates their ideas in the imagination. That is, in other words, whether in pronouncing concerning the identity of a person, we observe some real bond among his perceptions, or only feel one among the ideas we form of them. This question we might easily decide, if we wou'd recollect what has been already prov'd at large, that the understanding never observes any real connexion among objects, and that even the union of cause and effect, when strictly examin'd, resolves itself into a customary association of ideas. For from thence it evidently follows, that identity is nothing really belonging to these different perceptions, and uniting them together; but is merely a quality, which we attribute to them, because of the union of their ideas in the imagination, when we reflect upon them. Now the only qualities, which can give ideas an union in the imagination, are these three relations above-mentioned. These are the uniting principles in the ideal world, and without them every distinct object is separable by the mind, and may be separately consider'd, and appears not to have any more connexion with any other object, than if disjoin'd by the greatest difference and remoteness. 'Tis, therefore, on some of these three relations of resemblance, contiguity and causation, that identity depends; and as the very essence of these relations consists in their producing an easy transition of ideas; it follows, that our notions of personal identity, proceed entirely from the smooth and uninterrupted progress of the thought along a train of connected ideas, according to the principles above-explain'd.

The only question, therefore, which remains, is, by what relations this uninterrupted progress of our thought is produc'd, when we consider the successive existence of a mind or thinking person. And here 'tis evident we must confine ourselves to resemblance and causation, and must drop contiguity, which has little or no influence in the present case.

To begin with *resemblance*; suppose we cou'd see clearly into the breast of another, and observe that succession of perceptions, which constitutes his mind or thinking principle, and suppose that he always preserves the memory of a considerable part of past perceptions; 'tis evident that nothing cou'd more contribute to the bestowing a relation on this succession amidst all its variations. For what is memory, but a faculty, by which we raise up the images of past perceptions? And as an image necessarily resembles its object, must not the frequent placing of these resembling perceptions in the chain of thought, convey the imagination more easily from one link to another, and make the whole seem like the continuance of one object? In this particular, then, the memory not only discovers the identity, but also contributes to its production, by producing the relation of resemblance among the perceptions. The case is the same whether we consider ourselves or others.

As to *causation*; we may observe, that the true idea of the human mind, is to consider it as a system of different perceptions or different existences, which are link'd together by the relation of cause and effect, and mutually produce, destroy, influence, and modify each other. Our impressions give rise to their correspondent ideas; and these ideas in their turn produce other impressions. One thought chaces another, and draws after it a third, by which it is expell'd in its turn. In this respect, I cannot compare the soul more properly to any thing than to a republic or commonwealth, in which the several members are united by the reciprocal ties of government and subordination, and give rise to other persons, who propagate the same republic in the incessant changes of its parts. And as the same individual republic may not only change its members, but also its laws and constitutions; in like manner the same person may vary his character and disposition, as well as his impressions and ideas, without losing his identity...

4

On the Role of Symbolism in Political Thought

MICHAEL WALZER

"New philosophy calls all in doubt," wrote John Donne, and thereby suggested a theory of intellectual transformation. Because the universe was of a piece, all its parts harmoniously connected, the Copernican revolution seemed to call into question not only Ptolemaic astronomy but also a whole series of related ideas having to do with order, not in the heavens but on earth. With the sun lost and the cosmos "all in pieces," "Prince, Subject, Father, Son are things forgot."[1] Suddenly, the very categories of social and political thought seemed empty and useless. In a sense, Donne was right: later seventeenth-century writers like Hobbes and Locke were indeed compelled to work out anew the meanings of authority and subjection and to redefine political and familial obligation. But was he also right to suggest that this work was made necessary by the new philosophy?

For other writers, it was the new religious ideas which had destroyed the perceived coherence of the social world. Machiavellian "atheism" and Protestant voluntarism, thought Richard Hooker,[2] endangered the ancient, elaborate, and lawful structure of human life, giving rise to a kind of outlaw individualism which Donne also was to describe:

> For every man alone thinkes he hath got
> To be a Phoenix, and that there can bee
> None of that kinde, of which he is, but hee.
> (*The First Anniversary*)

Against the new man of his own time, Hooker reiterated the

This paper was read before the American Sociological Association, Chicago, August 30, 1965 and is reprinted by permission of the American Academy from *Political Science Quarterly*, LXXXI, 2 (June 1967), pp. 191–204.

traditional world view at great length and with enormous power, though not with any confidence that his heroic effort could stem the tide. For with the old religion, like the old cosmos some thirty years later, "all in pieces," the way seemed open for universal doubt and its frightening corollary, eagerness for novelty. Hooker sadly admitted the "aptness of men's minds to accept and believe" the new political doctrines.[3] But was he right to believe that these ideas followed directly from the collapse of ancient faith?

Certainly cosmology and theology were closely bound up with the politics of writers like Hooker and his predecessors. But they were bound up in a very complicated fashion. Scientific and religious thought on the one hand, and political thought on the other, were parts of a single system, but this was a system which even in the Middle Ages had frequently been subdivided, and whose various parts hung together in a way which implied no necessary logical connection. Hooker might write, for example, that it was "expedient" to understand the angelic hierarchy for the "more perfect direction" of mankind, but he did not mean that the best social order could be deduced from the structure of the angelic squadrons.[4] The connection between the two was not logical but analogical. The angels represented an order toward which human societies tended or might be directed. Similarly, the coherence of society was like the harmony of the planets; the rational, benevolent authority of the king and the father corresponded to that of God himself.[5] And so new ideas about God's government of the universe or about the orders of angels or the movements of planets did not necessarily call into question the social analogues of the old ideas. They merely made those analogues less persuasive than they had previously been; they undercut what for the moment may be called the symbolic reinforcement of such political ideas as harmony and hierarchy.

Consider another example: the traditional view of the state as a "body politic" was enormously strengthened and its effectiveness in political discourse greatly enhanced by the parallel view of the church as a divine body. Of course, the church was not thought to be *like* a body; it was thought to be a body, and Christ its actual head. But this mysterious identity could not be reproduced in politics, and so the unity and integration of the church, like that of the physical body itself, only symbolized a perfection which the state might approach or in terms of which it might convincingly be described. Protestant voluntarism, and the contracts and covenants to which it gave rise, weakened the force of this symbol but did not necessarily entail its rejection. For there might well be reasons, quite apart from religion, for continuing to use it; indeed, it would never have been used at all were there not such reasons.

Even Hooker's remarkable faith in human rationality and in the possible (or rather, the presumed) identity of positive and natural law did not logically depend upon his overarching vision of universal harmony. Imagine the heavens a chaos, the angels a band of skyborne scavengers and God himself their chieftain; it would still be possible for men to elaborate laws and organize communities. They would only require a set of images and models alternative to those they had just been so rudely denied. Barely twenty years after Hooker's death, Hugo Grotius argued, in effect, that such images and models were built into the human mind; man would be sociable even if there were no God. And the political theory based upon this insight was not so very different from Hooker's.

But if the rejection of the old political ideas did not follow logically from the new cosmology and theology, it followed nonetheless (and Grotius' revised traditionalism was only a temporary expedient). In order to understand why this was so, it is necessary to say something about the function of symbolism in political thought. For the old cosmology and theology provided not a set of propositions from which a political theory might be deduced, but rather a series of images and analogues out of which a theory might be fashioned. And once those images and analogues had been called into question, it was not impossible, but it was increasingly difficult, to think the old thoughts.

I

Politics is an art of unification; from many, it makes one. And symbolic activity is perhaps our most important means of bringing things together, both intellectually and emotionally, thus overcoming isolation and even individuality. "Whether verbal or iconographic," writes William York Tindall, "the religious symbol, and the political too, can unite man with man and man with something greater than he, society or God."[6] In a sense, the union of men can only be symbolized; it has no palpable shape or substance. The state is invisible; it must be personified before it can be seen, symbolized before it can be loved, imagined before it can be conceived. An image like the body politic, then, is not simply a decorative metaphor, applied by a writer who has already grasped the nature of political association and now wishes felicitously to convey his understanding. Rather, the image is prior to understanding or, at any rate, to theoretic understanding, as it is to articulation, and necessary to both.[7] When the state is imagined as a body politic, *then* a particular set of insights as to its nature are made available. The image does not so much reinforce existing political ideas (though it may later be used for that purpose) as underlie them. It provides an elementary sense of what the political community is like, of how physically distinct and solitary individuals are joined together. Or rather, in this case, it suggests that individuals are neither solitary nor distinct, but exist only as members of a body. Thus the image provides a starting point for political thinking, and so long as it is effective, no other starting point is possible. If symbolization does not by itself create unity (that is the function of political practice as well as of symbolic activity), it does create *units* — units of discourse which are fundamental to all thinking and doing, units of feeling around which emotions of loyalty and assurance can cluster.[8] But when the image becomes merely decorative, when it is "better left to the muses," as Milton wrote of the once vital symbol of the political father, then it has lost its unitive potency. It becomes a "conceit," still used by writers but no longer capable of engaging the intellect or the emotions.

Symbolic activity does more than provide the units of thought and feeling; it also connects those units with other structures: religious systems, planetary orders, physical bodies, man-made machines. It unifies the universe, provides politics with a series of references, links it closely with other realms of human experience. Thus the state, when seen as a body politic, is brought into close relation with the whole organic world. A single vocabulary describes animal bodies and political communities and makes the second appear almost as familiar, as natural, as well organized as the first. So kings become heads and soldiers arms; change is understood in terms of growth; disorder is described as a disease; decline as senility:

> States have degrees, as human bodies have,
> Spring, Summer, Autumn, Winter and the grave.[9]

If this is art, it is not merely artful; that is, it is not the creation of some crafty politician or hireling intellectual. It is rather a pervasive world-view, which cannot in its time be denied, though its parts can certainly be manipulated. Thus symbolic systems set (rough) limits to thought, supporting certain ideas, making others almost inconceivable.

Unit and reference symbols belong to a kind of public intellectual domain, like language itself. They cannot be ascribed to individual writers, though certain characteristic uses of them undoubtedly can be. The creative genius in political thought is not a man who invents new symbols, for that is an artificial and idiosyncratic business at best. He is rather a man like Hooker who elaborates old symbols with a new fullness and eloquence, or like Hobbes who explores the meaning of symbols just emerging in the thought and activity of his immediate predecessors and his contemporaries. But the symbols themselves seem to be a collective product, worked out by numberless men at many different levels of artistic and intellectual excellence over a long period of time.[10] Similarly, the decline of one or another set of symbols seems to be a gradual process involving the thought and activity of many men and imposing on all of them a certain strain and uneasiness. For this, in a minor way, is like losing a language, a loss which surely would be terrifying if we could properly imagine it.

If symbolization were a matter of logic only, "new philosophy" would quickly call all the old references into doubt. But images and analogues are matters of feeling as well; they shape our whole sensibility; they guarantee a sure place in a known world; they tell us more than we can easily repeat. And so their transformation encounters a resistance which logical demonstration does not or ought not to meet. This is a resistance especially strong in the realm of politics, for when all is said and done, the polity is more important (for most men) than the cosmos. Francis Bacon understood this well when he pleaded for scientific freedom and argued that the new discoveries would not affect political life:

> But surely there is a great distinction between matters of state and the arts; for the danger from new motion and from new light is not the same. In matters of state a change even for the better is distrusted, because it unsettles what is established; these things resting on authority, consent, fame and opinion, not on demonstration. But arts and sciences should be like mines, where the noise of new works and further advances is heard on every side. (*Novum Organum*, Bk. I, XC)

The contrast is a true one, though it is certainly over-exact. Nevertheless, changes in the way men conceived the cosmological reference-world did undermine conceptions of the polity. Whatever the intentions of the scientists, whatever the evasions of political writers, the new science had its subversive effects, for it called into question the very vocabulary with which fame and opinion work and the crucial symbols through which authority inspires consent.

At the same time, the evasions of publicists and philosophers like Bacon have their function in intellectual life; they slow down the process of transformation and make possible the development of alternative symbolic systems. If the earth was no longer at the center of the universe, if the planets did not move in perfect circles, then indeed it became easier to explore the parallel disharmonies of human life. And that exploration, carried on by dramatists, poets, preachers, and pamphleteers of all sorts, was simply the working out of images and analogues with which the new disharmony could be understood and even ordered – which is to say, theorized about.[11]

In a similiar fashion, the net impact of the new religion on political thought was significantly blunted, and time gained, by the genuine reluctance and (sometimes) the deliberate evasiveness of Puritan ministers. Most of them were undoubtedly sincere when they denied King James' dictum: no bishop, no king. They did not intend their defense of ministerial parity to be a defense of secular equality and they continued to employ the symbols of hierarchy in their occasional discussions of political and social life. Yet one can watch in their work the decay of those symbols, as a consequence of their reconstruction of the religious reference-world.[12] A direct attack upon the ancient authority of the king, however, did not occur until a new symbolic system had been fully developed. As Clifford Geertz has suggested with reference to the French Revolution, the principle of kingly authority "was destroyed long before the king: it was to the successor principle that he was, in fact, a ritual sacrifice."[13]

The process of destruction is very complex. What occurs is a slow erosion of the old symbols, a wasting away of the feelings they once evoked, an increasingly disjointed and inconsistent expression of political ideas, a nervous insistence upon the old units and references – all this accompanied, willy nilly, by a more and more arbitrary and extravagant manipulation of them – until finally the units cease to be accepted as intellectual givens and the references cease to be meaningful. But since men cannot orient themselves in the political world without unit and reference symbols, the systems are replaced even as they are called into question. And the more profound the questioning, the more adventurous is the search for replacements. The precise nature of the new symbols is by no means determined; it depends on the availability of new reference-worlds and on the artistic and intellectual success with which these are appropriated and the new references worked out.

Symbolic activity is thus not only a mediative, but also a creative process. It must be said again, however, that there is nothing *logically* necessary about this activity. The arbitrary reassertion of the old symbolism can offer intellectual and emotional sustenance for at least some time. Indeed, the official political theory during periods when symbolic forms are being questioned and replaced is likely to consist entirely of dogmatic reiterations and amazing elaborations of the old images and analogues. Experimental and innovative activity, which can often take place openly so far as the reference-worlds are concerned, takes place secretly, or at any rate beneath the public surface of intellectual life, so far as politics is concerned. And this is why systematic theorists like Hobbes claim such absolute originality; they have few if any public predecessors and may be quite unaware of their actual indebtedness.

But there is another reason for the extraordinary claims of the sixteenth- and seventeenth-century innovators which must briefly be considered. Whatever their hesitancy about politics, these men intended to call into doubt not merely the old images and analogues, but the very process of symbolization itself. This is how they viewed their attack upon the medieval system of "correspondences." They did not intend to replace that system with something more modern and so they had no eye to the tortuous processes by which they were enabled to do so — and by which, in some measure, the precise character of their own achievement was determined. Thus Martin Luther, announcing in one of his earliest pamphlets a recurrent Protestant theme, attacked the medieval writer Dionysius who had elaborated the symbols of hierarchy: "He plays with his allegories, but this does not make them realities . . . . This business of allegorizing is only for men who have nothing else to do."[14] Luther, presumably, had no time for such play. Similarly, Francis Bacon a hundred years later in his famous attack on intellectual Idols: "And though there be many things in nature which are singular and unmatched, yet [the human understanding] devises for them parallels and conjugates and relatives which do not exist."[15] In political thought, Hobbes waged a similar war against symbolism, defending a narrow conception of language and promising a science freed from the absurdities of metaphor. And yet Hobbes' thought, for all his careful definitions, is surely as symbolic as Hooker's. Despite the pretension of the opening chapters of *Leviathan*, the new science, like the old cosmology, did not provide a set of propositions, but a series of striking and suggestive images. So the body politic was replaced by the body-in-motion, harmonious integration by an anarchy of movement, authority by power, growth by construction. All this was profoundly important; it involved a major shift in sensibility and a fundamentally new political orientation. But it did not establish the absolute autonomy of politics, nor cut it off from all reference-worlds, nor terminate the human search for unity. Finally, it represented not linguistic clarification or scientific advance, but rather a transformation in symbolic expression. After all, what is Leviathan − "that mortal god" and perfect machine − but a new Idol?

II

The new symbols with which Hobbes worked have a history. In part this is the history of the modern science of physical and mechanical motion. But it remains a question why the world of motion became a reference-world for political thought, a new source of images and analogues. The answer lies not only in the success of the science, but also and more importantly in political and social transformations which literally set men moving and so made the new symbols appropriate. Indeed, the symbolism of clashing movement seems to have sources in political experience quite independent of its scientific sources. And the decline of the old symbols of harmony and hierarchy seems to have causes quite apart from and prior to the "new philosophy." Political images and analogues have, in fact, a double source and a double susceptibility: their rise and fall are related first to cultural change in the broadest sense, to new philosophies, theologies, and technologies; and secondly to political change, to new social problems and new methods of organizing and controlling human activity.

If this is true of the symbols as units of thought, it is equally true of them as units of feeling. Just as religious symbols need to be ritually acted out if they are fully to be felt, and just as the symbols change when the rituals do, so in the world of politics there is a continuous interaction between symbolic formation and enactment (and similarly, between theory and practice). The king will not long be acknowledged as head or father, for example, if he fails convincingly to act out the parts, or if other actions become more significant in communal life than the rituals of headship or fatherhood.[16]

What happened in sixteenth- and seventeenth-century England was that transformations in political experience directly paralleled transformations in the reference-worlds which had previously provided the terms of symbolic expression. The result was that new political practices were translated into new images and analogues, not quickly, but with relatively greater speed than anywhere else in Europe. And new theories were developed and systematically elaborated earlier there than anywhere else. In Italy, where changes in experience had preceded both "new philosophy" and religious reform, the new politics gave rise to no stable pattern of symbolic expression. Machiavelli had no Italian successors. But England's double transformation, complex and tortuous though it was, culminated in Hobbes' brilliant exploration of a symbolism which no later thinker — until the Romantics developed new images and analogues — could possibly avoid. For two hundred years there is hardly an English writer, hardly a coffee-house conversationalist, who is not a successor to Hobbes. Almost for that long, the new symbols seemed equally resonant with the religious and scientific worlds from which they had been drawn and with the political world to which they referred.

This double transformation probably cannot be precisely analyzed, but it can be illustrated — and with an example central to Hobbes' work. The body-in-motion upon which he builds his system is a symbolic figure. It represents the individual human being, but in a very special way: no longer is he a member of the body politic; no longer does he have a place in a hierarchical system of deference and authority; no longer do his movements conduce to universal harmony. Instead, the individual is alone, separated from his fellows, without a master or a secure social place; his movements, determined by no one but himself, clash with the movements of other, identical individuals; he acts out chaos. Now this extraordinary view of human activity was not invented by Hobbes. His creative achievement was to conceive the body-in-motion as the basis of a theoretical system and to offer his own map, so to speak, of the internal logic of the idea. But before the body-in-motion could be conceived, it had to be imagined, and before it could be imagined, it had to be experienced. The decay of the old cosmology and theology opened men to this experience, for if some sense it had always been available, the pervasive symbolism of harmony had made discordant motion difficult to accept. But at the same time, the experience itself had to become vastly more significant in communal life than it had been in previous ages before the collective imagination could center upon it. Center upon it that imagination surely did, as the sixteenth-century literature of vagabondage and ambition suggests. Here were the two sorts of motion — physical and social mobility, wandering and climbing — which Hobbes' single figure embodies. Indeed, the picaresque hero of the early novelists and the conquerors and usurpers of the dramatists would surely have called into question the old symbolic system even if its reference-worlds had never been transformed. Once again it must be said, however, that this would have been, as in any case it was, a very slow process. It was perfectly possible for a writer like Shakespeare to reaffirm the old cosmology and all its political references, while simultaneously exploring with extraordinary intensity the new man in motion. Harmony was his intention; disharmony his preoccupation: "Love cools, friendship falls off, brothers divide. In cities, mutinies; in countries, discord; in palaces, treason; and the bond cracked between son and father."[17]

And as in Shakespeare's plays, so in the political world itself the new man was first seen from within the loosening frame of the old symbolic system — that is, as a deviant and a threat. But the defense mounted against this threat — legislation, police, cruel punishments — was so massive as to call into question the harmony and naturalness of the order presumably being defended. Increasingly, political thinkers groped toward a vision of masterless men and sovereign power such as Hobbes was finally to describe.

But that vision could, literally, not be seen until the old symbols had been discarded. The villains of the dramas and the vagabonds, criminals, conspirators, and social climbers of the real world could be symbolically transformed into prototypes of man himself only with the assistance of new referential systems. Here social change and cultural innovation interconnect and the fallen Adam of Protestant theology and the moving bodies of the new physics both play their crucial part in the history of political ideas. They serve as universalizing images. They provide the basis for new theoretical analyses of the separated members and rebels against hierarchy who had previously been treated only as deviant figures. Donne's universalism — "*every man* . . . hath got to be a Phoenix" — has Protestant sources:

> For that first marriage was our funerall:
> One woman at one blow, that kill'd us all. . . .
> (*The First Anniversary*)

Hobbes, though he too drew upon the Calvinist tradition, owes far more to the scientists. His theory is presented to a large extent in the imagery of Galilean physics: "There be in animals two sorts of motions. . ." (*Leviathan*, Part I, VI). The availability of this imagery was of crucial importance not because it enabled him to express new ideas, but because it enabled him to treat theoretically a view of human behavior imminent, so to speak, in the minds of his predecessors, but concealed or distorted by an inadequate symbolic frame.

Once again, the comparison with Italy is useful. Sheldon Wolin has described how Machiavelli, who surely possessed a keen sense of men in motion, struggled to express himself through the old imagery: "The result was not a sharply defined picture, but a series of palimpsests."[18] This is true, but it does not go far enough. Machiavelli did not simply write his new ideas over the old symbols; rather his ideas were never fully developed because he had as yet no alternative symbols through which to work them out. Of course, he did possess new symbolic references – the images and analogues of warfare, for example, which he employed so brilliantly and which lie behind much that is original in his writings – but these did not include systems so complete, so alluring, so available for imitation, as the new theology and science of Hobbes' time. And this perhaps explains why Machiavelli's view of human nature was never systematically worked out. He himself seems uncertain whether he is talking about some or all men; his enemies all too easily pretended that he had justified occasional and desperate villainy rather than provided a serious psychology. It was Hobbes who first turned the *Prince* into *everyman* and explored the Machiavellianism of everyday life, and he was able to do so only with the help of a new symbolism. "Each individual appeared as an atom," writes Wolin, "somewhat different in composition, but having the same general appearance, hurtling across a flat social plane."[19]

III

The new political theories of the seventeenth century thus have two sources: cultural innovation and social change. But the ideas themselves are not in any direct sense a reflection of or even a response to innovation or change. Complex processes of symbolic transformation mediate the distance between cultural or social upheavals on the one hand and theoretical developments on the other – or, which is very nearly the same thing, between old and new theories. When new references-systems and new experiences coincide, as in seventeenth-century England, the mediative process may be shorter than in other cases and new theoretical work more quickly produced. But in any case that intervening moment of painful doubt and intellectual disarray — and of clandestine creativity — is enormously significant. It helps explain why theorists like Hobbes cannot carry on any meaningful debate with their predecessors. Their ideas have not been developed through any simple process of intellectual disagreement or rational response to changing conditions. Rather, they begin work with new unit and reference symbols; they see a different world; their reason has new tools at its disposal. Finally, they stand on the other side of a chasm like that which opens between men who no longer speak the same language.

Some 25 years after writing this, the word "chasm" makes me wince — a youthful anticipation of post-modernist hyperbole. What I was describing was a cultural and political *break*. It is wrong, however, to suggest that people cannot talk to one another across such a break. The talk requires new and difficult mediations (the work of historians, for example), and there are sure to be misunderstandings. But even if the meanings carried by the old symbols cannot be expressed by the new ones, they can, with effort, be understood by the people using the new ones. Hobbes himself understood them well enough to oppose them.

NOTES

1 John Donne, *The First Anniversary*. For some of the effects of the new science upon English thought and culture, see Marjorie Hope Nicolson, *The Breaking of the Circle* (New York, 1962).

2 Richard Hooker, *Of the Laws of the Ecclesiastical Polity*, Bk. V, I-III.

3 Hooker, *Ecclesiastical Polity*, Bk. I, I, 1.

4 Hooker, *Ecclesiastical Polity*, Bk. I, XVI, 4.

5 On the correspondences, see E.M.W. Tillyard, *The Elizabethan World Picture* (New York, 1944).

6 W. Y. Tindall, *The Literary Symbol* (Bloomington, 1955), p. 16.

7 See Susanne K. Langer, *Philospohy in a New Key* (Cambridge, Mass., 1957), p. 41.

8 Ernst Cassirer distinguishes mythical symbols which represent, he argues, an "objectification of feeling" from linguistic symbols which represent an "objectification of sense-impression." This is part of a more general distinction between mythical and rational thought which he defends in *The Myth of the State* (New York, 1955), p. 55. But it is the very essence of the symbol, as the term is used in this essay, that it simultaneously provokes thought and evokes feeling. Words alone may not do this, but words which have become part of the special vocabulary of politics — king, subject, citizen, duty, rights,

father of his country, checks and balances, and so on — obviously do.

9 Fulke Greville, *Treatie of Warres*. This search for references has, perhaps, a special cause in the history of political thought. Since antiquity, politics has been regarded as a realm about which only probabilistic statements could be made. So thinkers have been driven to escape this realm, to find some sort of certainty in religion, cosmology, science, and so on, and carry it back into politics. But this is not necessarily a self-conscious escape. It may be that certain sorts of statements about the state — vivid descriptions of or bold assertions about its essential qualities — such as human beings are prone to make, simply cannot be made, cannot even be thought, except metaphorically.

10 The argument here is based in part on Clifford Geertz's brilliant essay "Ideology as a Cultural System" in David Apter (ed.), *Ideology and Discontent* (Glencoe, 1964), p. 60.

11 It should be said that in any complex civilization there exist what might be called symbols-in-reserve, or symbols alternative to the dominant ones, to which men freed for one or another reason from the dominant ones can turn.

12 M. Walzer, *The Revolution of the Saints* (Cambridge, Mass., 1965), chap. V.

13 Geertz, "Ideology," p. 75, n. 43.

14 Luther, "The Pagan Servitude of the Church," in John Dillenberger (ed.), *Martin Luther, Selections from His Writings* (Garden City, N.Y., 1961), p. 343.

15 Bacon, *Novum Organum*, Bk. I, XLV.

16 See Geertz's discussion of Javanese kingship in "Ideology," pp. 66–7.

17 William Shakespeare, *King Lear*, I, ii.

18 Sheldon Wolin, *Politics and Vision* (Boston, 1960), p. 614.

19 Wolin, *Politics and Vision*, p. 282.

PART II
The (Non-)Individual Order

5

The Procedural Republic and the Unencumbered Self

MICHAEL J. SANDEL

Political philosophy seems often to reside at a distance from the world. Principles are one thing, politics another, and even our best efforts to "live up" to our ideals typically founder on the gap between theory and practice.[1]

But if political philosophy is unrealizable in one sense, it is unavoidable in another. This is the sense in which philosophy inhabits the world from the start; our practices and institutions are embodiments of theory. To engage in a political practice is already to stand in relation to theory.[2] For all our uncertainties about ultimate questions of political philosophy — of justice and value and the nature of the good life — the one thing we know is that we live *some* answer all the time.

In this essay I will try to explore the answer we live now, in contemporary America. What is the political philosophy implicit in our practices and institutions? How does it stand, as philosophy? And how do tensions in the philosophy find expression in our present political condition?

It may be objected that it is a mistake to look for a single philosophy, that we live no "answer," only answers. But a plurality of answers is itself a kind of answer. And the political theory that affirms this plurality is the theory I propose to explore.

THE RIGHT AND THE GOOD

We might begin by considering a certain moral and political vision. It is a liberal vision, and like most liberal visions gives pride of place to justice, fairness, and individual rights. Its core thesis is this: a just society seeks not to promote any particular ends, but enables

Reprinted by permission of SAGE Publications from *Political Theory* 12, 1 (February, 1984), pp. 81–96.

its citizens to pursue their own ends, consistent with a similar liberty for all; it therefore must govern by principles that do not presuppose any particular conception of the good. What justifies these regulative principles above all is not that they maximize the general welfare, or cultivate virtue, or otherwise promote the good, but rather that they conform to the concept of *right*, a moral category given prior to the good, and independent of it.

This liberalism says, in other words, that what makes the just society just is not the *telos* or purpose or end at which it aims, but precisely its refusal to choose in advance among competing purposes and ends. In its constitution and its laws, the just society seeks to provide a framework within which its citizens can pursue their own values and ends, consistent with a similar liberty for others.

The ideal I've described might be summed up in the claim that the right is prior to the good, and in two senses: the priority of the right means first, that individual rights cannot be sacrificed for the sake of the general good (in this it opposes utilitarianism), and second, that the principles of justice that specify these rights cannot be premised on any particular vision of the good life. (In this it opposes teleological conceptions in general.)

This is the liberalism of much contemporary moral and political philosophy, most fully elaborated by Rawls, and indebted to Kant for its philosophical foundations.[3] But I am concerned here less with the lineage of this vision than with what seem to me three striking facts about it.

First, it has a deep and powerful philosophical appeal. Second, despite its philosophical force, the claim for the priority of the right over the good ultimately fails. And third, despite its philosophical failure, this liberal vision is the one by which we live. For us in late twentieth-century America, it is our vision, the theory most thoroughly embodied in the practices and institutions most most central to our public life. And seeing how it goes wrong as philosophy may help us to diagnose our present political condition. So first, its philosophical power; second, its philosophical failure; and third, however briefly, its uneasy embodiment in the world.

But before taking up these three claims, it is worth pointing out a central theme that connects them. And that is a certain conception of the person, of what it is to be a moral agent. Like all political theories, the liberal theory I have described is something more than a set of regulative principles. It is also a view about the way the world is, and the way we move within it. At the heart of this ethic lies a vision of the person that both inspires and undoes it. As I will try to argue now, what make this ethic so compelling, but also, finally, vulnerable, are the promise and the failure of the unencumbered self.

The liberal ethic asserts the priority of right, and seeks principles of justice that do not presuppose any particular conception of the good.[4] This is what Kant means by the surpremacy of the moral law, and what Rawls means when he writes that "justice is the first virtue of social institutions."[5] Justice is more than just another value. It provides the framework that *regulates* the play of competing values and ends; it must therefore have a sanction independent of those ends. But it is not obvious where such a sanction could be found.

Theories of justice, and for that matter, ethics, have typically founded their claims on one or another conception of human purposes and ends. Thus Aristotle said the measure of a *polis* is the good at which it aims, and even J. S. Mill, who in the nineteenth century called "justice the chief part, and incomparably the most binding part of all morality," made justice an instrument of utilitarian ends.[6]

This is the solution Kant's ethic rejects. Different persons typically have different desires and ends, and so any principle derived from them can only be contingent. But the moral law needs a *categorical* foundation, not a contingent one. Even so universal a desire as happiness will not do. People still differ in what happiness consists of, and to install any particular conception as regulative would impose on some the conceptions of others, and so deny at least to some the freedom to choose their *own* conceptions. In any case, to govern ourselves in conformity with desires and inclinations, given as they are by nature or circumstance, is not really to be *self-governing* at all. It is rather a refusal of freedom, a capitulation to determinations given outside us.

According to Kant, the right is "derived entirely from the concept of freedom in the external relationships of human beings, and has nothing to do with the end which all men have by nature [i.e., the aim of achieving happiness] or with the recognized means of attaining this end."[7] As such, it must have a basis prior to all empirical ends. Only when I am governed by principles that do not presuppose any particular ends am I free to pursue my own ends consistent with a similar freedom for all.

But this still leaves the question of what the basis of the right could possibly be. If it must be a basis prior to all purposes and ends, unconditioned even by what Kant calls "the special circumstances of human nautre,"[8] where could such a basis conceivably by found? Given the stringent demands of the Kantian ethic, the moral law would seem almost to require a foundation in nothing, for any empirical precondition would undermine its priority. "Duty!" asks Kant at his most lyrical, "What origin is there worthy of thee, and where is to be found the root of thy noble descent which proudly rejects all kinship with the inlinations?"[9]

His answer is that the basis of the moral law is to be found in the *subject*, not the object of practical reason, a subject capable of an autonomous will. No empirical end, but rather "a subject of ends, namely a rational being himself, must be made the ground for all maxims of action."[10] Nothing other than what Kant calls "the subject of all possible ends himself" can give rise to the right, for only this subject is also the subject of an autonomous will. Only this subject could be that "something which elevates man above himself as part of the world of sense" and enables him to participate in an ideal, unconditioned realm wholly independent of our social and psychological inclinations. And only this thoroughgoing independence can afford us the detachment we need if we are ever freely to choose for ourselves, unconditioned by the vagaries of circumstance.[11]

Who or what exactly *is* this subject? It is, in a certain sense *us*. The moral law, after all, is a law we give *ourselves*; we don't *find* it, we *will* it. That is how it (and we) escape the reign of nature and circumstance and merely empirical ends. But what is important to see is that the "we" who do the willing are not "we" *qua* particular persons, you and me, each for ourselves — the moral law is not up to us as individuals — but "we" *qua* participants in what Kant calls "pure practical reason," "we" *qua* participants in a transcendental subject.

Now what is to guarantee that I *am* a subject of this kind, capable of exercising pure practical reason? Well, strictly speaking, there *is* no guarantee; the transcendental subject is only a possibility. But it is a possibility I must *presuppose* if I am to think of myself as a free moral agent. Were I wholly an empirical being, I would not be capable of freedom, for every exercise of will would be conditioned by the desire for some object. All choice would be heteronomous choice, governed by the pursuit of some end. My will could never be a first cause, only the effect of some prior cause, the instrument of one or another impulse or inclination. "When we think of ourselves as free," writes Kant, "we transfer ourselves into the intelligible world as members and recognize the autonomy of the will."[12] And so the notion of a subject prior to and independent of experience, such as the Kantian ethic requires, appears not only possible but indispensable, a necessary presupposition of the possibility of freedom.

How does all of this come back to politics? As the subject is prior to its ends, so the right is prior to the good. Society is best arranged when it is governed by principles that do not presuppose any particular conception of the good, for any other arrangement would fail to respect persons as being capable of choice; it would treat them as objects rather than subjects, as means rather than ends in themselves.

We can see in this way how Kant's notion of the subject is bound up with the claim for the priority of right. But for those in the Anglo-American tradition, the transcendental subject will seem a strange foundation for a familiar ethic. Surely, one may think, we can take rights seriously and affirm the primacy of justice without embracing the *Critique of Pure Reason*. This, in any case, is the project of Rawls.

He wants to save the priority of right from the obscurity of the transcendental subject. Kant's idealist metaphysic, for all its moral and political advantage, cedes too much to the transcendent, and wins for justice its primacy only by denying it its human situation. "To develop a viable Kantian conception of justice," Rawls writes, "the force and content of Kant's doctrine must be detached from its background in transcendental idealism" and recast within the "canons of a reasonable empiricism."[13] And so Rawls's project is to preserve Kant's moral and political teaching by replacing Germanic obscurities with a domesticated metaphysic more congenial to the Anglo-American temper. This is the role of the original position.

FROM TRANSCENDENTAL SUBJECT TO UNENCUMBERED SELF

The original position tries to provide what Kant's transcendental argument cannot − a foundation for the right that is prior to the good, but still situated in the world. Sparing all but essentials, the original position works like this: it invites us to imagine the principles we would choose to govern our society if we were to choose them in advance, before we knew the particular persons we would be − whether rich or poor, strong or weak, lucky or unlucky − before we knew even our interests or aims or conceptions of the good.

These principles — the ones we would choose in that imaginary situation — are the principles of justice. What is more, if it works, they are principles that do not presuppose any particular ends.

What they *do* presuppose is a certain picture of the person, of the way we must be if we are beings of whom justice is the first virtue. This is the picture of the unencumbered self, a self understood as prior to and independent of purposes and ends.

Now the unencumbered self describes first of all the way we stand toward the things we have, or want, or seek. It means there is always a distinction between the values I *have* and the person I *am*. To identify any characteristics as *my* aims, ambitions, desires, and so on, is always to imply some subject "me" standing behind them, at a certain distance, and the shape of this "me" must be given prior to any of the aims or attributes I bear. One consequences of this distance is to put the self *itself* beyond the reach of its experience, to secure its identity once and for all. Or to put the point another way, it rules out the possibility of what we might call *constitutive* ends. No role or commitment could define me so completely that I could not understand myself without it. No project could be so essential that turning away from it would call into question the person I am.

For the unencumbered self, what matters above all, what is most essential to our personhood, are not the ends we choose but our capacity to choose them. The original position sums up this central claim about us. "It is not our aims that primarily reveal our nature," writes Rawls, "but rather the principles that we would acknowledge to govern the background conditions under which these aims are to be formed... We should therefore reverse the relation between the right and the good proposed by teleological doctrines and view the right as prior."[14]

Only if the self is prior to its ends can the right be prior to the good. Only if my identity is never tied to the aims and interests I may have at any moment can I think of myself as a free and indenpendent agent, capable of choice.

This notion of independence carries consequences for the kind of community of which we are capable. Understood as unencumbered selves, we are of course free to join in voluntary association with others, and so are capable of community in the cooperative sense. What is denied to the unencumbered self is the possibility of membership in any community bound by moral ties antecedent to choice; he cannot belong to any community where the self *itself* could be at stake. Such a community — call it constitutive as against merely cooperative — would engage the identity as well as the interests of the participants, and so implicate its members in a citizenship more thoroughgoing than the unencumbered self can know.

For justice to be primary, then, we must be creatures of a certain kind, related to human circumstance in a certain way. We must stand to our circumstance always at a certain distance, whether as transcendental subject in the case of Kant, or as unencumbered selves in the case of Rawls. Only in this way can we view ourselves as subjects as well as objects of experience, as agents and not just instruments of the purposes we pursue.

The unencumbered self and the ethic it inspires, taken together, hold out a liberating vision. Freed from the dictates of nature and the sanction of social roles, the human subject is installed as sovereign, cast as the author of the only moral meanings there are. As participants in pure practical reason, or as parties to the original position, we are free to construct principles of justice unconstrained by an order of value antecedently given. And as actual, individual selves, we are free to construct principles of justice unconstrained by an order of value antecedently given. And as actual, individual selves, we are free to choose our purposes and ends unbound by such an order, or by custom or tradition or inherited status. So long as they are not unjust, our conceptions of the good carry weight, whatever they are, simply in virtue of our having chosen them. We are, in Rawls' words, "self-originating sources of valid claims."[5]

This is an exhilarating promise, and the liberalism it animates is perhaps the fullest expression of the Enlightenment's quest for the self-defining subject. But is it true? Can we make sense of our moral and political life by the light of the self-image it requires? I do not think we can, and I will try to show why not by arguing first within the liberal project, then beyond it.

JUSTICE AND COMMUNITY

We have focused so far on the foundations of the liberal vision, on the way it derives the principles it defends. Let us turn briefly now to the substance of those principles, using Rawls as our example. Sparing all but essentials once again, Rawls's two principles of justice are these: first, equal basic liberties for all, and second, only those social and economic inequalities that benefit the least-advantaged members of society (the difference principle).

In arguing for these principles, Rawls argues against two familiar alternatives — utilitarianism and libertarianism. He argues against utilitarianism that it fails to take seriously the distinction between persons. In seeking to maximize the general welfare, the utilitarian treats society as whole as if it were a single person; it conflates our many, diverse desires into a single system of desires, and tries to maximize. It is indifferent to the distribution of satisfactions among persons, except insofar as this may affect the overall sum. But this fails to respect our plurality and distinctness. It uses some as means to the happiness of all, and so fails to respect each as an end in himself. While utilitarians may sometimes defend individual rights, their defense must rest on the calculation that respecting those rights will serve utility in the long run. But this calculation is contingent and uncertain. So long as utility is what Mill said it is, "the ultimate appeal on all ethical questions,"[16] individual rights can never be secure. To avoid the danger that their life prospects might one day be sacrificed for the greater good of others, the parties to the original position therefore insist on certain basic liberties for all, and make those liberties prior.

If utilitarians fail to take seriously the distinctness of persons, libertarians go wrong by failing to acknowledge the arbitrariness of fortune. They define as just whatever distribution results from an efficient market economy, and oppose all redistribution on the grounds that people are entitled to whatever they get, so long as they do not cheat or steal or otherwise violate someone's rights in getting it. Rawls opposes this principle on the ground that the distribution of talents and assets and even efforts by which some get more and others get less is arbitrary from a moral point of view, a matter of good luck. To distribute the good things in life on the basis of these differences is not to do justice, but simply to carry over into human arrangements the arbitrariness of social and natural contingency. We deserve, as individuals, neither the talents our good fortune may have brought, nor the benefits that flow from them. We should therefore regard these talents as common assets, and regard one another as common beneficiaries of the rewards they bring. "Those who have been favored by nature, whoever they are, may gain from their good fortune only on terms that improve the situation of those who have lost out... In justice as fairness, men agree to share one another's fate.[17]

This is the reasoning that leads to the difference principle. Notice how it reveals, in yet another guise, the logic of the unencumbered self. I cannot be said to deserve the benefits that flow from, say, my fine physique and good looks, because they are only accidental, not essential facts about me. They describe attributes I *have*, not the person I *am*, and so cannot give rise to a claim of desert. Being an unencumbered self, this is true of *everything* about me. And so I cannot, as an individual, deserve anything at all.

However jarring to our ordinary understandings this argument may be, the picture so far remains intact; the priority of right, the denial of desert, and the unencumbered self all hang impressively together.

But the difference principle requires more, and it is here that the argument comes undone. The difference principle begins with the thought, congenial to the unencumbered self, that the assets I have are only accidentally mine. But it ends by assuming that these assets are therefore *common* assets and that society has a prior claim on the fruits of their exercise. But this assumption is without warrant. Simply because I, as an individual, do not have a privileged claim on the assets accidentally residing "here," it does not follow that everyone in the world collectively does. For there is no reason to think that their location in society's province or, for that matter, within the province of humankind, is any *less* arbitrary from a moral point of view. And if their arbitrariness within *me* makes them ineligible to serve *my* ends, there seems no obvious reason why their arbitrariness within any particular society should not make them ineligible to serve that society's ends as well.

To put the point another way, the difference principle, like utilitarianism, is a principle of sharing. As such, if must presuppose some prior moral tie among those whose assets it would deploy and whose efforts it would enlist in a common endeavor. Otherwise, it is simply a formula for using some as means to others' ends, a formula this liberalism is committed to reject.

But on the cooperative vision of community alone, it is unclear what the moral basis for this sharing could be. Short of the constitutive conception, deploying an individual's assets for the sake of the common good would seem an offense against the "plurality and distinctness" of individuals this liberalism seeks above all to secure.

If those whose fate I am required to share really are, morally speaking, *others*, rather than fellow participants in a way of life with which my identity is bound, the difference principle falls prey to the same objections as utilitarianism. Its claim on me is not the claim of a constitutive community whose attachments I acknowledge, but rather the claim of a concatenated collectivity whose entanglements I confront.

What the difference principle requires, but cannot provide, is some way of identifying those *among* whom the assets I bear are properly regarded as common, some way of seeing ourselves as mutually indebted and morally engaged to begin with. But as we have seen, the constitutive aims and attachments that would save and situate the difference principle are precisely the ones denied to the liberal self; the moral encumbrances and antecedent obligations they imply would undercut the priority of right.

What, then, of those encumbrances? The point so far is that we cannot be persons for whom justice is primary, and also be persons for whom the difference principle is a principle of justice. But which must give way? Can we view ourselves as independent selves, independent in the sense that our identity is never tied to our aims and attachments?

I do not think we can, at least not without cost to those loyalties and convictions whose moral force consists partly in the fact that living by them is inseparable from understanding ourselves as the particular persons we are — as members of this family or community or nation or people, as bearers of that history, as citizens of this republic. Allegiances such as these are more than values I happen to have, and to hold, at a certain distance. They go beyond the obligations I voluntarily incur and the "natural duties" I owe to human beings as such. They allow that to some I owe more than justice requires or even permits, not by reason of agreements I have made but instead in virtue of those more or less enduring attachments and commitments that, taken together, partly define the person I am.

To imagine a person incapable of constitutive attachments such as these is not to conceive an ideally free and rational agent, but to imagine a person wholly without character, without moral depth. For to have character is to know that I move in a history I neither summon nor command, which carries consequences nonetheless for my choices and conduct. It draws me closer to some and more distant from others; it makes some aims more appropriate, others less so. As a self-interpreting being, I am able to reflect on my history and in this sense to distance myself from it, but the distance is always precarious and provisional, the point of reflection never finally secured outside the history itself. But the liberal ethic puts the self beyond the reach of its experience, beyond deliberation and reflection. Denied the expansive self-understandings that could shape a common life, the liberal self is left to lurch between detachment on the one hand, and entanglement on the other. Such is the fate of the unencumbered self, and its liberating promise.

But before my case can be complete, I need to consider one powerful reply. While it comes from a liberal direction, its spirit is more practical than philosophical. It says, in short, that I am asking too much. It is one thing to seek constitutive attachments in our private lives; among families and friends, and certain tightly knit groups, there may be found a common good that makes justice and rights less pressing. But with public life − at least today, and probably always − it is different. So long as the nation-state is the primary form of political association, talk of constitutive community too easily suggests a darker politics rather than a brighter one; amid echoes of the moral majority, the priority of right, for all its philosophical faults, still seems the safer hope.

This is a challenging rejoinder, and no account of political community in the twentieth century can fail to take it seriously. It is challenging not least because it calls into question the status of political philosophy and its relation to the world. For if my argument is correct, if the liberal vision we have considered is not morally self-sufficient but parasitic on a notion of community it officially rejects, then we should expect to find that the political practice that embodies this vision is not *practically* self-sufficient either − that it must draw on a sense of community it cannot supply and may even undermine. But is that so far from the circumstance we face today? Could it be that through the original position darkly, on the far side of the veil of ignorance, we may glimpse an intimation of our predicament, a refracted vision of ourselves?

How does the liberal vision − and its failure − help us make sense of our public life and its predicament? Consider, to begin, the following paradox in the citizen's relation to the modern welfare state. In many ways, we in the 1980s stand near the completion of a liberal project that has run its course from the New Deal through the Great Society and into the present. But notwithstanding the extension of the franchise and the expansion on individual rights and entitlements in recent decades, there is a widespread sense that, individually and collectively, our control over the forces that govern our lives is receding rather than increasing. This sense is deepened by what appear simultaneously as the power and the powerlessness of the nation-state. On the one hand, increasing numbers of citizens view the state as an overly intrusive presence, more likely to frustrate their purposes than advance them. And yet, despite its unprecedented role in the economy and society, the modern state seems itself disempowered, unable effectively to control the domestic economy, to respond to persisting social ills, or to work America's will in the world.

This is a paradox that has fed the appeals of recent politicians (including Carter and Reagan), even as it has frustrated their attempts to govern. To sort it out, we need to identify the public philosophy implicit in our political practice, and to reconstruct its arrival. We need to trace the advent of the procedural republic, by which I mean a public life animated by the liberal vision and self-image we've considered.

The story of the procedural republic goes back in some ways to the founding of the republic, but its central drama begins to unfold around the turn of the century. As national markets and large-scale enterprise displaced a decentralized economy, the decentralized political forms of the early republic became outmoded as well. If democracy was to survive, the concentration of economic power would have to be met by a similar concentration of political power. But the Progressives understood, or some of them did, that the success of democracy requried more than the centralization of government; it also required the nationalization of politics. The primary form of political community had to be a recast on a national scale. For Herbert Croly, writing in 1909, the "nationalizing of American political, economic, and social life" was "an essentially formative and enlightening political transformation." We would become more of a democracy only as we became "more of a nation ... in ideas, in institutions, and in spirit."[18]

This nationalizing project would be consummated in the New Deal, but for the democratic tradition in America, the embrace of the nation was a decisive departure. From Jefferson to the populists, the party of democracy in American political debate had been, roughly speaking, the party of the provinces, of decentralized power, of small-town and small-scale America. And against them had stood the party of the nation — first Federalists, then Whigs, then the Republicans of Lincoln — a party that spoke for the consolidation of the union. It was thus the historic achievement of the New Deal to unite, in a single party and political program, what Samuel Beer has called "liberalism and the national idea."[19]

What matters for our purpose is that, in the twentieth century, liberalism made its peace with concentrated power. But it was understood at the start that the terms of this peace required a strong sense of national community, morally and politically to underwrite the extended involvements of a modern industrial order. If a virtuous republic of small-scale, democratic communities was no longer a possibility, a national republic seemed democracy's next best hope. This was still, in principle at least, a politics of the common good. It looked to the nation, not as a neutral framework for the play of competing interests, but rather as a formative community, concerned to shape a common life suited to the scale of modern social and economic forms.

But this project failed. By the mid- or late twentieth century, the national republic had run its course. Except for extraordinary moments, such as war, the nation proved too vast a scale across which to cultivate the shared self-understandings necessary to community in the formative, or constitutive sense. And so the gradual shift, in our practices and institutions, from a public philosophy of common purposes to one of fair procedures, from a politics of good to a politics of right, from the national republic to the procedural republic.

OUR PRESENT PREDICAMENT

A full account of this transition would take a detailed look at the changing shape of political institutions, constitutional interpretation, and the terms of political discourse in the broadest sense. But I suspect we would find in the *practice* of the procedural republic two broad tendencies foreshadowed by its philosophy: first, a tendency to crowd out democratic possibilities; second, a tendency to undercut the kind of community on which it nontheless depends.

Where liberty in the early republic was understood as a function of democratic institutions and dispersed power,[20] liberty in the procedural republic is defined in opposition to democracy, as an individual's guarantee against what the majority might will. I am free insofar as I am the bearer of rights, where rights are trumps.[21] Unlike the liberty of the early republic, the modern verison permits – in fact even requires – concentrated power. This has to do with the universalizing logic of rights. Insofar as I have a right, whether to free speech or a minimum income, its provision cannot be left to the vagaries of local preferences but must be assured at the most comprehensive level of political association. It cannot be one thing in New York and another in Alabama. As rights and entitlements expand, politics is therefore displaced from smaller forms of association and relocated at the most universal form – in our case, the nation. And even as politics flows to the nation, power shifts away from democratic institutions (such as legislatures and political parties) and toward institutions designed to be insulated from democratic pressures, and hence better equipped to dispense and defend individual rights (notably the judiciary and bureaucracy). /

These institutional developments may begin to account for the sense of powerlessness that the welfare state fails to address and in some ways doubtless deepens. But it seems to me a further clue to our condition recalls even more directly the predicament of the unencumbered self – lurching, as we left it, between detachment on the one hand, the entanglement on the other. For it is a striking feature of the welfare state that it offers a powerful promise of individual rights, and also demands of its citizens a high measure of mutual engagement. But the self-image that attends the rights cannot sustain the engagement.

/As bearers of rights, where rights are trumps, we think of ourselves as freely choosing, individual selves, unbound by obligations antecedent to rights, or to the agreements we make. And yet, as citizens of the procedural republic that secures these rights, we find ourselves implicated willy-nilly in a formidable array of dependencies and expectations we did not choose and recreasingly reject.

In our public life, we are more entangled, but less attached, than ever before. It is as though the unencumbered self presupposed by the liberal ethic had begun to come true – less liberated than disempowered, entangled in a network of obligations and involvements unassociated with any act of will, and yet unmediated by those common identifications or expansive self-definitions that would make them tolerable. As the scale of social and political organization has become more comprehensive, the terms of our collective identity have become more fragmented, and the forms of political life have outrun the common purpose needed to sustain them. /

Something like this, it seems to me, has been unfolding in America for the past half-century or so. I hope I have said at least enough to suggest the shape a fuller story might take. And I hope in any case to have conveyed a certain view about politics and philosophy and the relation between them – that our practices and institutions are themselves embodiments of theory, and to unravel their predicament is, at least in part, to seek after the self-image of the age.

NOTES

1 An excellent example of this view can be found in Samuel Huntington, *American Politics: The Promise of Disharmony* (Cambridge:

Harvard University Press, 1981). See especially his discussion of the "ideals versus institutions" gap, pp. 10–12, 39–41, 61–84, 221–62.

2   See, for example, the conceptions of a "practice" advanced by Alasdair MacIntyre and Charles Taylor. MacIntyre, *After Virtue* (Notes Dame: University of Notre Dame Press, 1981), pp. 175–209. Taylor, "Interpretation and the Sciences of Man", *Review of Metaphysics* 25, (1971) pp. 3–51.

3   John Rawls, *A Theory of Justice* (Oxford: Oxford University Press, 1971). Immanuel Kant, *Groundwork of the Metaphysics of Morals*, trans. H. J. Paton (1978; New York: Harper and Row, 1956). Kant, *Critique of Pure Reason*, trans. Norman Kemp Smith (1781, 1787; London: Macmillan, 1929). Kant, *Critique of Practical Reason*, trans. L. W. Beck (1788; Indianapolis: Bobbs-Merrill, 1956). Kant, "On the Common Saying: 'This May Be True in Theory, But It Does Not Apply in Practice,'" in Hans Reiss (ed.), *Kant's Political Writings* (1793; Cambridge: Cambridge University Press, 1970). Other recent versions of the claim for the priority of the right over good can be found in Robert Nozick, *Anarchy, State and Utopia* (New York: Basic Books, 1974); Ronald Dworkin, *Taking Rights Seriously* (London: Duckworth, 1977); Bruce Ackerman, *Social Justice in the Liberal State* (New Haven: Yale University Press, 1980).

4   This section, and the two that follow, summarize arguments developed more fully in Michael Sandel, *Liberalism and the Limits of Justice* (Cambridge: Cambridge University Press, 1982).

5   Rawls, *A Theory of Justice*, p. 3.

6   John Stuart Mill, *Utilitarianism*, in *The Utilitarians* (1893: Garden City: Doubleday, 1973), p. 465. Mill, *On Liberty*, in *The Utilitarians*, p. 485 (originally published 1849).

7   Kant (1793), p. 73.

8   Kant (1785), p. 92.

9   Kant (1788), p. 89.

10   Kant (1785), p. 105.

11   Kant (1788), p. 89.

12   Kant (1785), p. 121.

13   Rawls, "The Basic Structure as Subject," *American Philosophical Quarterly* (1977), p. 165.

14   Rawls, *A Theory of Justice*, p. 560.

15   Rawls, "Kantian Constructivism in Moral Theory," *Journal of philosophy* 77 (1980), p. 543

16   Mill, *The Utilitarians*, p. 485.

17   Rawls, *A Theory of Justice*, pp. 101–2.

18   Croly, *The Promise of American Life* (Indianapolis: Bobbs-Merrill, 1965), pp. 270–73.

19   Beer, "Liberalism and the National Idea," *The Public Interest*, Fall (1966), pp. 70–82.

20   See, for example, Laurence Tribe, *American Constitutional Law*

(Mineola: The Foundation Press, 1978), pp. 2–3.

21 See Ronald Dworkin, "Liberalism," in Stuart Hampshire (ed.), *Public and Private Morality* (Cambridge: Cambridge University Press, 1978), p. 136.

6

Justice as Fairness: Politic
Metaphysical

JOHN RAWLS

In this discussion I shall make some general remarks about how I now understand the conception of justice that I have called "justice as fairness" (presented in my book *A Theory of Justice*).[1] I do this because it may seem that this conception depends on philosophical claims I should like to avoid, for example, claims to universal truth, or claims about the essential nature and identity of persons. My aim is to explain why it does not. I shall first discuss what I regard as the task of political philosophy at the present time and then briefly survey how the basic intuitive ideas drawn upon in justice as fairness are combined into a political conception of justice for a constitutional democracy. Doing this will bring out how and why this conception of justice avoids certain philosophical and metaphysical claims. Briefly, the idea is that in a constitutional democracy the public conception of justice should be, so far as possible, independent of controversial philosophical and religious doctrines. Thus, to formulate such a conception, we apply the principle of toleration to philosophy itself: the public conception of justice is to be political, not metaphysical. Hence the title.

I want to put aside the question whether the text of *A Theory of Justice* supports different readings than the one I sketch here. Certainly on a number of points I have changed my views, and there are no doubt others on which my views have changed in ways that I am unaware of.[2] I recognize further that certain faults of exposition as well as obscure and ambiguous passages in *A Theory of Justice* invite misunderstanding; but I think these matters need not concern us and I shan't pursue them beyond a few footnote indications. For our purposes here, it suffices first, to show how a conception of justice with the structure and content of justice as fairness can be understood as political and not meta-

Reprinted by permission of Princeton University Press from *Philosophy and Public Affairs* 14, 3 (Fall, 1985), pp. 223–51.

...ysical, and second, to explain why we should look for such a conception of justice in a democratic society.

I

One thing I failed to say in *A Theory of Justice*, or failed to stress sufficiently, is that justice as fairness is intended as a political conception of justice. While a political conception of justice is, of course, a moral conception, it is a moral conception worked out for a specific kind of subject, namely, for political, social, and economic institutions. In particular, justice as fairness is framed to apply to what I have called the "basic structure" of a modern constitutional democracy [3] (I shall use "constitutional democracy" and "democratic regime," and similar phrases interchangeably.) By this structure I mean such a society's main political, social, and economic institutions, and how they fit together into one unified system of social cooperation. Whether justice as fairness can be extended to a general political conception for different kinds of societies existing under different historical and social conditions, or whether it can be extended to a general moral conception, or a significant part thereof, are altogether separate questions. I avoid prejudging these larger questions one way or the other.

It should also be stressed that justice as fairness is not intended as the application of a general moral conception to the basic structure of society, as if this structure were simply another case to which that general moral conception is applied.[4] In this respect justice as fairness differs from traditional moral doctrines, for these are widely regarded as such general conceptions. Utilitarianism is a familiar example, since the principle of utility, however it is formulated, is usually said to hold for all kinds of subjects ranging from the actions of individuals to the law of nations. The essential point is this: as a practical political matter no general moral conception can provide a publicly recognized basis for a conception of justice in a modern democratic state. The social and historical conditions of such a state have their origins in the Wars of Religion following the Reformation and the subsequent development of the principle of toleration, and in the growth of constitutional government and the institutions of large industrial market economies. These conditions profoundly affect the requirements of a workable conception of political justice: such a conception must allow for a diversity of doctrines and the plurality of conflicting, and indeed incommensurable, conceptions of the good affirmed by the members of existing democratic societies.

Finally, to conclude these introductory remarks, since justice as fairness is intended as a political conception of justice for a democratic society, it tries to draw solely upon basic intuitive ideas that are embedded in the political institutions of a constitutional democratic regime and the public traditions of their interpretation. Justice as fairness is a political conception in part becasue it starts from within a certain political tradition. We hope that this political conception of justice may at least be supported by what we may call an "overlapping consensus," that is, by a consensus that includes all the opposing philosophical and religious doctrines likely to persist and to gain adherents in a more or less just constitutional democratic society.[5]

II

There are, of course, many ways in which political philosophy may be understood, and writers at different times, faced with different political and social circumstances, understand their work differently. Justice as fairness I would now understand as a reasonably systematic and practicable conception of justice for a constitutional democracy, a conception that offers an alternative to the dominant utilitarianism of our tradition of political thought. Its first task is to provide a more secure and acceptable basis for constitutional principles and basic rights and liberties than utilitarianism seems to allow.[6] The need for such a political conception arises in the following way.

There are periods, sometimes long periods, in the history of any society during which certain fundamental questions give rise to sharp and divisive political controversy, and it seems difficult, if not impossible, to find any shared basis of political agreement. Indeed, certain questions may prove intractable and may never be fully settled. One task of political philosophy in a democratic society is to focus on such questions and to examine whether some underlying basis of agreement can be uncovered and a mutually acceptable way of resolving these questions publicly established. Or if these questions cannot be fully settled, as may well be the case, perhaps the divergence of opinion can be narrowed sufficiently so that political cooperation on a basis of mutual respect can still be maintained.

The course of democratic thought over the past two centuries or so makes plain that there is no agreement on the way basic institutions of a constitutional democracy should be arranged if they are to specify and secure the basic rights and liberties of citizens and answer to the claims of democratic equality when citizens are conceived as free and equal persons (as explained in the last three paragraphs of Section III). A deep disagreement exists as to how the values of liberty and equality are best realized in the basic structure of society. To simplify, we may think of this disagreement as a conflict within the tradition of democratic thought itself, between the tradition associated with Locke, which gives greater weight to what Constant called "the liberties of the moderns," freedom of thought and conscience, certain basic rights of the person and of property, and the rule of law, and the tradition associated with Rousseau, which gives greater weight to what Constant called "the liberties of the ancients," the equal political liberties and the values of public life. This is a stylized contrast and historically inaccurate, but it serves to fix ideas.

Justice as fairness tries to adjudicate between these contending traditions first, by proposing two priciples of justice to serve as guidelines for how basic institutions are to realize the values of liberty and equality, and second, by specifying a point of view from which these principles can be seen as more appropriate than other familiar principles of justice to the nature of democratic citizens viewed as free and equal persons. What it means to view citizens as free and equal persons is, of course, a fundamental question and is discussed in the following sections.What must be shown is that a certain arrangement of the basic structure, certain institutional forms, are more appropriate for realizing the values of liberty and equality when citizens are conceived as such persons, that is (very briefly), as having the requisite powers of moral personality that enable them to participate in society viewed as a system of fair cooperation for mutual advantage. So to continue, the two principles of justice (mentioned above) read as follows:

1 Each person has an equal right to a fully adequate scheme of equal baisc rights and liberties, which scheme is compatible with a similar scheme for all.
2 Social and economic inequalities are to satisfy two conditions: first, they must be attached to offices and positions open to all under conditions of fair equality of opportunity; and second, they must be to the greatest benefit of the least advantaged members of society.

Each of these principles applies to a different part of the basic structure; and both are concerned not only with basic rights, liberties, and opportunities, but also with the claims of equality;

while the second part of the second principle underwrites the worth of these institutional guarantees.[7] The two principles together, when the first is given priority over the second, regulate the basic institutions which realize these values. But these details, although important, are not our concern here.

We must now ask: how might political philosophy find a shared basis for settling such a fundamental question as that of the most appropriate institutional forms for liberty and equality? Of course, it is likely that the most that can be done is to narrow the range of public disagreement. Yet even firmly held convictions gradually change: religious toleration is now accepted, and arguments for persecution are no longer openly professed; similarly, slavery is rejected as inherently unjust, and however much the aftermath of slavery may persist in social practices and unavowed attitudes, no one is willing to defend it. We collect such settled convictions as the belief in religious toleration and the rejection of slavery and try to organize the basic ideas and principles implicit in these convictions into a coherent conception of justice. We can regard these convictions as provisional fixed points which any conception of justice must account for if it is to be reasonable for us. We look, then, to our public political culture itself, including its main institutions and the historical traditions of their interpretation as the shared fund of implicitly recognized basic ideas and principles. The hope is that these ideas and principles can be formulated clearly enough to be combined into a conception of political justice congenial to our most firmly held convictions. We express this by saying that a political conception of justice, to be acceptable, must be in accordance with our considered convictions, at all levels of generality, on due reflection (or in what I have called "reflective equilibrium").[8]

The public political culture may be of two minds even at a very deep level. Indeed, this must be so with such an enduring controversy as that concerning the most appropriate institutional forms to realize the values of liberty and equality. This suggests that if we are to succeed in finding a basis of public agreement, we must find a new way of organizing familiar ideas and principles into a conception of political justice so that the claims in conflict, as previously understood, are seen in another light. A political conception need not be an original creation but may only articulate familiar intuitive ideas and principles so that they can be recognized as fitting together in a somewhat different way than before. Such a conception may, however, go further than this: it may organize these familiar ideas and principles by means of a more fundamental intuitive idea within the complex structure of which the other familiar intuitive ideas are then systmeatically connected and related. In justice as fairness, as we shall see in the next section, this more fundamental idea is that of society as a system of fair social cooperation between free and equal persons. The concern of this section is how we might find a public basis of political agreement. The point is that a conception of justice will only be able to achieve this aim if it provides a reasonable way of shaping into one coherent view the deeper bases of agreement embedded in the public political culture of a constitutional regime and acceptable to its most firmly held considered convictions.

Now suppose justice as fairness were to achieve its aim and a publicly acceptable political conception of justice is found. Then this conception provides a publicly recognized point of view from which all citizens can examine before one another whether or not their political and social institutions are just. It enables them to do this by citing what are recognized among them as valid and sufficient reasons singled out by that conception itself. Society's main institutions and how they fit together into one scheme of social cooperation can be examined on the same basis by each citizen, whatever that citizen's social position or more particular interests. It should be observed that, on this view, justification is not regarded simply as valid argument from listed premises, even should these premises be true. Rather, justification is addressed to others who disagree with us, and therefore it must always proceed from some consensus, that is, from premises that we and others publicly recognize as true; or better, publicly recognize as acceptable to us for the purpose of establishing a working agreement on the fundamental questions of political justice. It goes without saying that this agreement must be informed and uncoerced, and reached by citizens in ways consistent with their being viewed as free and equal persons.[9]

Thus, the aim of justice as fairness as a political conception is practical, and not metaphysical or epistemological. That is, it presents itself not as a conception of justice that is true, but one that can serve as a basis of informed and willing political agreement between citizens viewed as free and equal persons. This agreement when securely founded in public political and social attitudes sustains the goods of all persons and associations within a just democratic regime. To secure this agreement we try, so far as we can, to avoid disputed philosophical, as well as disputed moral and religious, questions. We do this not because these questions are unimportant or regarded with indifference,[10] but because we think them too important and recognize that there is no way to resolve them politically. The only alternative to a principle of toleration is the autocratic use of state power. Thus, justice as fairness deliberately stays on the surface, philosophically speaking. Given the profound differences in belief and conceptions of the good at least since the Reformation, we must recognize that, just as on questions of religious and moral doctrine, public agreement on the basic questions of philosophy cannot be obtained without the state's infringement of basic liberties. Philosophy as the search for truth about an independent metaphysical and moral order cannot, I believe, provide a workable and shared basis for a political conception of justice in a democratic society.

We try, then, to leave aside philosophical controversies whenever possible, and look for ways to avoid philosophy's longstanding problems. Thus, in what I have called "Kantian constructivism," we try to avoid the problem of truth and the controversy between realism and subjectivism about the status of moral and political values. This form of constructivism neither asserts nor denies these doctrines.[11] Rather, it recasts ideas from the tradition of the social contract to achieve a practicable conception of objectivity and justification founded on public agreement in judgement on due reflection. The aim is free agreement, reconciliation through public reason. And similarly, as we shall see (in Section V), a conception of the person in a political view, for example, the conception of citizens as free and equal persons, need not involve, so I believe, questions of philosophical psychology or a metaphysical doctrine of the nature of the self. No political view that depends on these deep and unresolved matters can serve as a public conception of justice in a constitutional democratic state. As I have said, we must apply the principle of toleration to philosophy itself. The hope is that, by this method of avoidance, as we might call it, existing differences between contending political views can at least be moderated, even if not entirely removed, so that social cooperation on the basis of mutual respect can be maintained. Or if this is expecting too much, this method may enable us to conceive how, given a desire for free and uncoerced agreement, a public understanding could arise consistent with the historical conditions and constraints of our social world. Until we bring ourselves to conceive how this could happen, it can't happen.

III

Let's now survey briefly some of the basic ideas that make up justice as fairness in order to show that these ideas belong to a political conception of justice. As I have indicated, the overarching fundamental intuitive idea, within which other basic intuitive ideas are systematically connected, is that of society *as a fair system of cooperation* between free and equal persons. Justice as fairness starts from this idea as one of the basic intuitive ideas which we take to be implicit in the public culture of a democratic society. In their political thought, and in the context of public discussion of political questions, citizens do not view the social order as a fixed natural order, or as an institutional hierarchy justified by religious or aristocratic values. Here it is important to stress that from other points of view, for example, from the point of view of personal morality, or from the point of view of members of an association, or of one's religious or philosophical doctrine, various aspects of the world and one's relation to it, may be regarded in a different way. But these other points of view are not to be introduced into political discussion.

We can make the idea of social cooperation more specific by noting three of its elements:

1 Cooperation is distinct from merely socially coordinated activity, for example, from activity cooordinated by orders issued by some central authority. Cooperation is guided by publicly recognized rules and procedures which those who are cooperating accept and regard as properly regulating their conduct.
2 Cooperation involves the idea of fair terms of cooperation: these are terms that each participant may reasonably accept, provided that everyone else likewise accepts them. Fair terms of cooperation specify an idea of reciprocity or mutuality: all who are engaged in cooperation and who do their part as the rules and procedures require, are to benefit in some appropriate way as assessed by a suitable benchmark of comparison. A conception of political justice characterizes the fair terms of social cooperation. Since the primary subject of justice is the basic structure of society, this is accomplished in justice as fairness by formulating principles that specify basic rights and duties within the main institutions of society, and by regulating the institutions of background justice over time so that the benefits produced by everyone's efforts are fairly acquired and divided from one generation to the next.
3 The idea of social cooperation requires an idea of each participant's rational advantage, or good. This idea of good specifies what those who are engaged in cooperation, whether individuals, families, or associations, or even nation-states, are

trying to achieve, when the scheme is viewed from their own standpoint.

Now consider the idea of the person.[12] There are, of course, many aspects of human nature that can be singled out as especially significant depending on our point of view. This is witnessed by such expressions as *homo politicus, homo oeconomicus, homo faber* and the like. Justice as fairness starts from the idea that society is to be conceived as a fair system of cooperation and so it adopts a conception of the person to go with this idea. Since Greek times, both in philosophy and law, the concept of the person has been understood as the concept of someone who can take part in, or who can play a role in, social life, and hence exercise and respect its various rights and duties. Thus, we say that a person is someone who can be a citizen, that is, a fully cooperating member of society over a complete life. We add the phrase "over a complete life" because a society is viewed as a more or less complete and self-sufficient scheme of cooperation, making room within itself for all the necessities and activities of life, from birth until death. A society is not an association for more limited purposes; citizens do not join society voluntarily but are born into it, where, for our aims here, we assume they are to lead their lives.

Since we start within the tradition of democratic thought, we also think of citizens as free and equal persons. The basic intuitive idea is that in virtue of what we may call their moral powers, and the powers of reason, thought, and judgement connected with those powers, we say that persons are *free*. And in virtue of their having these powers to the requisite degree to be fully cooperating members of society, we say that persons are equal.[13] We can elaborate this conception of the person as follows. Since persons can be full participants in a fair system of social cooperation, we ascribe to them the two moral powers connected with the elements in the idea of social cooperation noted above: namely, a capacity for a sense of justice and a capacity for a conception of the good. A sense of justice is the capacity to understand, to apply, and to act from the public conception of justice which characterizes the fair terms of social cooperation. The capacity for a conception of the good is the capacity to form, to revise, and rationally to pursue a conception of one's rational advantage, or good. In the case of social cooperation, this good must not be understood narrowly but rather as a conception of what is valuable in human life. Thus, a conception of the good normally consists of a more or less determinate scheme of final ends, that is, ends we want to realize for their own sake, as well as of attachments to other persons and loyalties to various groups and associations. These attachments and loyalties give rise to affections and devotions, and therefore the flourishing of the persons and associations who are the objects of these sentiments is also part of our conception of the good. Moreover, we must also include in such a conception a view of our relation to the world – religious, philosophical, or moral – by reference to which the value and significance of our ends and attachments are understood.

In addition to having the two moral powers, the capacities for a sense of justice and a conception of the good, persons also have at any given time a particular conception of the good that they try to achieve. Since we wish to start from the idea of society as a fair system of cooperation, we assume that persons as citizens have all the capacities that enable them to be normal and fully cooperating members of society. This does not imply that no one ever suffers from illness or accident; such misfortunes are to be expected in the ordinary course of human life; and provision for these contingencies must be made. But for our purposes here I leave aside permanent physical disabilities or mental disorders so severe as to prevent persons from being normal and fully cooperating members of society in the usual sense.

Now the conception of persons as having the two moral powers, and therefore as free and equal, is also a basic intuitive idea assumed to be implicit in the public culture of a democratic society. Note, however, that it is formed by idealizing and simplifying in various ways. This is done to achieve a clear and uncluttered view of what for us is the fundamental question of political justice: namely, what is the most appropriate conception of justice for specifying the terms of social cooperation between citizens regarded as free and equal persons, and as normal and fully cooperating members of society over a complete life. It is this question that has been the focus of the liberal critique of aristocracy, of the socialist critique of liberal constitutional democracy, and of the conflict between liberals and conservatives at the present time over the claims of private property and the legitimacy (in contrast to the effectiveness) of social policies associated with the so-called welfare state.

IV

I now take up the idea of the orginal position.[14] This idea is introduced in order to work out which traditional conception of justice, or which variant of one of those conceptions, specifies the most appropriate principles for realizing liberty and equality once society is viewed as a system of cooperation between free and equal persons. Assuming we had this purpose in mind, let's see why we would introduce the idea of the original position and how it serves its purpose.

Consider again the idea of social cooperation. Let's ask: how are the fair terms of cooperation to be determined? Are they simply laid down by some outside agency distinct from the persons cooperating? Are they, for example, laid down by God's law? Or are these terms to be recognized by these persons as fair by reference to their knowledge of a prior and independent moral order? For example, are they regarded as required by natural law, or by a realm of values known by rational intuition? Or are these terms to be established by an undertaking among these persons themselves in the light of what they regard as their mutual advantage? Depending on which answer we give, we get a different conception of cooperation.

Since justice as fairness recasts the doctrine of the social contract, it adopts a form of the last answer: the fair terms of social cooperation are conceived as agreed to by those engaged in it, that is by free and equal persons as citizens who are born into the society in which they lead their lives. But their agreement, like any other valid agreement, must be entered into under appropriate conditions. In particular, these conditions must situate free and equal persons fairly and must not allow some persons greater bargaining advantages than others. Further, threats of force and coercion, deception and fraud, and so on, must be exclude.

So far so good. The foregoing considerations are familiar from everyday life. But agreements in everyday life are made in some more or less clearly specified situation embedded within the background institutions of the basic structure. Our task, however, is to extend the idea of agreement to this background framework itself. Here we face a difficulty for any political conception of justice that uses the idea of a contract, whether social or otherwise. The difficullty is this: we must find some point of view, removed from and not distorted by the particular features and circumstances of the all-encompassing background framework, from which a fair agreement between free and equal persons can be reached. The original position, with the feature I have called "the veil of ignorance," is this point of view.[15] And the reason why the original position must abstract from and not be affected by the contingencies of the social world is that the conditions for a fair agreement on the principles of political justice between free and equal persons must eliminate the bargaining advantages which inevitably arise within background institutions of any society as the result of cumulative social, historical, and natural tendencies. These contingent advantages and accidental influences from the past should not influence an agreement on the principles which are to regulate the institutions of the basic structure itself from the present into the future.

Here we seem to face a second difficulty, which is, however, only apparent. To explain: from what we have just said it is clear that the original position is to be seen as a device of representation and hence any agreement reached by the parties must be regarded as both hypothetical and non-historical. But if so, since hypothetical agreements cannot bind, what is the significance of the original position?[16] The answer is implicit in what has already been said: it is given by the role of the various features of the original position as a device of representation. Thus, that the parties are symmetrically situated is required if they are to be seen as representatives of free and equal citizens who are to reach an agreement under conditions that are fair. Moreover, one of our considered convictions, I assume, is this: the fact that we occupy a particular social position is not a good reason for us to accept, or to expect others to accept, a conception of justice that favors those in this position. To model this conviction in the original position the parties are not allowed to know their social position; and the same idea is extended to other cases. This is expressed figuratively by saying that the parties are behind a veil of ignorance. In sum, the original position is simply a device of representation: it describes the parties, each of whom are responsible for the essential interests of a free and equal person, as fairly situated and as reaching an agreement subject to appropriate restrictions on what are to count as good reasons.[17]

Both of the above mentioned difficulties, then, are overcome by viewing the original position as a device of representation: that is, this position models what we regard as fair conditions under which the representatives of free and equal persons are to specify the terms of social cooperation in the case of the basic structure of society; and since it also models what, for this case, we regard as acceptable restrictions on reasons available to the parties for favoring one agreement rather than another, the conception of justice the parties would adopt identifies the conception we regard — *here and now* — as fair and supported by the best reasons. We try to model restrictions on reasons in such a way that it is perfectly evident which agreement would be made by the parties in the original position as citizens' representatives. Even if there should be, as surely there will be, reasons for and against each conception of justice available, there may be an overall balance of reasons plainly favoring one conception over the rest. As a device of representation the idea of the original position serves as a means of public reflection and self-clarification. We can use it to help us work out what we now think, once we are able to take a clear and uncluttered view of what justice requries when society is conceived as a scheme of cooperation between free and equal persons over time from one generation to the next.The original position serves as a unifying idea by which our considered convictions at all levels of generality are brought to bear on one another so as to achieve greater mutual agreement and self-understanding.

To conclude: we introduce an idea like that of the original position because there is no better way to elaborate a political conception of justice for the basic structure from the fundamental intuitive idea of society as a fair system of cooperation between citizens as free and equal persons. There are, however, certain hazards. As a device of representation the original position is likely to seem somewhat abstract and hence open to misunderstanding. The description of the parties may seem to presuppose some metaphysical conception of the person, for example, that the essential nature of persons is independent of and prior to their contingent attributes, including their final ends and attachments, and indeed, their character as a whole. But this is an illusion caused by not seeing the original position as a device of representation. The veil of ignorance, to mention one prominent feature of that position, has no metaphysical implications concerning the nature of the self; it does not imply that the self is ontologically prior to the facts about persons that the parties are excluded from knowing. We can, as it were, enter this position any time simply by reasoning for principles of justice in accordance with the enumerated restrictions. When, in this way, we simulate being in this position, our reasoning no more commits us to a metaphysical doctrine about the nature of the self than our playing a game like Monopoly commits us to thinking that we are landlords engaged in a desperate rivalry, winner take all. We must keep in mind that we are trying to show how the idea of society as a fair system of social cooperation can be unfolded so as to specify the most appropriate principles for realizing the institutions of liberty and equality when citizens are regarded as free and equal persons.

V

I just remarked that the idea of the original position and the description of the parties may tempt us to think that a metaphysical doctrine of the person is presupposed. While I said that this interpretation is mistaken, it is not enough simply to disavow reliance on metaphysical doctrines, for despite one's intent they may still be involved. To rebut claims of this nature requires discussing them in detail and showing that they have no foothold. I cannot do that here.

I can, however, sketch a positive account of the political conception of the person, that is, the conception of the person as citizen (discussed in Section III), involved in the original position as a device of representation. To explain what is meant by describing a conception of the person as political, let's consider how citizens are represented in the original position as free persons. The representation of their freedom seems to be one source of the idea that some metaphysical doctrine is presupposed. I have said elsewhere that citizens view themselves as free in three respects, so let's survey each of these briefly and indicate the way in which the conception of the person used is political.[18]

First, citizens are free in that they conceive of themselves and of one another as having the moral power to have a conception of the good. This is not to say that, as part of their political conception of themselves, they view themselves as inevitably tied to the pursuit of the particular conception of the good which they affirm at any given time. Instead, as citizens, they are regarded as capable of revising and changing this conception on reasonable and rational grounds, and they may do this if they so desire. Thus, as free persons, citizens claim the right to view their persons as independent from and as not identified with any particular conception of the good, or scheme of final ends. Given their moral power to form, to revise, and rationally to pursue a conception of the good, their public identity as free persons is not affected by changes over time in their conception of the good. For example, when citizens convert from one religion to another, or no longer affirm an established religious faith, they do not cease to be, for questions of political justice, the same persons they were before. There is no loss of what we may call their public identity, their identity as a matter of basic law. In general, they still have the same basic rights and duties; they own the same property and can make the same claims as before, except insofar as these claims were connected with their previous religious affiliation. We can imagine a society (indeed, history offers numerous examples) in which basic rights and recognized claims depend on religious affiliation, social class, and so on. Such a society has a different political conception of the person. It may not have a conception of citizenship at all; for this conception, as we are using it, goes with the conception of society as a fair system of cooperation for mutual advantage between free and equal persons.

It is essential to stress that citizens in their personal affairs, or in the internal life of asssociations to which they belong, may regard their final ends and attachments in a way very different from the way the political conception involves. Citizens may have, and normally do have at any given time, affections, devotions, and loyalties that they believe they would not, and indeed could and should not, stand apart from and objectively evaluate from the point of view of their purely rational good. They may regard it as simply unthinkable to view themselves apart from certain religious, philosophical, and moral convictions, or from certain enduring attachments and loyalties. These convictions and attachments are part of what we may call their "non-public identity." These convictions and attachments help to organize and give shape to a person's way of life, what one sees oneself as doing and trying to accomplish in one's social world. We think that if we were suddenly without these particular convictions and attachments we would be disoriented and unable to carry on. In fact, there would be, we might think, no point in carrying on. But our conceptions of the good may and often do change over time, usually slowly but sometimes rather suddenly. When these changes are sudden, we are particularly likely to say that we are no longer the same person. We know what this means: we refer to a profound and pervasive shift, or reversal, in our final ends and character; we refer to our different nonpublic, and possibly moral or religious, identity. On the road to Damascus Saul of Tarsus becomes Paul the Apostle. There is no change in our public or political identity, nor in our personal identity as this concept is understood by some writers in the philosophy of mind.

The second respect in which citizens view themselves as free is that they regard themselves as self-originating sources of valid claims. They think their claims have weight apart from being derived from duties or obligations specified by the political conception of justice, for example, from duties and obligations owed to society. Claims that citizens regard as founded on duties and obligations based on their conception of the good and the moral doctrine they affirm in their own life are also, for our purposes here, to be counted as self-originating. Doing this is reasonable in a political conception of justice for a constitutional democracy; for provided the conceptions of the good and the moral doctrines citizens affirm are compatible with the public conception of justice, these duties and obligations are self-originating from the politcal point of view.

When we describe a way in which citizens regard themselves as free, we are describing how citizens actually think of themselves in a democratic society should questions of justice arise. In our conception of a constitutional regime, this is an aspect of how citizens regard themselves. That this aspect of their freedom belongs to a particular political conception is clear from the contrast with a different political conception in which the members of society are not viewed as self-originating sources of valid claims. Rather, their claims have no weight except insofar as they can be derived from their duties and obligations owed to society, or from their ascribed roles in the social hierarchy justified by religious or aristocratic values. Or to take an extreme case, slaves are human beings who are not counted as sources of claims, not even claims based on social duties or obligations, for slaves are not counted as capable of having duties or obligations. Laws that prohibit the abuse and maltreatment of slaves are not founded on claims made by slaves on their own behalf, but on claims originating either from slaveholders, or from the general interests of society (which does not include the interests of slaves). Slaves are, so to speak, socially dead: they are not publicly recognized as persons at all.[19] Thus, the contrast with a political conception which allows slavery makes clear why conceiving of citizens as free persons in virtue of their moral powers and their having a conception of the good, goes with a particular political conception of the person. This conception of persons fits into a political conception of justice founded on the idea of society as a system of cooperation between its members conceived as free and equal.

The third respect in which citizens are regarded as free is that they are regarded as capable of taking responsibility for their ends and this affects how their various claims are assessed.[20] Very roughly, the idea is that, given just background institutions and given for each person a fair index of primary goods (as required by the principles of justice), citizens are thought to be capable of adjusting their aims and aspirations in the light of what they can reasonably expect to provide for. Moreover, they are regarded as capable of restricting their claims in matters of justice to the kinds of things the principles of justice allow. Thus, citizens are to recognize that the weight of their claims is not given by the strength and psychological intensity of their wants and desires (as opposed to their needs and requirements as citizens), even when their wants and desires are rational from their point of view.

I cannot pursue these matters here. But the procedure is the same as before: we start with the basic intuitive idea of society as a system of social cooperation. When this idea is developed into a conception of political justice, it implies that, viewing ourselves as persons who can engage in social cooperation over a complete life, we can also take responsibility for our ends, that is, that we can adjust our ends so that they can be pursued by the means we can reasonably expect to acquire given our prospects and situation in society. The idea of responsibility for ends is implicit in the public political culture and discernible in its practices. A political conception of the person articulates this idea and fits it into the idea of society as a system of social cooperation over a complete life.

To sum up, I recapitulate three main points of this and the preceding two sections:

First, in Section III persons were regarded as free and equal in virtue of their possessing to the requisite degree the two powers of moral personality (and the powers of reason, thought, and judgement connected with these powers), namely, the capacity for a sense of justice and the capacity for a conception of the good. These powers we associated with two main elements of the idea of cooperation, the idea of fair terms of cooperation and the idea of each participant's rational advantage, or good.

Second, in this section (Section V), we have briefly surveyed three respects in which persons are regarded as free, and we have noted that in the public political culture of a constitutional democratic regime citizens conceive of themselves as free in these respects.

Third, since the question of which conception of political justice is most appropriate for realizing in basic institutions the values of liberty and equality has long been deeply controversial within the very democratic tradition in which citizens are regarded as free and equal persons, the aim of justice as fairness is to try to resolve this question by starting from the basic intuitive idea of society as a fair system of social cooperation in which the fair terms of cooperation are agreed upon by citizens themselves so conceived. In Section IV, we saw why this approach leads to the idea of the original position as a device of representation.

VI

I now take up a point essential to thinking of justice as fairness as a liberal view. Although this conception is a moral conception, it is not, as I have said, intended as a comprehensive moral doctrine. The conception of the citizen as a free and equal person is not a moral ideal to govern all of life, but is rather an ideal belonging to a conception of political justice which is to apply to the basic structure. I emphasize this point because to think otherwise would be incompatible with liberalism as a political doctrine. Recall that as such a doctrine, liberalism assumes that in a constitutional democratic state under modern conditions there are bound to exist conflicting and incommensurable conceptions of the good. This feature characterizes modern culture since the Reformation. Any viable political conception of justice that is not to rely on the autocratic use of state power must recognize this fundamental social fact. This does not mean, of course, that such a conception cannot impose constraints on individuals and associations, but that when it does so, these constraints are accounted for, directly or indirectly, by the requirements of political justice for the basic structure.

Given this fact, we adopt a conception of the person framed as part of, and restricted to, an explicitly political conception of justice. In this sense, the conception of the person is a political one. As I stressed in the previous section, persons can accept this conception of themselves as citizens and use it when discussing questions of political justice without being committed in other parts of their life to comprehensive moral ideals often associated with liberalism, for example, the ideals of autonomy and individuality. The absence of commitment to these ideals and indeed to any particular comprehensive ideal, is essential to liberalism as a political doctrine. The reason is that any such ideal, when pursued as a comprehensive ideal, is incompatible with other conceptions of the good, with forms of personal, moral, and religious life consistent with justice and which, therefore, have a proper place in a democratic society. As comprehensive moral ideals, autonomy and individuality are unsuited for a political conception of justice. As found in Kant and J. S. Mill, these comprehensive ideals, despite their very great importance in liberal thought, are extended too far when presented as the only appropriate foundation for a constitutional regime.[21] So understood, liberalism becomes but another sectarian doctrine.

This conclusion requires comment: it does not mean, of course, that the liberalisms of Kant and Mill are not appropriate moral conceptions from which we can be led to affirm democratic institutions. But they are only two such conceptions among others, and so but two of the philosophical doctrines likely to persist and gain adherents in a reasonably just democratic regime. In such a regime the comprehensive moral views which support its basic institutions may include the liberalisms of individuality and autonomy; and possibly these liberalisms are among the more prominent doctrines in an overlapping consensus, that is, in a consensus in which, as noted earlier, different and even conflicting doctrines affirm the publicly shared basis of political arrangements. The liberalisms of Kant and Mill have a certain historical pre-eminence as among the first and most important philosophical views to espouse modern constitutional democracy and to develop its underlying ideas in an influential way; and it may even turn out that societies in which the ideals of autonomy and individuality are widely accepted are among the most well-governed and harmonious.[22]

By contrast with liberalism as a comprehensive moral doctrine, justice as fairness tries to present a conception of political justice rooted in the basic intuitive ideas found in the public culture of a constitutional democracy. We conjecture that these ideas are likely to be affirmed by each of the opposing comprehensive moral doctrines influential in a reasonably just democratic society. Thus justice as fairness seeks to identify the kernel of an overlapping consensus, that is, the shared intuitive ideas which when worked up into a political conception of justice turn out to be sufficient to underwrite a just constitutional regime. This is the most we can expect, nor do we need more.[23] We must note, however, that when justice as fairness is fully realized in a well-ordered society, the value of full autonomy is likewise realized. In this way justice as fairness is indeed similar to the liberalisms of Kant and Mill; but in contrast with them, the value of full autonomy is here specified by a political conception of justice, and not by a comprehensive moral doctrine.

It may appear that, so understood, the public acceptance of justice as fairness is no more than prudential; that is, that those who affirm this conception do so simply as a modus vivendi which allows the groups in the overlapping consensus to pursue their own good subject to certain constraints which each thinks to be for its advantage given existing circumstances. The idea of an overlapping consensus may seem essentially Hobbesian. But against this, two remarks: first, justice as fairness is a moral conception: it has conceptions of person and society, and concepts of right and fairness, as well as principles of justice with their complement of the virtues through which those principles are embodied in human character and regulate political and social life. This conception of justice provides an account of the cooperative virtues sutiable for a political doctrine in view of the conditions and requirements of a constitutional regime. It is no less a moral conception because it is restricted to the basic structure of society, since this restriction is what enables it to serve as a political conception of justice given our present circumstances. Thus, in an overlapping consensus (as understood here), the conception of justice as fairness is not regarded merly as a modus vivendi.

Second, in such a consensus each of the comprehensive philosophical, religious, and moral doctrines accepts justice as fairness in its own way; that is, each comprehensive doctrine, from within its own point of view, is led to accept the public reasons of justice specified by justice as fairness. We might say that they recognize its concepts, principles, and virtues as theorems, as it were, at which their several views coincide. But this does not make these points of concidence any less moral or reduce them to mere means. For, in general, these concepts, principles, and virtues are accepted by each as belonging to a more comprehensive philosophical, religious, or moral doctrine. Some may even affirm justice as fairness as a natural moral conception that can stand on its own feet. They accept this conception of justice as a reasonable basis for political and social cooperation, and hold that it is as natural and fundamental as the concepts and principles of honesty and mutual trust, and the virtues of cooperation in everyday life. The doctrines in an overlapping consensus differ in how far they maintain a further foundation is necessary and on what that further foundation should be. These differences, however, are compatible with a consensus on justice as fairness as a political conception of justice.

VI

I shall conclude by considering the way in which social unity and stability may be understood by liberalism as a political doctrine (as opposed to a comprehensive moral conception).[24]

One of the deepest distinctions between political conceptions of justice is between those that allow for a plurality of opposing and even incommensurable conceptions of the good and those that hold that there is but one conception of the good which is to be recognized by all persons, so far as they are fully rational. Conceptions of justice which fall on opposite sides of this divide are distinct in many fundamental ways. Plato and Aristotle, and the Christian tradition as represented by Augustine and Aquinas, fall on the side of the one rational good. Such views tend to be teleological and to hold that institutions are just to the extent that they effectively promote this good. Indeed, since classical times the dominant tradition seems to have been that there is but one rational conception of the good, and that the aim of moral philosophy, together with theology and metaphysics, is to determine its nature. Classical utilitarianism belongs to this dominant tradition. By contrast, liberalism as a political doctrine supposes that there are many conflicting and incommensurable conceptions of the good, each compatible with the full rationality of human persons, so far as we can ascertain within a workable political conception of justice. As a consequence of this supposition, liberalism assumes that it is a characteristic feature of a free democratic culture that a plurality of conflicting and incommensurable conceptions of the good are affirmed by its citizens. Liberalism as a political doctrine holds that the question the dominant tradition has tried to answer has no practicable answer; that is, it has no answer suitable for a political conception of justice for a democratic society. In such a society a teleological political conception is out of the question: public agreement on the requisite conception of the good cannot be obtained.

As I have remarked, the historical origin of this liberal supposition is the Reformation and its consequences. Until the Wars of Religion in the sixteenth and seventeenth centuries, the fair terms of social cooperation were narrowly drawn: social cooperation on the basis of mutual respect was regarded as impossible with persons of a different faith; or (in the terminology I have used) with persons who affirm a fundamentally different conception of the good. Thus one of the historical roots of liberalism was the development of various doctrines urging religious toleration. One theme in justice as fairness is to recognize the social conditions that give rise to these doctrines as among the so-called subjective circumstances of justice and then to spell out the implications of the principle of toleration. As liberalism is stated by Constant, de Tocqueville, and Mill in the nineteenth century, it accepts the plurality of incommensurable conceptions of the good as a fact of modern democratic culture, provided, of course, these conceptions respect the limits specified by the appropriate principles of justice. One task of liberalism as a political doctrine is to answer the question: how is social unity to be understood, given that there can be no public agreement on the one rational good, and a plurality of opposing and incommensurable conceptions must be taken as given? And granted that social unity is conceivable in some definite way, under what conditions is it actually possible?

In justice as fairness, social unity is understood by starting with the conception of society as a system of cooperation between free and equal persons. Social unity and the allegiance of citizens to their common institutions are not founded on their all affirming the same conception of the good, but on their publicly accepting a political conception of justice to regulate the basic structure of society. The concept of justice is independent from and prior to the concept of goodness in the sense that its principles limit the conceptions of the good which are permissible. A just basic structure and its background institutions establish a framework within which permissible conceptions can be advanced. Elsewhere I have called this relation between a conception of justice and conceptions of the good the priority of right (since the just falls under the right). I believe this priority is characteristic of liberalism as a political doctrine and something like it seems essential to any conception of justice reasonable for a democratic state. Thus to understand how social unity is possible given the historical conditions of a democratic society, we start with our basic intuitive idea of social cooperation, an idea present in the public culture of a democratic society, and proceed from there to a public conception of justice as the basis of social unity in the way I have sketched.

As for the question of whether this unity is stable, this importantly depends on the content of the religious, philosophical, and moral doctrines available to constitute an overlapping consensus. For example, assuming the public political conception to be justice as fairness, imagine citizens to affirm one of three views: the first view affirms justice as fairness because its religious beliefs and understanding of faith lead to a principle of toleration and underwrite the fundamental idea of society as a scheme of social cooperation between free and equal persons; the second view affirms it as a consequence of a comprehensive liberal moral conception such as those of Kant and Mill; while the third affirms justice as fairness not as a consequence of any wider doctrine but as in itself sufficient to express values that normally outweigh whatever other values might oppose them, at least under reasonably favorable conditions. This overlapping consensus appears far more stable than one founded on views that express skepticism and indifference to religious, philosophical, and moral values, or that regard the acceptance of the principles of justice simply as a prudent modus vivendi given the existing balance of social forces. Of course, there are many other possibilities.

The strength of a conception like justice as fairness may prove to be that the more comprehensive doctrines that persist and gain adherents in a democratic society regulated by its principles are likely to cohere together into a more or less stable overlapping consensus. But obviously all this is highly speculative and raises questions which are little understood, since doctrines which persist and gain adherents depend in part on social conditions, and in particular, on these conditions when regulated by the public conception of justice. Thus we are forced to consider at some point the effects of the social conditions required by a conception of political justice on the acceptance of that conception itself. Other things equal, a conception will be more or less stable depending on how far the conditions to which it leads support comprehensive religious, philosophical, and moral doctrines which can constitute a stable overlapping consensus. These questions of stability I cannot discuss here.[33] It suffices to remark that in a society marked by deep divisions between opposing and incommensurable conceptions of the good, justice as fairness enables us at least to conceive how social unity can be both possible and stable.

NOTES

1   J. Rawls, *A Theory of Justice* (Cambridge, Mass.: Harvard University Press, 1971).
2   A number of these changes, or shifts of emphasis, are evident in three lectures entitled "Kantian Constructivism in Moral Theory," *Journal of Philosophy* 77 (September 1980).
3   *A Theory of Justice*, Sec. 2 and see the Index: see also "The Basic Structure as Subject" in Alvin Goldman and Jaegwon Kim (eds), *Values and Morals* (Dordrecht: Reidel, 1978), pp. 47–71.
4   Rawls, "The Basic Structure as Subject," pp. 48–50.
5   This idea was introduced in *A Theory of Justice*, pp. 387f. as a way to weaken the conditions for the reasonableness of civil disobedience in a nearly just democratic society. Here and later in Sections VI and VII it is used in a wider context.
6   *A Theory of Justice*, Preface, p. viii.
7   The statement of these principles differs from that given in *A Theory of Justice* and follows the statement in Rawls, "The Basic Liberties and Their Priority," *Tanner Lectures on Human Values*, Vol. III (Salt Lake City: University of Utah Press, 1982), p. 5.
8   *A Theory of Justice*, pp. 20f., 48–51 and 120f.
9   *A Theory of Justice*, pp. 580–3.
10 *A Theory of Justice*, pp. 214f.

11 On Kantian constructivism, see especially the third lecture referred to in footnote 2.

12 It should be emphasized that a conception of the person, as I understand it here, is a normative conception, whether legal, political or moral, or indeed also philosophical or religious, depending on the overall view to which it belongs. In this case the conception of the person is a moral conception, one that begins from our everyday conception of persons as the basic units of thought, deliberation and responsibility, and adapted to a political conception of justice and not to a comprehensive moral doctrine. It is in effect a political conception of the person, and given the aims of justice as fairness a conception of citizens. Thus, a conception of the person is to be distinguished from an account of human nature given by natural science or social theory. On this point see "Kantian Constructivism," pp. 534f.

13 *A Theory of Justice*, Sec. 77.

14 *A Theory of Justice*, Sec. 4, chap. 3, and the Index.

15 On the veil of ignorance see *A Theory of Justice*, Sec. 24 and the Index.

16 This question is raised by Ronald Dworkin in the first part of his very illuminating and to me, highly instructive, essay "Justice and Rights" (1973), reprinted in *Taking Rights Seriously* (Cambridge, Mass.: Harvard University Press, 1977).

17 The original position models a basic feature of Kantian constructivism, namely the distinction between the Reasonable and the Rational, with the Reasonable as prior to the Rational. (For an explanation of this distinction, see "Kantian Constructivism," pp. 528–32 and *passim*).

18 For the first two respects see "Kantian Constructivism," pp. 544f. (For the third respect, see footnote 20 below.)

19 For the idea of social death, see Orlando Patterson, *Slavery and Social Death* (Cambridge, Mass.: Harvard University Press, 1982), esp. pp. 5–9, 38–45, 337. This idea is interestingly developed in this book and has a central place in the author's study of slavery.

20 See "Social Unity and Primary Goods" in Amartya Sen and Bernard Williams (eds), *Utilitarianism and Beyond* (Cambridge: Cambridge University Press, 1982), Sec. IV, pp. 167–70.

21 For Kant, see *The Foundations of the Metaphysics of Morals* and *The Critique of Practical Reason*. For Mill, see *On Liberty*, particularly chap. 3 where the ideal of individuality is most fully discussed.

22 This point has been made with respect to the liberalisms of Kant and Mill, but for American culture one should mention the important conceptions of democratic individuality expressed in the works of Emerson, Thoreau and Whitman. These are instructively discussed by George Kateb in his "Democratic Individuality and the Claims of Politics", *Political Theory* 12 (August 1984).

23 For the idea of the kernel of an overlapping consensus see *A Theory of Justice*, last para. of Sec. 35, pp. 220f. For the idea of full autonomy see "Kantian Constructivism," pp. 528ff.

24 This account of social unity is found in "Social Unity and Primary Goods," Sen and Williams (eds), esp. pp. 160f., 170−3, 183f.

7

Rational Fools: A Critique of the Behavioral Foundations of Economic Theory

AMARTYA K. SEN

I

In his *Mathematical Psychics*, published in 1881, Edgeworth asserted that "the first principle of Economics is that every agent is actuated only by self-interest."[1] This view of man has been a persistent one in economic models, and the nature of economic theory seems to have been much influenced by this basic premise. In this essay I would like to examine some of the problems that have arisen from this conception of human beings.

I should mention that Edgeworth himself was quite aware that this so-called first principle of economics was not a particularly realistic one. Indeed, he felt that "the concrete nineteenth century man is for the most part an impure egoist, a mixed utilitarian."[2] This raises the interesting question as to why Edgeworth spent so much of his time and talent in developing a line of inquiry the first principle of which he believed to be false. The issue is not why abstractions should be employed in pursuing general economic questions − the nature of the inquiry makes this inevitable − but why would one choose an assumption which he himself believed to be not merely inaccurate in detail but fundamentally mistaken?...

[Sen now describes one answer characteristic of economics. Citing a number of writers, including Kenneth Arrow and F. H. Hahn, he shows that for them the assumption of purely self-seeking individuals, within the structure of a limited economic model, provides fairly clear-cut responses to questions that econ-

Reprinted by permission of Princeton University Press from *Philosophy and Public Affairs* 6, 4 (Summer, 1977), pp. 317−44.

omists want to ask, including those that would deal with the relationship between egoism and the general good.]

The primary concern here is not with the relation of postulated models to the real economic world, but with the accuracy of answers to well-defined questions posed with preselected assumptions which severely constrain the nature of the models that can be admitted into the analysis. A specific concept of man is ingrained in the question itself, and there is no freedom to depart from this conception so long as one is engaged in answering this question. The nature of man in these current economic models continues, then, to reflect the particular formulation of certain general philosophical questions posed in the past. The realism of the chosen conception of man is simply not a part of this inquiry.

II

There is another non-empirical — and possibly simpler — reason why the conception of man in economic models tends to be that of a self-seeking egoist. It is possible to define a person's interests in such a way that no matter what he does he can be seen to be furthering his own interests in every isolated act of choice. While formalized relatively recently in the context of the theory of revealed preference, this approach is of respectable antiquity, and Joseph Butler was already arguing against it in the Rolls Chapel two and a half centuries ago.[3] The reduction of man to a self-seeking animal depends in this approach on careful definition. If you are observed to choose x rejecting y, you are declared to have "revealed" a preference for x over y. Your personal utility is then defined as simply a numerical representation of this "preference," assigning a higher utility to a "preferred" alternative. With this set of definitions you can hardly escape maximizing your own utility, except through inconsistency. Of course, if you choose x and reject y on one occasion and then promptly proceed to do the exact opposite, you can prevent the revealed preference theorist from assigning a preference ordering to you, thereby restraining him from stamping a utility function on you which you must be seen to be maximizing. He will then have to conclude that either you are inconsistent or your preferences are changing. You can frustrate the revealed-preference theorist through more sophisticated inconsistencies as well.[4] But if you are consistent, then no matter whether you are a single-minded egoist or a raving altruist or a class conscious militant, you will appear to be maximizing your own utility in this enchanted world of definitions. Borrowing from the terminology used in connection with taxation, if the Arrow-Hahn justification of the assumption of egoism amounts to an *avoidance* of the issue, the revealed preference approach looks more like a robust piece of *evasion*.

This approach of definitional egoism sometimes goes under the name of rational choice, and it involves nothing other than internal consistency. A person's choices are considered "rational" in this approach if and only if these choices can *all* be explained in terms of some preference relation consistent with the revealed preference definition, that is, if all his choices can be explained as the choosing of "most preferred" alternatives with respect to a postulated preference relation.[5] The rationale of this approach seems to be based on the idea that the only way of understanding a person's real preference is to examine his actual choices, and there is no choice-independent way of understanding someone's attitude towards althernatives. (This view, by the way, is not confined to economists only. When, many years ago, I had to take my qualifying examination in English Literature at Calcutta University, one of the questions we had to answer concerning *A Midsummer Night's Dream* was: Compare the characters of Hermia and Helena. Whom would you choose?)

I have tried to demonstrate elsewhere that once we eschew the curious definitions of preference and welfare, this approach presumes both too little and too much: too little because there are non-choice sources of information on preference and welfare as these terms are usually understood, and too much because choice may reflect a compromise among a variety of considerations of which personal welfare may be just one.[6]

The complex psychological issues underlying choice have been forcefully brought out by a number of penetrating studies dealing with consumer decisions and production activities. It is very much an open question as to whether these behavioral characteristics can be at all captured within the formal limits of consistent choice on which the welfare-maximization approach depends.[7]

III

Paul Samuelson has noted that many economists would "separate economics from sociology upon the basis of rational or irrational behavior, where these terms are defined in the penumbra of utility theory."[8] This view might well be resented, for good reasons, by sociologists, but the cross that economists have to bear in this view of the dichotomy can be seen if we note that the approach of "rational behavior," as it is typically interpreted, leads to a remarkably mute theory. Behavior, it appears, is to be "explained in terms of preferences, which are in turn defined only by behavior." Not surprisingly excursions into circularities have been frequent. Nevertheless, Samuelson is undoubtedly right in asserting that the theory "is not in a technical sense *meaningless*."[9] The reason is quite simple. As we have already discussed, the approach does impose the requirement of internal consistercy of observed choice, and this might well be refuted by actual observations, making the theory "meaningful" in the sense in which Samuelson's statement is intended.

The requirement of consistency does have surprising cutting power. Various general characteristics of demand relations can be derived from it. But in the present context, the main issue is the possibility of using the consistency requirement for actual *testing*. Samuelson specifies the need for "ideal observational conditions" for the implications of the approach to be "refuted or verified." This is not, however, easy to satisfy since, on the one hand, our love of variety makes it illegitimate to consider individual acts of choice as the proper units (rather than *sequences* of choices) while, on the other hand, lapse of time makes it difficult to distinguish between inconsistencies and changing tastes. There have, in fact, been very few systematic attempts at testing the consistency of people's day-to-day behavior, even though there have been interesting and useful contrived experiments on people's reactions to uncertainty under laboratory conditions. What counts as admissible evidence remains unsettled. If today you were to poll economists of different schools, you would almost certainly find the coexistence of beliefs (i) that the rational behavior theory is unfalsifiable, (ii) that it is falsifiable and so far unfalsified, and (iii) that it is falsifiable and indeed patently false.

However, for my purposes here this is not the central issue. Even if the required consistency were seen to obtain, it would still leave the question of egoism unresolved except in the purely definitional sense, as I have already noted. A consistent chooser can have any degree of egoism that we care to specify. It is, of course, true that in the special case of pure consumer choice over private goods, the revealed preference theorist tries to relate the person's "preference" or "utility" to his *own* bundle of commodities. This restriction arises, however, not from any guarantee that he is concerned only with his own interests, but from the fact that his own consumption bundle — or that of his family — is the only bundle over which he has direct *control* in his acts of choice. The question of egoism remains completely open.

I believe the question also requires a clearer formulation than it tends to receive, and to this question I shall now turn.

IV

As we consider departures from "unsympathetic isolation abstractly assumed in Economics," to use Edgeworth's words, we must distinguish between two separate concepts: (i) sympathy and (ii) commitment. The former corresponds to the case in which the concern for others directly affects one's own welfare. If the knowledge of torture of others makes you sick, it is a case of sympathy; if it does not make you feel personally worse off, but you think it is wrong and you are ready to do something to stop it, it is a case of commitment. I do not wish to claim that the words chosen have any very great merit, but the distinction is, I think, important. It can be argued that behavior based on sympathy is in an important sense egoistic, for one is oneself pleased at others' pleasure and pained at others' pain, and the pursuit of one's own utility may thus be helped by sympathetic action. It is action based on commitment rather than sympathy which would be non-egoistic in this sense. (Note, however, that the *existence* of sympathy does not imply that the action helpful to others must be *based on* sympathy in the sense that the action would not take place had one got less or no comfort from others' welfare. This question *of causation* is to be taken up presently.)

Sympathy is, in some ways, an easier concept to analyze than commitment. When a person's sense of well-being is psychologically dependent on someone else's welfare, it is a case of sympathy; other things given, the awareness of the increase in the welfare of the other person then makes this person directly better off. (Of course, when the influence is negative, the relation is better named "antipathy," but we can economize on terminology and stick to the term "sympathy," just noting that the relation can be positive or negative.) While sympathy relates similar things to each other — namely, welfares of different persons — commitment relates choice to anticipated levels of welfare. One way of defining commitment is in terms of a person choosing an act that he believes will yield a lower level of personal welfare to him than an alternative

that is also available to him. Notice that the comparison is between *anticipated* welfare levels, and therefore this definition of
commitment excludes acts that go against self-interest resulting
purely from a failure to foresee consequences.

A more difficult question arises when a person's choice happens
to coincide with the maximization of his anticipated personal
welfare, but that is not the *reason* for his choice. If we wish to
make room for this, we can expand the definition of commitment
to include cases in which the person's choice, while maximizing
anticipated personal welfare, would be unaffected under at least
one counterfactual condition in which the act chosen would cease
to maximize personal welfare. Commitment in this more inclusive
sense may be difficult to ascertain not only in the context of others'
choices but also in that of one's own, since it is not always clear
what one would have done had the circumstances been different.
This broader sense may have particular relevance when one acts
on the basis of a concern for duty which, if violated, could cause
remorse, but the action is really chosen out of the sense of duty
rather than just to avoid the illfare resulting from the remorse
that would occur if one were to act otherwise. (Of course, even
the narrower sense of commitment will cover the case in which the
illfare resulting from the remorse, if any, is *outweighed* by the
gain in welfare.)

I have not yet referred to uncertainty concerning anticipated
welfare. When this is introduced, the concept of sympathy is
unaffected, but commitment will require reformulation. The
necessary modifications will depend on the person's reaction to
uncertainty. The simplest case is probably the one in which the
person's idea of what a "lottery" offers to him in terms of personal
gain is captured by the "expected utility" of personal welfare
(that is, adding personal welfares from different outcomes weighted
by the probability of occurrence of each outcome). In this case,
the entire discussion is reformulated simply replacing personal
welfare by *expected* personal welfare; commitment then involves
choosing an action that yields a lower expected welfare than
an alternative available action. (The broader sense can also be
correspondingly modified.)

In the terminology of modern economic theory, sympathy is a
case of "externality." Many models rule out externalities, for
example, the standard model to establish that each competitive
equilibrium is a Pareto optimum and belongs to the core of the
economy. If the existence of sympathy were to be permitted in
these models, some of these standard results would be upset,

though by no means all of them.[10] But this would not require a serious revision of the basic structure of these models. On the other hand, commitment does involve, in a very real sense, counter-preferential choice, destroying the crucial assumption that a chosen alternative must be better than (or at least as good as) the others for the person choosing it, and this would certainly require that models be formulated in an essentially different way.

The contrast between sympathy and commitment may be illustrated with the story of two boys who find two apples, one large, one small. Boy *A* tells boy *B*, "You choose." *B* immediately picks the larger apple. *A* is upset and permits himself the remark that this was grossly unfair. "Why?" asks *B*. "Which one would you have chosen, if you were to choose rather than me?" "The smaller one, of course," *A* replies. *B* is now triumphant: "Then what are you complaining about? That's the one you've got!" *B* certainly wins this round of the argument, but in fact *A* would have lost nothing from *B*'s choice had his own hypothetical choice of the smaller apple been based on sympathy as opposed to commitment. *A*'s anger indicates that this was probably not the case.

Commitment is, of course, closely connected with one's morals. But moral this question is in a very broad sense, covering a variety of influences from religious to political, from the ill-understood to the well-argued. When, in Bernard Shaw's *The Devil's Disciple*, Judith Anderson interprets Richard Dudgeon's willingness to be hanged in place of her husband as arising from sympathy for him or love for her, Richard is adamant in his denial: "What I did last night, I did in cold blood, caring not half so much for your husband, or for you as I do for myself. I had no motive and no interest: all I can tell you is that when it came to the point whether I would take my neck out of the noose and put another man's into it, I could not do it."[11]

The characteristic of commitment with which I am most concerned here is the fact that it drives a wedge between personal choice and personal welfare, and much of traditional economic theory relies on the identity of the two. This identity is sometimes obscured by the ambiguity of the term "preference," since the normal use of the word permits the identification of preference with the concept of being better off, and at the same time it is not quite unnatural to define "preferred" as "chosen." I have no strong views on the "correct" use of the word "preference," and I would be satisfied as long as both uses are not *simultaneously* made, attempting an empirical assertion by virtue of two definitions. The basic link between choice behavior and welfare achievements in the traditional models is severed as soon as commitment is admitted as an ingredient of choice.

V

"Fine," you might say, "but how relevant is all this to the kind of choices with which economists are concerned? Economics does not have much to do with Richard Dudgeon's march to the gallows." I think one should immediately agree that for many types of behavior, commitment is unlikely to be an important ingredient. In the private purchase of many consumer goods, the scope for the exercise of commitment may indeed be limited and may show up rather rarely in such exotic acts as the boycotting of South African avocados or the eschewing of Spanish holidays. Therefore, for many studies of consumer behavior and interpretations thereof, commitment may pose no great problem. Even sympathy may not be extremely important, the sources of interpersonal interdependence lying elsewhere, for example, in the desire to keep up with the Joneses or in being influenced by other people's habits.

But economics is not concerned only with consumer behavior; nor is consumption confined to "private goods." One area in which the question of commitment is most important is that of the so-called public goods. These have to be contrasted with "private goods" which have the characteristic that they cannot be used by more than one person: if you ate a piece of apple pie, I wouldn't consider devouring it too. Not so with "public goods," for example, a road or a public park, which you and I may both be able to use. In many economic models private goods are the only ones around, and this is typically the case when the "invisible hand" is given the task of doing visible good. But, in fact, public goods are important in most economies and cover a wide range of services from roads and street lighting to defense. There is much evidence that the share of public goods in national consumption has grown rather dramatically in most countries in the world.

The problem of optimal allocation of public goods has also been much discussed, especially in the recent economic literature. A lot of attention, in particular, has been devoted to the problem of correct revelation of preferences. This arises most obviously in the case of subscription schemes where a person is charged according to benefits received. The main problem centers on the fact that it is in everybody's interest to understate the benefit he expects, but this understatement may lead to the rejection of a public project which would have been justified if true benefits were known. Analysis of this difficulty, sometimes referred to as the "free rider" problem, has recently led to some extremely ingenious proposals for circumventing this inefficiency within the framework of egoistic action. The reward mechanism is set up with such ungodly cunning that people have an incentive to reveal exactly their true willingness to pay for the public good in question. One difficulty in this solution arises from an assumed limitation of strategic possibilities open to the individual, the removal of which leads to an impossibility result. Another difficulty concerns the fact that in giving people the incentive to reveal the truth, money is handed out and the income distribution shifts in a way unguided by distributional considerations. This effect can, of course, be undone by a redistribution of initial endowments and profit shares, but that action obviously raises difficulties of its own.

Central to this problem is the assumption that when asked a question, the individual gives that answer which will maximize his personal gain. How good is this assumption? I doubt that in general it is very good. ("Where is the railway station?" he asks me. "There," I say, pointing at the post office, "and would you please post this letter for me on the way?" "Yes," he says, determined to open the envelope and check whether it contains something valuable.) Even in the particular context of revelation of preferences for public goods the gains-maximizing behavior may not be the best assumption. Leif Johansen, one of the major contributors to public economics, is, I think, right to question the assumption in this context:

> Economic theory in this, as well as in some other fields, tends to suggest that people are honest only to the extent that they have economic incentives for being so. This is a homo oeconomicus assumption which is far from being obviously true, and which needs confrontation with observed realities. In fact, a simple line of thought suggests that the assumption can hardly be true in its most extreme form. No society would be viable without some norms and rules of conduct. Such norms and rules are necessary for viability exactly in fields where strictly economic incentives are absent and cannot be created.[12]

What is at issue is not whether people invariably give an honest answer to every question, but whether they always give a gains-maximizing answer, or at any rate, whether they give gains-maximizing answers often enough to make that the appropriate general assumption for economic theory. The presence of non-gains-maximizing answers, including truthful ones, immediately brings in commitment as a part of behavior.

The question is relevant also to the recent literature on strategic voting. A number of beautiful analytical results have recently been established showing the impossibility of any voting procedure satisfying certain elementary requirements and making honest voting the gains-maximizing strategy for everyone. The correctness of these results is not in dispute, but is it appropriate to assume that people always do try to maximize personal gains in their voting behavior? Indeed, in large elections, it is difficult to show that any voter has any real prospect of affecting the outcome by his vote, and if voting involves some cost, the expected net gain from voting may typically be negative. Nevertheless, the proportion of turnout in large elections may still be quite high, and I have tried to argue elsewhere that in such elections people may often be "guided not so much by maximization of expected utility, but something much simpler, viz, just a desire to record one's true preference."[13] If this desire reflects a sense of commitment, then the behavior in question would be at variance with the view of man in traditional economic theory.

VI

The question of commitment is important in a number of other economic contexts. It is central to the problem of work motivation, the importance of which for production performance can hardly be ignored.

It is certainly costly and may be impossible to devise a system of supervision with rewards and punishment such that everyone has the incentive to exert himself. Every economic system has, therefore, tended to rely on the existence of attitudes toward work which supersedes the calculation of net gain from each unit of exertion. Social conditioning plays an extremely important part here. I am persuaded that Britain's present economic difficulties have a great deal to do with work-motivation problems that lie outside the economics of rewards and punishments, and one reason why economists seem to have so little to contribute in this area is the neglect in traditional economic theory of this whole issue of commitment and the social relations surrounding it.

These questions are connected, of course, with ethics, since moral reasoning influences one's actions, but in a broader sense these are matters of culture, of which morality is one part. Indeed, to take an extreme case, in the Chinese "cultural revolution" one of the primary aims was the increase of the sense of commitment with an eye on economic results: "the aim of the Great Proletarian Cultural Revolution is to revolutionize people's ideology and as a consequence to achieve greater, faster, better and more economical results in all fields of work.[14] Of course, China was experimenting with reducing dramatically the role of material incentives in production, which would certainly have increased the part that commitment was meant to play, but even within the traditional systems of payments, much reliance is usually placed on rules of conduct and modes of behavior that go beyond strictly economic incentives. To run an organization *entirely* on incentives to personal gain is pretty much a hopeless task.

I will have a bit more to say presently on what might lie behind the sense of commitment, but I would like to emphasize at this stage that the morality or culture underlying it may well be of a limited kind — far removed from the grandeur of approaches such as utilitarianism. The "implicit collusions" that have been observed in business behavior in oligopolies seem to work on the basis of a system of mutual trust and sense of responsibility which has well-defined limits, and attempts at "universalization" of the same kind of behavior in other spheres of action may not go with it at all. There it is strictly a question of business ethics which is taken to apply within a fairly limited domain.

Similarly, in wage negotiations and in collective bargaining the sense of solidarity on either side may have well-defined limits, and may not fit in at all with an approach such as that of general utilitarianism. Edgeworth's implicit assumption, on which I commented earlier, that egoism and utilitarianism exhaust the possible alternative motivations, will be especially unhelpful in this context. While the field of commitment may be large, that of commitment based on utilitarianism and other universalized moral systems may well form a relatively small part of it.

VII

The economic theory of utility, which relates to the theory of rational behavior, is sometimes criticized for having too much structure; human beings are alleged to be "simpler" in reality. If our argument so far has been correct, precisely the opposite seems to be the case: traditional theory has *too little* structure. A person is given *one* preference ordering, and as when the need arises this is supposed to reflect his interests, represent his welfare, summarize his idea of what should be done, and describe his actual choices and behavior. Can one preference ordering do all these things? A person thus described may be "rational" in the limited sense of revealing no inconsistencies in his choice behavior, but if he has no use for these distinctions between quite different concepts, he must be a bit of a fool. The *purely* economic man is indeed close to being a social moron. Economic theory has been much preoccupied with this rational fool decked in the glory of his *one* all-purpose preference ordering. To make room for the different concepts related to his behavior we need a more elaborate structure.

What kind of a structure do we need? A bit more room up top is provided by John Harsanyi's important distinction between a person's "ethical" preferences and his "subjective" preferences: "the former must express what this individual prefers (or, rather would prefer), on the basis of impersonal social considerations alone, and the latter must express what he actually prefers, whether on the basis of his personal interests or on any other basis."[15] This dual structure permits us to distinguish between what a person thinks is good from the social point of view and what he regards as good from his own personal point of view. Presumably sympathy enters directly into the so-called subjective preference, but the role of commitment is left somewhat unclear. Insofar as a person's "subjective" preferences are taken to "define his utility function," the intention seems to be to exclude commitment from it, but an ambiguity arises from the fact that these are defined to "express his preferences in the full sense of the word as they actually are." Is this in the sense of choice, or in the sense of his conception of his own welfare? Perhaps Harsanyi intended the latter, since "ethical" preferences are by contrast given the role of expressing "what he prefers only in those possibly rare moments when he forces a special impartial and impersonal attitude on himself." But what if he departs from his personal welfare maximization (including any sympathy), not through an impartial concern for all, but through a sense of commitment to some particular group, say to the neighborhood or to the social class to which he belongs? The fact is we are still short of structure.

Even in expressing moral judgements from an impersonal point of view, a *dual* structure is deficient. Surely a preference ordering can be *more* ethical than another but *less* so than a third. We need more structure in this respect also. I have proposed elsewhere – at the 1972 Bristol conference on "practical reason" – that we need to consider *rankings of preference rankings* to express our moral judgements.[16] I would like to discuss this structure a bit more. A particular morality can be viewed, not just in terms of the "most moral" ranking of the set of alternative actions, but as a moral ranking of the rankings of actions (going well beyond the identification merely of the "most moral" ranking of actions). Let X be the set of alternative and mutually exclusive combinations of actions under consideration, and let Y be the set of rankings of the elements of X. A ranking of the set Y (consisting of action-rankings) will be called a meta-ranking of action-set X. It is my claim that a particular ranking of the action-set X is not articulate enough to express much about a given morality, and a more robust format is provided by choosing a meta-ranking of actions (that is, a ranking of Y rather than of X). Of course, such a meta-ranking may include *inter alia* the specification of a particular action-ranking as the "most moral," but insofar as actual behavior may be based on a compromise between claims of morality and the pursuit of various other objectives (including self-interest), one has to look also at the relative moral standings of those action-rankings that are *not* "most moral."

To illustrate, consider a set X of alternative action combinations and the following three rankings of this action-set X: ranking A representing my personal welfare ordering (thus, in some sense, representing my personal interests), ranking B reflecting my "isolated" personal interests ignoring sympathy (when such a separation is possible, which is not always so),[17] and ranking C in terms of which actual choices are made by me (when such choices are representable by a ranking, which again is not always so.) The "most moral" ranking M can, conceivably, be any of these rankings A, B, or C. Or else it can be some other ranking quite distinct from all three. (This will be the case if the actual choices of actions are not the "most moral" in terms of the moral system in question, and if, furthermore, the moral system requires sacrifice of some self-interest and also of "isolated" self-interest.) But even when some ranking M distinct from A, B and C is identified as being at the top of the moral table, that still leaves open the question as to how A, B, and C may be ordered vis-á-vis each other. If, to take a particular example, it so happens that the pursuit of self-interest, including pleasure and pain from sympathy, is put morally above the pursuit of "isolated" self-interest (thereby leading to a partial coincidence of self-interest with morality), and the actual choices reflect a morally superior position to the pursuit of self-interest (perhaps due to a compromise in the moral direction), then the morality in question precipitates the meta-ranking M, C, A, B, in descending order. This, of course, goes well beyond specifying that M is "morally best."

The technique of meta-ranking permits a varying extent of moral articulation. It is not being claimed that a moral meta-ranking must be a *complete* ordering of the set Y, that is, must completely order all rankings of X. It can be a *partial* ordering, and I expect it often will be incomplete, but I should think that in most cases there will be no problem in going well beyond the limited expression permitted by the twofold specification of "ethical" and "subjective" preferences.

The rankings of action can, of course, be ordered also on grounds other than a particular system of morality: meta-ranking is a general technique usable under alternative interpretations of the meta-ranking relation. It can be used to describe a particular ideology or a set of political priorities or a system of class interests. In quite a different context, it can provide the format for expressing what preferences one would have preferred to have ("I wish I liked vegetarian foods more," or "I wish I didn't enjoy smoking so much"). Or it can be used to analyze the conflicts involved in addiction ("Given my current tastes, I am better off with heroin, but having heroin leads me to addiction, and I would have preferred not to have these tastes"). The tool of meta-rankings can be used in many different ways in distinct contexts.

This is clearly not the occasion to go into a detailed analysis of how this broader structure permits a better understanding of preference and behavior. A structure is not, of course, a theory, and alternative theories can be formulated using this structure. I should mention, however, that the structure demands much more information than is yielded by the observation of people's actual choices, which would at most reveal only the ranking C. It gives a role to introspection and to communication. To illustrate one use of the apparatus, I may refer to some technical results. Suppose I am trying to investigate your conception of your own welfare. You first specify the ranking A which represents your welfare ordering. But I want to go further and get an idea of your *cardinal* utility function, that is, roughly speaking, not only which ranking gives you more welfare but also by how much. I now ask you to order the different rankings in terms of their "closeness" to your actual welfare ranking A, much as a policeman uses the technique of photofit: is this more like him, or is that? If your answers reflect the fact that reversing a stronger preference makes the result more distant than reversing a weaker intensity of preference, your replies will satisfy certain consistency properties, and the order of rankings will permit us to compare your welfare *differences* between pairs. In fact, by considering higher and higher order rankings, we can determine your cardinal welfare function as closely as you care to specify. I am not saying that this type of dialogue is the best way of discovering your welfare function, but it does illustrate that once we give up the assumption that observing choices is the only source of data on welfare, a whole new world opens up, liberating us from the informational shackles of the traditional approach.

This broader structure has many other uses, for example, permitting a clearer analysis *of akrasia* — the weakness of will — and clarifying some conflicting considerations in the theory of liberty, which I have tried to discuss elsewhere.[18] It also helps in analyzing the development of behavior involving commitment in situations characterized by games such as the Prisoners' Dilemma.[19] This game is often treated, with some justice, as the classic case of failure of individualistic rationality. There are two players and each has two strategies, which we may call selfish and unselfish to make it easy to remember without my having to go into too much detail. Each player is better off personally by playing the selfish strategy *no* matter what the other does, but both are better off if both choose the unselfish rather than the selfish strategy. It is individually optimal to do the selfish thing: one can only affect one's own action and not that of the other, and given the other's strategy — no matter what — each player is better off being selfish. But this combination of selfish strategies, which results from self-seeking by both, produces an outcome that is worse for both than the result of both choosing the unselfish strategy. It can be shown that this conflict can exist even if the game is repeated many times.

Some people find it puzzling that individual self-seeking by each should produce an inferior outcome for all, but this, of course, is a well-known conflict, and has been discussed in general terms for a very long time. Indeed, it was the basis of Rousseau's famous distinction between the "general will" and the "will of all."[20] But the puzzle from the point of view of rational behavior lies in the fact that in actual situations people often do not follow the selfish strategy. Real life examples of this type of behavior in complex circumstances are well known, but even in controlled experiments in laboratory conditions people playing the Prisoners' Dilemma frequently do the unselfish thing.

In interpreting these experimental results, the game theorist is tempted to put it down to the lack of intelligence of the players: "Evidently the run-of-the-mill players are not strategically sophisticated enough to have figured out that strategy DD [the selfish strategy] is the only rationally defensible strategy, and this intellectual short-coming saves them from losing." A more fruitful approach may lie in permitting the possibility that the person is *more* sophisticated than the theory allows and that he has asked himself what type of preference he would like the other player to have, and on somewhat Kantian grounds has considered the case for himself having those preferences, or behaving *as if* he had them. This line of reasoning requires him to consider the modifications of the game that would be brought about by acting through commitment (in terms of "revealed preferences," this would look as if he had different preferences from the ones he actually had), and he has to assess alternative behavior norms in that light. I have discussed these issues elsewhere; thus I shall simply note here that the apparatus of *ranking of rankings* assists the reasoning which involves considering the merits of having different types of preferences (or of acting as if one had them).

VIII

Admitting behavior based on commitment would, of course have far-reaching consequences on the nature of many economic models. I have tried to show why this change is necessary and why the consequences may well be serious. Many issues remain unresolved, including the empirical importance of commitment as a part of behavior, which would vary, as I have argued, from field to field. I have also indicated why the empirical evidence for this cannot be sought in the mere observation of actual choices, and must involve other sources of information, including introspection and discussion.

There remains, however, the issue as to whether this view of man amounts to seeing him as an irrational creature. Much depends on the concept of rationality used, and many alternative characterizations exist. In the sense of *consistency* of choice, there is no reason to think that admitting commitment must imply any departure from rationality. This is, however, a weak sense of rationality.

The other concept of rationality prevalent in economics identifies it with the possibility of justifying each act in terms of self-interest: when act x is chosen by person i and act y rejected, this implies that i's personal interests are expected by i to be better served by x than by y. There are, it seems to me, three distinct elements in this approach. First, it is a consequentialist view: judging acts by consequences only.[21] Second, it is an approach of *act* evaluation rather than *rule* evaluation. And third, the only consequences considered in evaluating acts are those on one's own interests, everything else being at best an intermediate product. It is clearly possible to dispute the claims of each of these elements to being a necessary part of the conception of rationality in the dictionary sense of "the power of being able to exercise one's reason." Moreover, arguments for rejecting the straightjacket of each of these three principles are not hard to find. The case for actions based on commitment can arise from the violation of any of these three principles. Commitment sometimes relates to a sense of obligation going beyond the consequences. Sometimes the lack of personal gain in particular *acts* is accepted by considering the value of *rules* of behavior. But even within a consequentialist act-evaluation framework, the exclusion of any consideration other than self-interest seems to impose a wholly arbitrary limitation on the notion of rationality.

Henry Sidgwick noted the arbitrary nature of the assumption of egoism:

> If the Utilitarian has to answer the question, "Why should I sacrifice my own happiness for the greater happiness of another?" it must surely be admissible to ask the Egoist, "Why should I sacrifice a present pleasure for one in the future? Why should I concern myself about my own future feelings any more than about the feelings of other persons?" It undoubtedly seems to Common Sense paradoxical to ask for a reason why one should seek one's own happiness on the whole; but I do not see how the demand can be repudiated as absurd by those who adopt views of the extreme empirical school of psychologists, although those views are commonly supposed to have a close affinity with Egoistic Hedonism. Grant that the Ego is merely a system of coherent phenomena, that the permanent identical "I" is not a fact but a fiction, as Hume and his followers maintain; why, then, should one part of the series of feelings into which the Ego is resolved be concerned with another part of the same series, any more than with any other series?[22]

The view of rationality that identifies it with consequentialist act-evaluation using self-interest can be questioned from any of these three angles. Admitting commitment as a part of behavior implies no denial of reasoned assessment as a basis for action.

There is not much merit in spending a lot of effort in debating the "proper" definition of rationality. The term is used in many different senses, and none of the criticisms of the behavioral foundations of economic theory presented here stands or falls on the definition chosen. The main issue is the acceptability of the assumption of the invariable pursuit of self-interest in each act. Calling that type of behavior rational, or departures from it irrational, does not change the relevance of these criticisms, though it does produce an arbitrarily narrow definition of rationality. This paper has not been concerned with the question as to whether human behavior is better described as rational or irrational. The main thesis has been the need to accommodate commitment as a part of behavior. Commitment does not presuppose reasoning, but it does not exclude it; in fact, insofar as consequences on others have to be more clearly understood and assessed in terms of one's values and instincts, the scope for reasoning may well expand. I have tried to analyze the structural extensions in the conception of preference made necessary by behavior based on reasoned assessment of commitment. Preferences as rankings have to be replaced by a richer structure involving meta-rankings and related concepts.

I have also argued against viewing behavior in terms of the traditional dichotomy between egoism and universalized moral systems (such as utilitarianism). Groups intermediate between oneself and all, such as class and community, provide the focus of many actions involving commitment. The rejection of egoism as description of motivation does not, therefore, imply the acceptance of some universalized morality as the basis of actual behavior. Nor does it make human beings excessively noble.

Nor, of course, does the use of reasoning imply remarkable wisdom.

> It is as true as Caesar's name was Kaiser,
> That no economist was ever wiser,

said Robert Frost in playful praise of the contemporary economist. Perhaps a similarly dubious tribute can be paid to the economic man in our modified conception. If he shines at all, he shines in comparison — in contrast — with the dominant image of the rational fool.

NOTES

1 F. Y. Edgeworth, *Mathematical Psychics: An Essay on the Application of Mathematics to the Moral Sciences* (London, 1881), p. 16.
2 Edgeworth, *Mathematical Psychics*, p. 104. In fact, he went on to make some interesting remarks on the results of "impure" egoism, admitting an element of sympathy for each other. The remarks have been investigated and analyzed by David Collard, "Edgeworth's Propositions on Altruism," *Economic Journal* 85 (1975).
3 J. Butler, *Fifteen Sermons Preached at the Rolls Chapel* (London, 1726); see also T. Nagel, *The Possibility of Altruism* (Oxford, 1972), p. 81.
4 See H. S. Houthakker, "Revealed Preference and the Utility Function," *Economica* 17 (1950); P. A. Samuelson, "The Problem of Integrability in Utility Theory," *Economica* 17 (1950).
5 For the main analytical results see M. K. Richter, "Rational Choice," in J. S. Chipman et al. (eds), *Preference, Utility and Demand Theory* (New York, 1971).
6 A. K. Sen, "Behaviour and the Concept of Preference," *Economica* 40 (1973). See also S. Körner's important study, *Experience and Conduct* (Cambridge, 1971).
7 On the required conditions of consistency for viewing choice in terms of a binary relation see A. K. Sen, "Choice Functions and Revealed Preference," *Review of Economic Studies* 38 (1971).
8 P. A. Samuelson, *The Foundations of Economics* (Cambridge, Mass., 1955), p. 90.
9 Samuelson, *The Foundations of Economics*, p. 91.
10 See A. K. Sen, "Labour Allocation in a Co-operative Enterprise," *Review of Economic Studies* 33 (1966).
11 G. B. Shaw, *Three Plays for Puritans* (Harmondsworth, 1966), p. 94.
12 L. Johansen, "The Theory of Public Goods: Misplaced Emphasis" (Institute of Economics, University of Oslo, 1976).
13 See A. K. Sen, *Collective Choice and Social Welfare* (Edinburgh and San Francisco, 1970), p. 195.
14 "The Decision of the Central Committee of the Chinese Communist Party concerning the Great Proletarian Cultural Revolution," adopted on 8 August 1966, reproduced in Joan Robinson, *The Cultural Revolution in China* (Harmondsworth, 1969). See also A. K. Sen, *On Economic Inequality* (Oxford, 1973).
15 J. Harsanyi, "Cardinal Welfare, Individualistic Ethics, and Interpersonal Comparisons of Utility," *Journal of Political Economy* 63 (1955), p. 315.
16 A. K. Sen, "Choice, Orderings and Morality," in S. Körner (ed.), *Practical Reason* (Oxford, 1974).
17 This presupposes some "independence" among the different elements influencing the level of overall welfare, implying some "separability." See W. M. Gorman, "Tricks with Utility Functions," in M. Artis and

A. R. Nobay (eds), *Essays in Economic Analysis* (Cambridge, 1975).

18 See Sen, "Choice, Orderings and Morality;" and also Sen, "Liberty, Unanimity and Rights," *Economica* 43 (1976). Note also the relevance of this structure in analyzing the incompleteness of the conception of liberty in terms of the ability to do what one *actually wishes*. Cf. "If I find that I am able to do little or nothing of what I wish, I need only contract or extinguish my wishes, and I am made free. If the tyrant (or 'hidden persuader') manages to condition his subjects (or customers) into losing their original wishes and embrace ('internalize') the form of life he has invented for them, he will, on this definition, have succeeded in liberating them." I. Berlin, "Two Concepts of Liberty," in *Four Essays on Liberty* (Oxford, 1969), pp. 139–40.

19 See R. D. Luce and H. Raiffa, *Games and Decisions* (New York, 1958); A. Rapoport and A. M. Chammah, *Prisoner's Dilemma: A Study in Conflict and Cooperation* (Ann Arbor, 1965); W. G. Runciman and A. K. Sen, "Games, Justice and the General Will," *Mind* 74 (1965); N. Howard, *Paradoxes of Rationality* (Cambridge, Mass., 1971).

20 See Runciman and Sen, "Games, Justice and the General Will."

21 On the nature of "consequentialism" and the problems engendered by it, see B. Williams, "A Critque of Utilitarianism," in J. J. C. Smart and B. Williams, *Utilitarianism: For and Against* (Cambridge, 1973).

22 H. Sidgwick, *The Method of Ethics* (London, 1874; 7th ed., 1907), pp. 418–19. See also Nagel's forceful exposition of the thesis that "altruism itself depends on a recognition of the reality of other persons, and on the equivalent capacity to regard oneself as merely one individual among many." *The Possibility of Altruism*, p. 1.

Part III
The (Dis-)Ordered Individual

8
Discipline, Politics, Ambiguity

WILLIAM CONNOLLY

UNCONSCIOUS CONTRIVANCES OF CONTROL

Is there a sense in which liberal and radical thought together obscure modes of disciplinary control in modernity? A sense, that is, in which the conceptions of self held by radical proponents of civic virtue and liberal defenders of human interests and rights combine to conceal the violence required to produce and maintain the modern self? Michel Foucault thinks there is. He treats liberalism and radicalism as two complementary doctrines; together they enter into those discursive practices which constitute "disciplinary society."

I will explore this question, first, by offering a brief account of contemporary modes of disciplinary control, which, though surely contestable, coheres with a conception of self common to liberals and radicals; second, by presenting the Foucauldian case for extension of the account into new corners of institutional life; and third, by responding to the Foucauldian reading with one that both profits and deviates from it. The dialectic to be pursued expresses the conviction that liberal and radical doctrines are most in need of redefinition at those obscure junctures where their differences merge into commonalities.

In an era characterized by doctrines of "reindustrialization," "supply-side economics," "rational choice," "incentive systems," "zerosum economics," and "legitimacy deficits" a broad doctrinal drift toward the problem of managing, regulating, and controlling the behavior of people and institutions can be discerned. The liberal drive to devise means to coordinate more aspects of public and private life indeed meshes with the radical understanding that

Reprinted by permission of the University of Wisconsin Press from William Connolly, *Politics and Ambiguity* (Madison: University of Wisconsin Press, 1987), pp. 99–115.

operative citizen allegiance to the roles and ends of the political economy is weak. The drive to extend discipline over those who do not discipline themselves — discernible in the programs of liberal economists such as Charles Schultze and Lester Thurow — represents an effort to close the gap between the imperatives of social coordination built into the political economy and disposition of workers, owners, welfare dependents, taxpayers, children, and parents to evade, elude, resist, and oppose those imperatives.[1]

The pressures to extend disciplinary control are perhaps most prominent in the doctrine of "reindustrialization" — a loose constellation of policies and proposals designed to foster capital accumulation, deregulate business, foster worker productivity, impose austerity on low-income households, and restore rapid economic growth. Within it is discernible the drift toward militarization of welfare as young clients are told they can get the job experience they need in the army, navy, air force, and marines, and as students, facing cutbacks in civilian funds for higher education, are informed of the expansion of ROTC scholarships committing them to future military duty. Welfare is thus shifted into a bureaucracy that renders its beneficiaries more susceptible to disciplinary control. There is the corollary shift from public welfare to private philanthropy, allowing private patrons to set the terms of aid away from the glare of public accountability; the use of inflation to force those workers without effective bargaining power to accept real reductions in income; the relaxation of restrictions on domestic state surveillance; the intimidation of public- and some private-sector unions; the rapid growth of private security systems to monitor workers and consumers; the visible acts of police brutality against isolated members of the underclass; the hardening line against blue-collar crime; the campaigns to censor library books and regulate school curricula; the effort to isolate decaying cities in the Northeast and Midwest from a political coalition large enough to govern the nation; the tax revolts that eventually provoke governmental cutbacks in the budget for civilian welfare and services.

But these visible modes of control are limited in effectiveness unless they are complemented by what we might describe as unconscious contrivances of social discipline. The latter emerge when allegiance to the purposes and priorities of the political economy is low among particular constituencies, the demands for central coordination remain high, and opportunities to elude or evade sacrifices and obligations imposed by private and public authorities are relatively plentiful.

Consider, by way of example, the illegal alien. Castigated by many as a thief of American jobs, the alien is a valuable commodity to labor-intensive businesses. Because the alien is illegal, he or she is a possessor of labor power without political rights. The alien is thus in a weak position to complain about wages or working conditions, to establish roots in the broader community, to organize collectively, or to participate in the political life of the society. Illegality in this instance depoliticizes; it subjects the alien to a self-imposed discipline and silence designed to shield him from the eye of the public authorities. The anonymous presence of the alien further inhibits the demands citizen workers make; and it reminds marginal citizens that they could become aliens in their own country if they step too far outside the accepted bounds of political propriety. There is thus reason in the hostility many marginal workers feel toward the alien; he both poses a threat to them and symbolizes starkly a condition they experience darkly and imperfectly. The drive of the marginal worker/citizen to maintain psychological distance from the alien contains the fear that the actual condition of the one group is too close for comfort to the possible status of the other.

Consider, to bring things closer to home, the citizen who is also a tax evader. In the 1981 Federal Income Tax Form the taxpayer is instructed to report all earnings, including "bartering income (fair market value of goods and services you returned in return for your services) ... business expense reimbursements that cover more than you spent for those services ... gains from the sale of ... securities, coins, gold, silver or other property, gambling winnings, embezzled or other illegal income." The formal rules of tax payment, the difficulties of enforcement, and the intimate connection between disposable income and participation in the good life available in America combine to convert a large percentage of American citizens into low-grade criminals. A nation of tax evaders is a nation of people who, to varying degrees, have an incentive to keep a low public profile, to keep their visible life unexceptionable so that nothing unusual will excite the interest of the Internal Revenue Service or the citizens who are invited to report suspicious behavior to it.

The alien and the tax evader, as agents of self-discipline and self-depoliticization, are threads woven into the fabric of the political economy. Large sections of the political economy are woven from the same spool. The army recruit who learns to "beat the system" by seeking anonymity within it unwittingly provides support for the military as an order sustained by anonymous role bearers. The welfare freeloader, the small-time participant in the underground economy, the gambler, the drug user or dealer, the street person, the sexually perverse, the draft or draft-registration evader, the divorcee striving to retain child custody or evade child support, the informant seeking protection from organized crime, the academic researcher adapting to stringent criteria for grant support, the hooker, the professional adjusting to narrow standards for career advancement in a tight economy, the employee who has falsified educational credentials or a police record or an official history of mental instability to get a job, the alcoholic, the public official on the take – all these people, when the appropriate background conditions are operative, are drawn into the web of social control through the self-pursuit of anonymity and conventionality. Some of them literally become resident aliens, while others merely maintain a low profile to hook into the regular or irregular economy.

In each of these cases the evasion of laws or social norms in one respect operates to discipline the self in others; those who, from need or ambition, rip off the system in one way strip from themselves as well a measure of freedom and effective citizenship.

Certain attributes of these unconscious contrivances of social control need attention. First, these artifices of self-discipline are unplanned. They emerge initially as a miscellany of dispersed tactics to evade official laws and regulations. They then function as unorganized modes of social control whenever the primary strategies of control are tightly enforced; and some of them eventually become deployed as conscious instruments of control by public and private authorities. The ambiguous relation between the state and the citizen/taxpayer exemplifies this pattern of development. Individual members of the underclass, for instance, develop multiple strategies to evade payments to the state. As the phenomenon spreads it functions to reduce total revenue available to the state and to depoliticize the evaders. Finally, particular authorities realize that they can use the veiled threat of tightened enforcement to keep these potential elements of disruption in line.

Second, these unconscious contrivances do not function well as modes of social control during periods of prosperity and tolerance for social diversity. They solidify when the reins of conscious social coordination are drawn more tightly. Thus gays may participate openly in the life of the community until public knowledge of their sexual orientation threatens their livelihoods or community status; then they must either go underground or accept the prospect of a marginal status. Academic grantspersons can maintain congruence between their own standards and the criteria of granting agencies as long as the latter appreciate diversity in research orientation, but when the criteria are narrowly defined they must either drop out of the race or adapt their orientation to officially prescribed standards.

Third, though these mechanisms, in cumulative effect, help to displace political articulation of disaffection, they do not normally help the political economy to function efficiently. These are contrivances of order rather than efficiency, of discipline rather than state revenue, of depoliticization rather than realization of a good life shared by citizens in common. These unconscious contrivances of order proliferate when operative allegiance to role assignments is low, when belief in the future promised by the civilization of productivity has been suspended, and when no insurgent movement has crystallized to articulate the deeper discontents of disaffected constituencies. The gap opened between the order's expanded need for the coordination of individual conduct and the contracted civic virtue among subordinate sections of the populace is filled, though imperfectly and ambiguously, by these unconscious contrivances of social discipline. The mechanisms of social discipline are thus extended in tandem with the extension of social disaffection. And the dimensions of these practices that help to maintain overt social peace also support economic deterioration.

DISCIPLINE AND SUBJECTIVITY

Foucault, the consummate theorist of modernity as disciplinary society, would detect major defects in the foregoing account. The conceptions of self and rationality it presupposes prohibit it from probing the mechanisms that generate the particular structures of self, rationality, virtue, sexuality, criminality, and madness appropriate to modernity. And it seems to endorse, in its opposition to the incentive systems and police powers of the present, an ideal of collectivity in which people freely identify with the ends and norms of their way of life. Its basic flaw resides in its insistence on treating an effect of disciplinary society — the unified subject as a bearer of rights, interests, and virtues — as an epistemically privileged center to be protected from repression or unjust coercion. The account thus perceives disciplines that limit the subject but not those that constitute the subject, and it misses these latter pressures because it insists on construing the unified subject as a rational achievement of modernity.

Modernity, on Foucault's reading, is sustained by drawing the self systematically into the orbit of social discipline. It is not coincidental that paranoia — the constant sense of being under surveillance by others — is the paradigmatic mental illness of modernity. For the politics of control through visibility of the self to agents of normalization encourages self-protection of one's status as a free, responsible agent through self-containment of impulses and inclinations that do not conform to established standards of normality. The normalized self is, for Foucault, the self that maintains self-surveillance to avoid treatment for delinquency, mental illness, or sexual perversity; disciplinary society is the order that extends strategies of normalization into new frontiers of social life. The humanist critics of repressive politics and the overt agents of coercive control are, on this reading, Siamese twins. Facing in different directions, they are bound together at the back; strategies of normalization pursued by the advocates of civic virtue, sexual liberation, client-centered therapy, and prison reform complement the overt forms of coercion pursued by police and intelligence bureaucracies as well as the incentive systems forged by policy scientists. As Foucault's genealogies of madness, therapy, medicine, crime, and sexuality are designed to show, these twin strategies function together (behind the backs of the intellectuals who constitute them as oppositional) to extend the tentacles of order more deeply into the self.

The logic of Foucault's account is exhibited in his history of madness.[2] The literature and art of the late Middle Ages were preoccupied with folly. Lodged within a world alive with the signs of God's purpose and will, folly signified a self both fallen from humanity and possessed by a truth beyond the powers of human articulation. Since the phenomenon was suspended in ambiguity, the social response to madness was ambiguous. It was simultaneously an object of fear and fascination, a danger to be avoided and a dark sign to be read for clues about the human condition and its relation to the larger cosmos. The Ship of Fools, a symbol of significance beyond its actual use, embodied this ambiguity. On these ships the mad were at once separated from society and free to travel on water in pursuit of their lost humanity; they could seek purification on the waterways and provide ordinary people, when the ships pulled into the harbor, with glimpses into the mysteries of human life and the limits of human reason.

What does it presage, this wisdom of fools? Doubtless since it is a forbidden wisdom, it presages both the reign of Satan and the end of the world; ultimate bliss and supreme punish-

ment; omnipotence on earth and the infernal fall. The Ship
of Fools sails through a landscape of delights, where all is
offered to desire, a sort of renewed paradise, since there no
man knows either suffering or need; and yet has not recovered
his innocence .... When man deploys the arbitrary nature
of his madness he confronts the dark necessity of the world;
the animal that haunts his nightmares and his nights of
privation in his own nature, which will lay bare hell's piti-
less truth.[3]

But modernity, through a series of stages launched during
the Enlightenment, has squeezed the ambiguity out of madness.
Madness is now constituted as unreason, and the processes by
which we confine, exclude, medicalize and cure it ensure that
reason, in its modern guise, can avoid awareness of limits or
antinomies it may contain. The agents of control and confinement
unite with their unwitting allies, the agents of rehabilitation and
treatment, to define the mad as victims of a disease to be cured
or controlled, never as *signs* that the norms from which they
deviate are too demanding or destructive of the self to which
they are applied. The occurrence of mental illness, in the modern
era of persons, freedom, and responsibility, authorizes officials to
suspend rights to self-control; and the knowledge that such a
suspension might be invoked encourages one to contain those
aspects of self that do not fit into established standards. Madness
is, on the Foucauldian reading, a real phenomenon, and its bearers
do suffer immensely. But its modern mode functions politically
to ward off deconstructions of established standards of reason
and normality and to establish the modern self as a locus of
disciplinary normalization.

A corollary shift occurs in the modern orientation to criminality.
In late medieval Europe torture was a closely regulated means of
discovering the truth of crime, and punishment was a public
spectacle through which the sovereign displayed his power and
vengeance to the assembled crowd. The spectacle expressed a
certain ambiguity; for here the crowd might listen to the condemned
man denounce the sovereign, and here on occasion the crowd
might support the condemned against the sovereign. The political
dimension of crime – its ambiguous embodiment of avarice and
opposition to the order – could emerge in these spectacles. People
could glimpse arbitrary elements in their own order through the
spectacle of crime and punishment.

But here too ambiguity has now been subdued. The criminal is either a person who has voluntarily broken a just code to which he had previously consented or a delinquent who has lost self-control. He is either an agent to be punished or the bearer of an illness to be treated.

It is well known that modern prisons breed hardened criminals. That effect, Foucault insists, is not one of its failures but the sign of its greatest success. Modern penality depoliticizes crime; it draws attention to the character of the criminal and away from the power of the regime; and it separates the criminal from other disaffected elements of the population. The spread of crime thus seldom jeopardizes the order. Rather it constantly renews the cry for law and order or, when that cycle has exhausted itself, for the rehabilitation of delinquents. In either event, the contemporary constitution of crime fosters the perfection and extension of techniques for surveillance, treatment and coercive control, which increasingly typify disciplinary society. To use a non-Foucauldian vocabulary, the range of legitimate political issues is constricted by these social disciplines even while the formal channels of democratic politics remain open.

These shifts in the constitution of madness and criminality, along with a corollary series of shifts in the organization of medicine, sexuality, and education, correlate with the persistent drift of modernity toward a more tightly articulated order. The emergence of modern practices of bureaucratic control, market discipline, therapeutic help, democratic virtue, and sexual liberation, though each often defines itself in opposition to others, meshes with the global tendency of modern orders to organize the self into an agent of self-containment. Neither Rousseau nor Hobbes, Bentham nor Locke, Marx nor Hegel, has understood the dynamics of this process in all its complexity. Each in opposing the others has obscured the ways in which his own ideals anticipate some dimension of disciplinary society.

Disciplinary society is perpetuated through the production and deployment of the bifurcated self, while public life pulsates with debates over which side of this bifurcation should receive priority in the treatment of crime, perversity, welfare cheating, and personal instability. One side of the self – the site of the free, self-interested, rational, and responsible agent – endorses the norms of the order as its own postulates of reason and morality; it contains those aspects of the self that do not correspond to these constructions; and when it breaks one of the codes to which it has consented, it is worthy of being held responsible for the infringement. The second side is "the other" in the self, which does not fit neatly into this affirmative construction; it is the locus of wishes, feelings, and desires that escape articulation. To give these impulses verbal expression today is to translate them into the language of therapy, medicine, psychiatry, and moral perversity. This other side of the self is also a site of political control; for behavior that escapes the self-control of reason, interest, and responsibility is located within categories that require bureaucratic intervention to control, reform or prevent it.

The bifurcated self of modernity, then, is susceptible to multiple strategies of discipline; each side is penetrated by social discipline; and the side receiving the most attention in a particular case is the one that appears most vulnerable to available tactics of control. That is why Foucault can contend that modern "individualization" is really a complex set of processes by which the bifurcated self is produced. Its behavior is recorded in "individualized" files, and its conduct is normalized through a heterogeneous ensemble of disciplinary tactics. Bureaucratization and individualization, incentive systems governing self-interested agents, and moral codes internalized by virtuous citizens are, on this reading, complementary mechanisms of disciplinary control.

SELF-REFLEXIVITY AND AMBIGUITY

This is an incomplete account of Foucault's picture of disciplinary society and the modern self. It ignores, for instance, counterpressures spawned within those parts of the self (and especially those selves defined as others) which resist these mechanisms of normalization and subjectification. It will suffice to allow us to pose some pertinent issues about the alternatives to disciplinary politics; for when modernity is characterized in this way it appears that we must either give up any aspiration to a society in which democracy flourishes or reject this entire archeology of disciplinary society. We can be democrats or nihilists; we can criticize the present from the perspective of alternative ideals or join Foucault in repudiating every ideal imaginable today as the tyrannical extension of "our participation in the present system."[4]

But perhaps these options have been posed too starkly by both Foucault and his humanist adversaries. It may be possible to articulate a vision of democratic life that consciously maintains tension between these two tendencies, affirming the legitimacy of limits and conventions essential to democratic politics while otherwise exposing and opposing the modern drift toward rationalization, normalization and dependency. Acknowledging intractable points of opposition between the drive to disturb forces of normalization and the quest to sustain preconditions of democratic life, it might show how each, properly understood, is a precondition and a limit to the other. To proceed in this direction it would be necessary both to tame the priorities and imperatives of the political economy of private productivity and to redefine the counte-rideal of collectivity, which has inspired the left since the inception of capitalism.

Foucault's genealogies embody a critique of the ideal of self-consciousness or reflexivity that has governed critical thought in the modern age. The pursuit of self-consciousness is the pursuit of a future in which all impulses that govern the self and all forces that govern the order are fully transparent to the participants. This ideal, crystallized most purely in the thought of Marx and Habermas, also finds more restrained expression in the thought of Hegel, Mill and Freud. In its most optimistic formulations it is connected to radical understandings of community, legitimacy, and freedom. A legitimate society on this radical reading is one in which participants are conscious of its principles of operation and freely internalize them as premises of their own conduct.

Foucault must see this ideal of self-consciousness and collectivity as the tyrannical twin of the liberal ideal of individuality. Reflexivity is a trap. It obligates us to bring the self more completely under the control of historically constructed standards of reason and morality; it draws us into confessional relationships in which therapeutic authorities first translate our dreams, wishes, and anxieties into clinical vocabularies and then hand them back to us as officially prescribed avenues to freedom; and it sets the stage for political authorities to impose virtue on those who have not internalized the officially sanctioned standards of self-consciousness. "Western man has become the confessing animal," Foucault insists, and our ideals of freedom and self-consciousness function to bring us more thoroughly within the orbit of normalization.

It is sometimes claimed against Foucault that his opposition to reflexivity at one level is contradicted by his contribution to it at another. Do not his genealogies make us more reflective about the ways in which the organized pursuit of self-consciousness functions to organize the self? Does he not endorse reflexivity in the act of opposing it? While this objection may be formally correct, the theorists who catch Foucault in this trap merrily return to those in which they themselves are caught; they remain untouched by new possibilities of reflection *they* acknowledge him to have opened. We can break out of this sterile circle of refutation and counter-refutation by *modifying* the ideal of reflexivity that has governed the left since the nineteenth century and by revising as well the ideas of legitimacy, freedom and community to which it is linked.

By comparing the ambiguous orientations to madness and punishment in the late Middle Ages to the enclosures operative today, we can glimpse the elements of political conquest inscribed in contemporary practices. This is Foucault's contribution to reflexivity. And while we are immersed in the constructs and institutions that sustain these definitions, there is enough slippage, anomaly, and incoherence discernible inside them to support the suspicion that they mix together timeless standards of reason and defensive attempts to stabilize historically particular readings of the dualities of reason/unreason, self/other, virtue/vice, and normality/abnormality. One comes away from a Foucauldian encounter suspicious of the claim that these constructions represent universal truth and wary of any critique of them couched in the name of countertruths eventually susceptible to transparent formulation.

The modified idea of reflexivity suggested by these considerations does not pursue a future in which normalization, self-transparency, and freedom sustain one another. Reflexivity, rather, allows us to glimpse the limits of our own categories of classification and treatment and to confront, if obliquely, the defensive impulses that help to sustain them. We reflexively acknowledge that we lack sufficient resources to comprehend "the other" (those other people and aspects of our own conduct that escape established categories or transgress established standards). We acknowledge that there is much about the self that does and must elude us. If the Enlightenment struggled to dissolve the mysteries about the self and its world celebrated by traditional religious doctrines, the idea of reflexivity supported here brings us through genealogy to a secular appreciation of limits, antinomies and mysteries lodged in the historical constructions through which social relations are organized. The point is to divorce secularism from the Enlightenment's hostility to mystery and ambiguity. Instead of treating deviations from established norms always as evidence against the deviants, we allow the persistent emergence of the other to bring us into touch with arbitrary elements in our own constructions. Instead of joining critiques of bourgeois or technocratic reason to a vision of a fully rational society, we allow genealogical deconstructions of past and present constructions to encourage us to oppose any future ideals of collectivity that promise to be governed purely by the light of reason. For the more fully we insist on standing in the light of pure reason, the more completely we are obliged to shove that which is out of place into the darkness.

Such an orientation does not entail rejection of all standards now available to us; for we could not live in any society if all standards were to be rejected. It does encourage us to adopt a more ironic stance toward standards we endorse, striving to detect arbitrary elements within necessary limits and to discern the shadow of injustice haunting existing norms of rationality. It also encourages us to project an ideal of order that can sustain itself without drawing so massively on the forces of punishment, incentive systems, therapy, self-containment, and civic virtue.

If the ideal of order suggested by these abstract statements acknowledges the need for limitation and constraint even while questioning the standards invoked to *identify* constraints and to *justify* the means of their protection, does it not deconstruct itself even before it has descended to earth from the heaven of theory? What *political* difference could be made by this appreciation of limits, ambiguity, and mystery?

We can consider these questions initially by recalling the tribal ritual practices mentioned earlier. Victor Turner in *The Ritual Process* has characterized these tribal rites of reversal:

> Each person plays and for the moment may experience the role of his opposite; the servile wife acts the domineering husband, and vice versa; the ravisher acts the ravished; the menial acts the master; the enemy acts the friend, the strictured youths act the rulers of the republic.... Each actor playfully takes the role of others in relation to his own usual self. Each may thereby learn to play his own routine roles afresh, surely with renewed understanding, possibly with greater grace, perhaps with reciprocated love.[5]

One's initial reaction to these tribal rites is to paint a picture of an actual or possible mode of modernity in which they are superfluous, to insist that the elimination of established injustices is infinitely preferable to their consolidation through periodic rites of renewal. This reaction, though, mirrors the Enlightenment dream of complete rationality, justice, and transparency in social relations. It is as if *we* must pounce on the most obvious defect in the alien culture to ensure that *they* cannot help us to glimpse the madness in our dreams. I agree that it is imperative today to reduce inequalities of class and gender. However, once we acknowledge that the ideal of social life implicit in the demand to eliminate all limitation and darkness is a dangerous mystification, we must also suspect that our best efforts on these fronts will leave a residue of violence and resentment. Perhaps the extension of legal norms into new frontiers of social life both reduces the most blatant forms of injustice and diminishes the quality of those social relations newly absorbed into these forms. Perhaps the extension of litigiousness into new corners of life submerges one set of virtues while it realizes another.

The message for modernity within these tribal rites resides in the appreciation of the irony and ambiguity they embody. Acknowledgment of ambiguity within modernity tends to be reduced to a single-minded demand for justice. This devaluation of ambiguity in turn supports the denial, exclusion, and suppression of that which does not "fit" neatly within our norms and ideals. The rites express reflexively what reflexive impulses honed by the Enlightenment suppress: the norms and standards appropriate to the good life we prize together are also destructive in their impact on the other in oneself and other selves; the rites of reversal affirm this ambiguity and offer some degree of redress for the human losses incurred. The participants cannot articulate all the denials hidden in their affirmations because they swim in the culture which contains them; but they can set aside occasions in which the alien elements find some mode of expression by those who experience them most intensely.

Once we acknowledge that the technocratic ideal of reason and the radical ideal of collectivity share inflated conceptions of rationality, the unity of self, and social harmony, we can adopt an ironic stance toward norms worthy of endorsement.

Consider the treatment of the modern self as a subject. This self-identity, crucial to modern practices of freedom, knowledge, responsibility, and democracy, is a socially engendered organization that could have been (and has been) otherwise. But this acknowledgment does not require elimination of the formation. We may be particularly receptive, or at least receptive in important respects, to this form of identity. Since the human is incomplete without any socially established identity, there may be good reason to cherish this identity by comparison to previous and thinkable alternatives. And this appreciation may sustain itself even as we come to terms with ambiguities lodged in the self-identity of the subject.

We might come to see the subject as an essentially ambiguous achievement of modernity to be cherished while we modify our understanding and experience of it. It enables the democratization of social life (for the citizen is the subject at the level of politics); it provides an organization of self responsive to the human quest to examine the terms of our own existence. But the formation, imposed upon a being not predesigned to fit perfectly within it, inevitably spawns otherness in the self and in those other selves who deviate significantly from the standard it imposes. It is thus an ambiguous achievement.

To constitute the self as a subject, understood in some transcendental sense as the natural or true self, is to treat deviation from subjectivity as a lack, incapacity, or defect *itself* in need of correction or help. But to understand one's own subjectivity to be a partial and historical achievement imposed upon a bring not predesigned to fit neatly into this mold is to understand that one's self-formation helps to create the otherness to which it reacts. To adopt this self-interpretation − this distinctive mode of self-consciousness − is to interrogate the relation between subjectivity and deviations from it in new ways; it is to question the single-minded interpretation of deviation as incapacity, defect, sickness, delinquency, irrationality itself in need of help. Such a formulation of self as subject heightens sensitivity to ways in which "help" given to others and to otherness flows first from the socially established need to fix the self's identity as a subject and second and problematically from internalization by the other of the need for this help.

Perhaps a modest example will illuminate this point. As social pressures to facilitate speed and suppleness in communication have intensified (pressures themselves worthy of explanation), those whose speech facility or reading comprehension does not mesh with this imperative become identified as victims who suffer from "stuttering" or "dyslexia." Former inconveniences now become "disabilities" or even "illnesses." We silently produce new disabilities and loudly debate whether their new victims should be helped to overcome them or penalized because they lack critical skills. But the defect here is not simply in the self: it is located in the form of life now requiring these skills to get along within it.

The best help we can give these parties, if we think about them alone, is to revise the rules of discourse so that such deviations from the standard become only modest inconveniences. Failing that, perhaps because it is concluded that the social good requires this speed and mode of communication, we can at least come to see that we have engendered the problem we seek to resolve and that redress is owed to those whose incapacities have been socially produced.

When the account appropriate to this modest example is applied to a larger array of phenemona such as sexual deviance, delinquency, "underground" economic activity, irrationality, irresponsibility, and retardation, they also assume a different appearance. We begin to ask how the tightening of social imperatives helps to create new abnormalities, deviations, incapacities, and delinquencies and how it might be possible to loosen or relax the circumstances that being new forms of otherness into being.

The idea of the subject as an essentially ambiguous achievement of modernity is bound up, then, with appreciation of the need to rethink aspects of life that deviate from this standard, perhaps by seeking to enhance the social space in which difference can be without constituting a danger to the standard itself. The provision of institutional space for difference at once enhances the prospect for the subject to appreciate ambiguities in its own formation and encourages it to come to terms with the debt it owes to that in itself and other selves diverging from it.

But this space cannot be simply given as a permission. Such permission can always be rescinded, and those who receive it are constantly aware of their dependence on the sufferance of the donor. It must be established politically by actions that create what I called earlier greater "slack" in the institutional order itself.

An order that can afford to relax the reins of social control is one that can allow a rather broad range of behavior to *be*, only lightly touched by the pressure of normative standards. Where normative standards are essential, it still enables a large portion of negatively appraised conduct to be defined as odd, strange, eccentric, or wayward, finding it less necessary to convert so many of these negative judgements into operational concepts of illegality, delinquency, abnormality, irrationality, perversity, and obsolescence. The latter characterizations irresistibly link judgement to institutional routines of decision, regulation, and control. They draw slack out of the order.

It will be said that the current American order provides considerable slack already, and that this condition (depending on the liberal or conservative stance from which the assertion is made) is already one of its greatest virtues or greatest vices. I agree that we are not stuck in a "one-dimensional society," but the United States is today marked by tendencies to rationalize and control broader areas of life, and these tendencies do not *merely* express the will of some to compel others to conform to their standards. The contemporary imperative to generate economic growth under adverse conditions of realization intensifies pressures to extend disciplinary control into new corners of life. If these imperatives are not met the order will stumble along dangerously, and if they are met it will be necessary to squeeze more slack out of the order.

In an order with slack the imperatives themselves are loosened. Because the imperatives are relaxed there is more room for us, first, to define our lives outside the medium of politics, second, for politics to serve as the medium through which we confront ambiguities within those limits. Modern politics, at its best, embodies its own rites of reversal, but it cannot be at its best under current conditions.

This idea of slack, serving as a counterpoint to the logic of disciplinary control, itself stands in an ambiguous relation to radical and liberal doctrines. Echoes from an earlier liberalism reverberate within it. The classical liberal doctrine — in its support for constitutionalism, human rights, fallibilism, privacy, and the market as invisible coordinator of economic life — sought to protect the self from close dependence on state power and to restrict the space for political contestation. But while the doctrine of constitutionalism retains its importance, several other institutions and economic priorities in which liberalism placed its faith have become enlisted today as vehicles of disciplinary control.

The extension of private and public modes of disciplinary control flows to a great extent from the dual effort to foster economic expansion and to control elements inessential or disruptive to that course. Today slack in the order must be nourished by reconstituting the interdependent complexes of consumption, production, profit, economic growth, and resource dependence, which extend both underground evasions and disciplinary controls. The old liberal ideal of private space is now too tenuously connected to institutions and priorities historically defined by liberalism as essential to it.

The relation to established radical doctrine is similarly ambiguous. The position sketched here endorses much of the radical understanding of the sources of our economic condition while modifying the ideal of collectivity informing leftist opposition to capitalism. Once the contours of contemporary discipline have been delineated it is clear that a collective regime, not only through specific historic contingencies that block realization of its ideals, but also in its essential conception, contains the logic of disciplinary control. The collectivist ideal promises social unity and legitimacy through civic virtue; but while a measure of civic virtue is essential to a well-governed state, it is asked to bear far too much weight in collectivist ideals of life. It is not merely that the collectivist ideal implies unjustified confidence in the human capacity to achieve coordination through rational consensus, but also that it presupposes too close a harmony between the dictates of a well-ordered society and the character of the selves within it. Since the self is not "designed" to fit perfectly into any way of life, we must anticipate that every good way of life will both realize something in the self and encounter elements in the self resistant to its form; and we should thereby endorse the idea of slack as part of our conception of the good life. An order with slack can sustain itself well without the need to organize the self so completely into a creature of virtue. For the more an order needs virtue the more it eventually authorizes the extension of disciplinary strategies to secure it.

The experience of the twentieth century does not suggest that virtue should be expunged from politics, for a double dialectic of corruption and regimentation moves in to fill the gap opened by the disappearance of virtue. Virtue, though, is most likely to be sustained in a way of life that can flourish without having to extend the tentacles of order into so many corners of life. Slack in the order enables a broader range of behavior merely to be because the imperative to assimilate repugnant or eccentric conduct to the categories of irrationality or illegality has been relaxed. Slack at once reduces the space virtue must cover and enhances the prospects for civic virtue within the space appropriate to it.

Slack in the order thus provides the antidote to those conscious and unconscious contrivances of social discipline emerging in the United States today to fill the gap created by the contraction of civic virtue and expansion of imperatives for social coordination. The key to its attainment surely resides in strategies to curtail the dual imperative for economic expansion and selective austerity that haunts the American political economy.[6]

Neither welfare liberalism nor radicalism today, taken in their dominant forms, speaks sensitively to the wish of citizens to participate in the common life while maintaining a degree of freedom from thorough entanglement in the forces of community and order. Each of these movements has lost touch with deep aspirations among constituencies it seeks to represent, and each now sees elements of its previous support drifting toward the right. Each must therefore cultivate new sensibilities to re-establish contact with its natural constituencies.

NOTES

1 See Charles Schultze, *The Public Use of Private Interest* (Washington, D.C.: Brookings Institution, 1977) and Lester Thurow, *The Zero-Sum*

Society (New York: Basic Books, 1980). I agree that these two texts do not exhaust the range of ideas located today under the umbrella "liberalism". But they do represent a powerful strand of liberal thought when it turns its attention to the political economy. And, I would argue, those liberals who focus on the doctrine of rights either appeal covertly to such an economic doctrine to provide the state with the dividend needed to fund welfare and protect rights, or retreat to an abstract doctrine of rights, which becomes more and more detached from the actual life of its day. I have developed the latter arguments in *Appearance and Reality in Politics* (Cambridge: Cambridge University Press, 1981), chaps. 4 and 6.

2   There have been notable shifts in Foucault's theory between the early work exemplified by *Madness and Civilization* (New York: Random House, 1965) and the later position represented by *Discipline and Punish* (New York: Pantheon, 1977) and *The History of Sexuality* (New York: Vintage Press, 1980), but my point now is to delineate common themes that cut across these divisions.

3   Foucault, *Madness and Civilization*, pp. 22–3.

4   Michel Foucault, *Language, Counter-memory, Practice* (Oxford: Basil Blackwell, 1977), p. 230.

5   Victor Turner, *The Ritual Process* (Ithaca, N.Y.: Cornell University Press, 1969), pp. 185–6.

6   How could the twin imperatives of economic expansion and selective austerity be relaxed? My own guess is to revise the infrastructure of consumption so that the constant expansion of consumption *needs*, which fuels electoral pressures for constant economic growth and the imposition of austerity on marginal constituencies, could be curtailed. However, my point in this essay is less to consider how to foster these ends and more to argue that these are ends worthy of endorsement and exploration by liberals and radicals today.

9

Text and Pretexts: Reflections on Perspectivism in Nietzsche

TRACY B. STRONG

> Only knowledge of a language that possesses another mode
> of conceiving the world can lead to the appropriate knowl-
> edge of one's own language.
> (Cited from U. von Wilamowitz-Moellendorff, *Platon*, vol. I in
> M. M. Bakhtin, "From the Prehistory of Novelistic Discourse" in
> *The Dialogic Imagination*)

The most natural response to the question "what is Nietzsche's
doctrine of perspectivism about?" is to begin a discussion of
epistemology. Most commentators have assumed that perspectivism
is Nietzsche's attempt to give an account of how knowledge of the
world is (or is not) possible. An obvious range of conclusions has
been reached: for some Nietzsche is successful in that he establishes a
credible epistemological position; for others the position is coherent
but incorrect; for still others his is an impossible and self-contra-
dictory enterprise.[1]

There is no doubt but that this response has a certain plausibility
to it. Nietzsche's doctrine of perspectivism often is textually associated with his remarks on the possibility of truth, with his
claims as to the status knowledge can have in human affairs, with
his critique of the clearly epistemological writings of other philosophers, and, most notably, with his attacks on Kant's concept
of the thing-in-itself.

There is, however, reason to doubt that epistemology is what
Nietzsche has in mind. I take epistemology to be that branch of
philosophy that is concerned either to ground knowledge in a
realm that is "objective," that is, not affected by the act of knowing,
or to establish "objectively" that this aim is impossible in at least

Reprinted by permission of SAGE Publications from *Political Theory*
13, 2 (May, 1985), pp. 164–82.

certain realms of human experience. In both cases the aim is to delineate a realm secure from the phenomenal vagaries of the knower: the benefit for Kant, for instance, was to make room for faith; for early positivists, it clearly was to separate the world of science from the mists of moral judgements.

In any case, epistemology must center itself around the attempt to discover a permanent framework for inquiry. More precisely, it consists in an attempt to discover how a thinker can associate him- or herself with the transcendent pattern that makes "objective" thought possible.[2] Of a necessity, epistemology must either seek to establish a knowing self that transcends the vagaries of phenomenal life or despair of attaining knowledge at all.

When Nietzsche talks about perspectivism, however, he clearly speaks of it as a doctrine that *encompasses* epistemology:

> What I paid attention to was much more the fact that no epistemological skepticism or dogmatics has ever appeared without ulterior motives; that they had a value of second rank as soon as one considered *what* in fact *compelled* this position.[3]

> Fundamental innovation: in the place of epistemology a perspective theory of affects.[4]

These and other passages attack the possibility of achieving a position in which knowledge might be treated as if it were liberated from the knower. They suggest that Nietzsche thinks the final project of epistemology to be ultimately untenable. None of this implies that Nietzsche is, as some have argued, a "noncognitivist;" but it does imply that knowledge cannot for Nietzsche be epistemologically grounded.

I wish to argue here that for Nietzsche the whole epistemological enterprise is flawed in that it misconstrues the nature of the self. Perspectivism is Nietzsche's attempt at replacing epistemology with an understanding of the self and of knowledge that does not posit any particular position (or self) as final. It teaches us not only that we always are masked but that we must be if we wish to know at all. If, as Nietzsche remarks in the first book of *Morgenröte*, nature is always silent and we are condemned to error when we speak, perspectivism is the solution to that dilemma. It is the recognition that speech and thought are disguises, even and perhaps especially for ourselves, but that they are not to be rejected as lesser for all of that; it is the enforcement on ourselves of the dialectical recognition to the self and to the hearer and reader that we are in disguise. The most aristocratic of modern thinkers deconstructs himself repeatedly into the most democratic.[5]

There is perhaps no better place to begin this investigation than with the recent paper by Alexander Nehamas, "Immanent and Transcendent Perspectivism in Nietzsche."[6] Nehamas argues that Nietzsche uses perspectivism in a number of ways, only one of which is ultimately interesting and philosophically tenable (which come to the same thing here).

Nehamas claims that Nietzsche alternates between or confuses two versions of perspectivism.[7] In the first version Nietzsche asserts that no one human understanding of the world can coherently claim to be an "ultimate" or "privileged" understanding. This is because Nietzsche understands (almost as well, one might say, as Wilfrid Sellars) that the world is not *given* to human beings and that the activity of knowing is a formulating of the world.[8] Nehamas calls this "immanent perspectivism" and notes that it implies neither that there are not knowable rules as to how humans understand the world nor that the world is without structure or regularity. Rather, it merely asserts that it is the nature both of understanding and of the world that the world cannot be exhausted by any number of acts of understanding. There always is a first word, but never a last.

Nehamas also sees in Nietzsche a second version of perspectivism that he calls "transcendent." This includes two separate propositions: first, Nehamas argues that Nietzsche wants to say that there is such a thing as a "human" perspective, understood in the sense of *Gattungswesen*; second, according to Nehamas again, Nietzsche thinks this human perspective is incommensurable and radically untranslatable into any other possible species perspective.

Nehamas's central argument is that the two forms of perspectivism are incompatible with each other. The proposition that the world is not exhausted by the knowing of it in no way implies and is in fact contradictory to the claim that we never know another point of view. This argument clearly is logically true, but I believe it to commit Nehamas to a number of propositions about Nietzsche, none of which I think correct; the exploration of Nehamas's argument, however, is a fruitful entry into a different understanding of the place of perspectivism in Nietzsche's thought.

The following conclusions seem to me to be entailed by Nehamas's argument. First, in relation to "transcendent" perspectivism Nietzsche would be falling back into the trap he consistently seeks to escape. The "human" perspective becomes a grounding, by default, it is true; it is an unsatisfactory but paradoxically secure basis for human knowledge.

Second, in this view perspectivism describes something that a subject *has*: for instance, Nehamas assumes that to know another's point of view one must have it. This is a logical imputation; it corresponds to a point of view whereby the world is something that we suffer and knowledge becomes a kind of burden of the species. It is true, of course, that Nietzsche often speaks of knowledge as suffering; but he does so most often when talking about the kind of knowledge characteristic of a world "infected" by Socratic epistemology or when he suggests that there still lurks a Christian understanding in Kant. As we shall see, this is a view that Nietzsche seeks to undermine, not one that he holds.

Nietzsche spends a good deal of time arguing that it is wrong to think of the world as "appearing" *to* us. In the summer of 1888 he noted that "the apparent world" reduces itself to a specific manner of action on the world, emanating from a center. He goes on to say that the interaction of all such actions constitutes what we mean by the world. After that, "no shadowy right remains such that one might here speak of appearance .... The specific manner of reacting is the only manner of reacting; we do not know how many and what kinds there are in all."[9] The conclusion of this passage is the well-known epigram that the "antithesis of the apparent world and the true world has reduced itself into the antithesis [of] world and nothing." That is, there is only the world and no thing is "behind" or "above" (or even "below") it.

I do not think that by this somewhat Hesiodic vision Nietzsche wants to say that the world is simply that which we have created in our seeing. Such a facile radical Kantianism still would commit Nietzsche to the claim that all knowledge is knowledge *for* the knower and, therefore, that there is something called a subject *before* there is knowledge. Knowledge would be something that one *had* and philosophy would consist, as it has since Socrates, in coming to know oneself.

It is important to note here that a self that had a "transcendent" perspective would also have to be a self that did not change. It would involve "what it means to be an X" where X is understood as a species with some kind of permanent enduring characteristics that in turn ensure its definition. Much of the writing from the period during which Nietzsche explores perspectivism – from 1884 onward – is occupied with a critique of the idea of a unitary self.

I think there is an important difficulty with an implication such as Nehamas's that Nietzsche thinks that knowing the world constitutes a reduction of the world to something less that it "is" and that knowledge of the world, therefore, is something flawed. When Nehamas writes that for Nietzsche "physical realities are . . . fundamentally flawed and take us no closer to understanding real nature," both the implication that there is a flaw and the implication that there is a "real nature" are misleading. The passage he is discussing comes in a criticism of the presuppositions of physicists.[10] Nietzsche is arguing that these scientists forget that when they reduce the "apparent world" to atoms, the atoms are themselves constructions. They make this mistake, he indicates, because they have forgotten that it is in the nature of being such a subject (a physicist) to come to such conclusions about the world.

Nietzsche, if I read him correctly, is not saying that physics is per se flawed, but that as a science it cannot, any more than anything else, claim to be a foundation for other knowledge. Physics, like anything else, requires a knowing subject, in this case one whose knowledge is what we call physics. Physicists are what we are in the conversation of humankind when we do physics. (Here I might note somewhat gnomically that Nietzsche speaks of becoming "*what* one is," not "who.")

This is a preliminary reason for the argument that the self may not know itself in any final or complete fashion. When Nietzsche notes in the preface to the *Genealogy of Morals* that "we are unknown to ourselves" as men of knowledge,[11] he is claiming that any self that claims to know itself is necessarily self-defeating. This constant theme in Nietzsche — it already was the burden of the *Birth of Tragedy* to argue against the Aristotelian notion of *anagnorisis* (recognition) — finds a direct expression in another note from early 1888: "First mark of the great psychologist: he never seeks himself, he has not eyes for himself . . . . We have neither the time nor the curiosity to rotate about ourselves."[12]

Thus, for Nietzsche there is not only no point of view that is privileged in relation to the outer world (which Nehamas acutely points out is a consequence of immanent perspectivism), but also none privileged in relation to the "inner self," in relation to consciousness. Indeed, the whole relation between outer and inner is denied. There is neither a kind of internal self positing a self — a la Fichte — nor a given noumenal self. Nietzsche remarks: "The apparent 'inner world' is governed by just the same forms and procedures as the 'outer world.' We never encounter facts."[13]

Perspectivism, then, cannot mean that everything is "in the eye of the beholder," or that all is "subjective." This is what we might think it meant if we read perspectivism to imply merely that what we see is shaped by our point of view. To such a claim, Nietzsche explicitly responds that "even this is interpretation. The 'subjective' is not something given, it is something added and invented and projected behind what there is .... In so far as the word 'knowledge' has any meaning, the world is knowable ...; it has no meaning behind it; it has countless meanings."[14] Nietzsche's point here is that it is a mistake to look behind or underneath the world for its true sense. As he notes in 1888, the world of becoming is of "equivalent value every moment." All we need to know and all we can know is present in the world as we encounter it. This is the meaning of the "Midnight" poem in *Zarathustra*; to paraphrase Robert Frost, all meaning is already ours.[15]

Ever since the sixth book of the *Republic*, the dominant theme and presupposition of epistemology has been that there is one layer of the self and of the understanding that is somehow deeper and closer to unchanging "reality" than any other. Nietzsche's response to this is categorical: "The 'subject' is a fiction that many similar states in us are the effects of one substratum; but it is we who first created the 'similarity' of these states; our adjusting them and making them similar is the fact, not their similarity — which had rather ought to be denied." Nietzsche then proceeds to compare the "subject" to a regent at the head of a commonality and never so sure of its position that it can simply ignore the world and wreak its will. Elsewhere, he speaks of the world and the self as centers of power that have entered into alliances with each other. None of this is a denial that there "is" such a thing as a subject, but rather a critique of the presupposition that the subject has a natural and given unity of any kind. Thus, Nietzsche continues and asserts that if our "'ego' is for us the sole being, there is also good reason to doubt if it be not a 'perspectival illusion,' an 'apparent' unity in which all is gathered as if bonded by an horizon."[16]

If knowlege is possible only by virtue of a "belief in being," this does not imply that for Nietzsche there is no such thing as knowledge, nor that knowledge depends on "point of view," but only that for knowledge to be possible some grounding has been accepted and recognized. Previous thinkers had assumed that knowledge depended on the nature of the knower; in Nietzsche's "*umgedrehter Platonismus*," knowing produces the self and addition modes of knowing produce additional selves.

What concerns Nietzsche is the fact that for many people the very possibility of a secure and confident knowledge of the world has disappeared — or is in the process of doing so. Their selves, therefore, are also dissolving, such that like those at the end of the *Genealogy of Morals*, they would rather "will the void than be void of will." Many of us, for instance, are now or are in the process of becoming what Max Weber called "religiously unmusical." We know what religion is, but it makes no sense for us, we cannot sing in tune. Part of what Nietzsche is trying to accomplish is to impress on us that the subject that might have been "religiously musical" has been called into radical question. We — some of us — are no longer and can no longer be that person. Although the particular reasons for such a disintegration derive from historical and genealogical factors, the process itself derives from the general nature of the self. Nietzsche writes: "The subject is itself ... a construct ...: a simplification in order to designate (*bezeichnen*) the *force*, which posits, invents, thinks as something distinct from all other particular positings, discoverings, thinkings as such."[17]

With this we can arrive at a new understanding of Nietzsche's advocacy of "having many points of view."[18] In 1884, Nietzsche had noted the following as an "insight":

> All estimations of values (*Wertschätzungen*) are a matter of a definite perspective: the maintenance of the individual, a commonality, a race, a state, a church, a belief, a culture. *Due to the forgetfulness that there are only perspectival evaluations* [my italics], all sorts of contradictory evaluations and thus contradictory drives swarm (*wimmeln*) inside *one person*. This is the expression of the diseased condition in man, in opposition to the condition in animals, where all instincts play particular roles. This contradictory creature has however in his nature a great method of knowing: he feels many fors and againsts — he raises himself up to *justice* — to a comprehension beyond the valuation of good and evil. The wisest man would be the richest in contradictions, who as it were, has feelers (*Tastorganen*) for all kinds of men: and right among them [has] his great moments of *grandiose harmony*.[19]

This is a difficult and important passage. Two broad perspectival categories appear, the first that of "good and evil" (i.e., moral) and "justice" (i.e., doing that which is appropriate to that which one encounters). The move to justice is something Nietzsche considers to be beyond the valuation of good and evil. Justice itself seems not to depend on the "unity" of a self, but on the ability of an organism to contain what one might call "nonantagonistic" contradictions within itself.

Nietzsche is engaged in a radical reconceptualization of the subject. We are not to think of the subject as a unity but as a multiplicity, what Nietzsche calls a *Vielheit*.[20] This conclusion clearly is preliminary, as even to assert that the subject is a multiplicity is still to assert that there is something that it is. That said, exploration still is rewarding. Most individuals, and here Nietzsche means both philosophers and the rest of us, assume that the unity of the world is derived from the unity of the archetectonics of the faculty that makes knowing possible — from the nature of the self. (This is what Kant had demonstrated.) Such a unity would have its origins in the unity of the self which knows. Against this, Nietzsche argues that the unity of the known and the unity of the knower are derived from the activity of knowing. As an activity, knowing — understanding the world — is something that humans and perhaps other species do; perhaps we have done it as a species since, say, the "discovery of mind" around 1400 BC, or since the development of what Karl Jaspers has called the "axial period." For Nietzsche, knowing is not a consequence of the self but, rather, productive of what we have come to call the self. (Part of the source of Nietzsche's repeated strictures against Socrates derive from this source.)[21]

Most people, according to Nietzsche, have "forgotten" that the unity of the world is a double imputation, first from the unity of the knower derived from the act of knowing and then, in turn, by the transfer of the unity of the knower into the world. "We put value into things," writes Nietzsche in the late summer of 1886, "and this value has an effect on us, after we have forgotten that we were the donors."[22] In those who rise up to justice, the knower remains multiple, even in his or her own understanding. In them life is an "experiment of the thinker ... not a duty, not a fatality, not a deceit."[23]

We will look more closely at what it means to think of life as an experiment, but let us note here that it does not mean precisely what Jean Granier refers to as "multiple ontologies."[24] Rather, life as a *Versuch* carries all of the means of *Versuch*; it is an experiment, and an "endeavor," but also always subject to the "temptation" that one may call oneself finished, given, and final. (One thinks here, not inappropriately, of Whitman.)

Nietzsche does not then alternate between two versions of perspectivism but, rather, gives us a hierarchy. The perspectivism of justice and that of morality do not correspond to points of view, nor to some kind of natural species differentiation (as in being a bat, or an ant, or a human), but to the differences in the way that a perspective affects the knower's understanding of him- or herself in the world. Some lack the ability to have "a basis, a condition of existence" for their judgements, and their judgements therefore are "chaos." They have no world(s) but simply nothing, even though they may not know it (yet).[25] Some kinds of perspective may ultimately not make a sense for the knower but, rather, produce a lack of sense; indeed, Nietzsche's formulation and critique of nihilism is of the consequences of one such perspective (the moral), perhaps the most important consequence for contemporary Europeans.

It is worth noting in passing here that this is not a theory of false consciousness. False consciousness, as Michael Holquist has noted, implies that all claims to knowledge "can never express the actual place they occupy among the reigning myths of their own time and place."[26] Nihilism is not a false consciousness whereby our knowledge of ourselves would be incomplete because of our own involvement in the inevitability of our misrecognitions of our own place in the world. The theory of a hierarchy of perspective places the emphasis not on "truth" but on the consequences of a perspective on the knower. Nietzsche presents far fewer epistemological problems than does Marx.

In any case, it is against a perspective such as that of nihilism that Nietzsche sets this statement: "Task: to see things *as they are*. Means: to look on them from a hundred eyes, from many persons."[27] Given what has been said, Nietzsche must mean by this that things can only be seen as they are if they are seen multiply and as multiple. The more composite a knower is — that is, the more that one is not subject in a "forgetful" fashion to one's own creations and valuations — and the more that we do not insist that we be a unity, the more eyes the "subject" will have, the more it will see things "as they are," not as given, but as multiple themselves.

It is central to realize that the move to justice has no "accomplishment": there can be no *Vollendung*. There is, in fact, a danger that we will want to think or pretend that we have accomplished ourselves. As Nietzsche writes in *Beyond Good and Evil*:

It might be a basic character of existence that those who would know it completely would perish, in which case the strength of a spirit should be measured according to how much 'truth' one could still barely endure — to put it more clearly, to what degree one would *require* that it be thinned down, shrouded, sweetened, blinded, falsified.[28]

The (neo-Calvinist?) claim that humans are beings whose nature it is to be limited shapes much of Nietzsche's work. *The Birth of Tragedy* is a text in the theory of understanding; it is the answer to the question of how the Greeks came to be who they were and how they attained that mode of life without falling either into "asiatic chaos" or into the rigid prose of Rome.[29] From 1872 onward Nietzsche insists explicitly on the incompatibility of truth and life and of the necessity of "horizons" in making meaning possible. In *Beyond Good and Evil* he notes: "Let at least this much be admitted: there would be no life at all if not on the basis of perspective estimates and appearances."[30] We are caught, we might say, in danger of establishing a "fetishism of persons," in which we project the "conditions of our preservation as the predicates of being in general."[31]

Perspectivism is at the center of Nietzsche's thought. To have a perspective is to have horizons, and such limitation is what we mean by life and having a definition as (a) being. The fact that we are alive — and that we die — means that we are unable to do full justice to the world, which would be to have so transparent a contact with the world ("as it is," in all its becoming) that there would be "no simplification of it." We must then accept as a predicate of human existence that it is "unjust." In the 1886 preface to *Human-all-too-human* Nietzsche argues that human beings can never experience the world as other than unjust and that it is a sign of health that one forgo any attempt to conceive of experience in the world as other than tragic. Indeed, already in his 1870 lectures on *Oedipus Rex* Nietzsche had made the point that tragedy presents the "deepest conflict between life and thought." (Greek) tragedy consists of the manner in which the Greeks managed to accept the fact that all knowledge, including that of themselves, was perspectival and yet not call that acceptance into question.[32]

If there is nothing besides perspective (for humans at least),[33] then the obvious conclusion is not that the world cannot be known but, rather, that it is in the nature of the world as we experience it to be known. There is no action in the world that does not embody all that we need to understand it, providing only that we do not insist on understanding it according to a mistaken and arrogant notion of the subject.[34] Nietzsche warns us against the temptation of assuming that the world is not or cannot be known or that we are not and cannot be known. Knowledge is not flawed, even if it is not perfect.

If the above is true, then everything must be understood in terms of the whole of which it is a part. Yet the characteristic of that whole must be what the Russian critic M. M. Bakhtin has called "heteroglossia." For Bakhtin, heteroglossia is a fundamental characteristic not only of the novel but also of society. It means simply that at any given place or time the totality of the conditions that give an utterance meaning will ensure that it will necessarily have a meaning somewhat different at any other time and place.

Such a position is entailed by Nietzsche's conclusion that it is in the nature of the world to be known. Yet Nietzsche has established two fundamental perspectives that characterize attitudes toward the world. For his writing to be successful he must at the same time express both of those perspectives and seek to bring them into an "alliance" one with the other. On the face to it this would seem impossible. A careful exploration of the relation between the doctrine of perspectivism and the will to power shows, I think, the opposite.

One might well raise the question here of *why* humans insist on seeing the world otherwise: the answer can be found in a study of Nietzsche's genealogical investigations, but cannot be addressed here.[35] One can, however, raise the question of what condemns us to experience the world as known and thus ensures that we will experience the world as a self. The answer comes in the doctrine of the will to power.

As is known, Nietzsche insists several times that the "world is and is only will to power." The will to power is in fact the "operating principle" of perspectivism. There is not space here to fully discuss the will to power; in any case, I have done so elsewhere.[36] A few short reminders: all forms of life are/have a will to power. It "interprets" and that interpretation is "a means to become master of something."[37] The will to power understands (interprets) the new in terms of the old; it extends the the understanding and the categories of the life and action of a particular being over that which is not yet that being.

The will to power is that by which the world has the quality of being intelligible. The rhetoric of Nietzsche's approach to this question is important. In the second section of *Beyond Good and Evil* he notes that "there would be no life at all if not on the basis of perspectival estimates and appearances."[38] Two aphorisms later, he introduces the notion of a "text without an author," and then deepens his earlier statements by suggesting that to view the world as will to power is to view it from the "inside," that is, on its own terms. The perspectival world thus is a text without an author and is "determined and characterized according to its 'intelligible character.'"[39] Hence, when we speak of the world as will to power we mean that the world as it presents itself to us is completely intelligible – that is its nature, so to speak.[40] The question of what a perspective is cannot be answered or, indeed, even asked. It asks for something that has no conceptual substance.

Does not, however, the assertion that the world *is* will to power constitute an assertion that there is something that the world is? And can this assertion be without contradiction a perspective? To address this problem requires a detour through the discussion, alluded to above, of a text without an author.

On a preliminary basis, let us note that Nietzsche is aware of this question. In a note not included in the *Will to Power* he raises what he calls a basic question as follows:

> Basic question: if the perspectival belongs to essence (*Wesen*) as such? As is not only a form of considering (*Behauptungsform*), a relation between different beings (*Wesen*)? Do the different powers stand in relation, such that this relation is tied to the observations-optics (*Observations-Optik*)? This would be possible if all being (*Sein*) were *essentially* some kind of observation (*Wahrnehmenden*).[41]

Perspectivism thus cannot be understood as the perspective of some*thing*, for there can be no thing without perspective, which is not a perspective. Indeed, "there would be nothing called knowledge, if thought did not reform the world into 'things.'"[42]

Knowing consists in forming, in making the world, and in making known. (Here the English misses the resonances of *machen*.) In a "complicated" way, Nietzsche explains, knowing makes for "specificity." "My notion," he continues, "is that each particular body tries to becomes master over the whole territory and to expand its strength (its will to power) and to push back all which resists its expansion."[43]

In this "turned around Platonism" that which is, is the result of human action rather than its premise. Thus: "To *impress* upon becoming the character of being – that is the highest will to power."[44] Nietzsche emphasizes "impress" (*aufzuprägen*) because the will to power will be the highest when the subject in question actively "impresses being," that is, takes becoming out of the river of time and gives it being. The aphorism continues: "That everything recurs is the closest approximation of a world of becoming to a world of being." It is precisely because of perspectivism that eternal return is possible. (There are, of course, also different forms of eternal return that in turn correspond to the different forms of perspectivism.)[45]

If the above is the case, there can be no transcendent persectivism for Nietzsche. We are inevitably meaningful to and for all creatures that we encounter. That we want to deny this is the source of the disease of transcendent perspectivism, of the desire to believe that we are unknowable to others. (In fact, for Nietzsche we are meaningful even to the inorganic, given that Nietzsche cannot on these grounds refuse to make a clear cut differentiation between such entities and ourselves.) What Nietzsche is struck by is the fact that we make sense all the time, whether we want to or not, and how fragile yet compelling is our description of ourselves. There is no need to erect defenses against not making sense, as do, for instance, those scientists who, panicked by the possibiity of incalculability, turn calculability into a general a priori of knowledge.[46]

Is the world (and, indeed, we ourselves) a text of which we are the continual author? In a later essay Alexander Nehamas has argued that Nietzsche holds to this position, but that no life can ever be lived completely in this mode — we cannot be identical as both text and autobiographer.[47] The basis of his argument is akin to that advanced in his earlier essay: we always are more than that which we make of the world; hence, as authors we always are more than the text that we would that ourself be.

Again, Nehamas's argument is an important route into Nietzsche. Clearly, for Nietzsche what something "is" is what is made of it (that is, the relations that it enters into). Anything that is the case is just as great as the number of the relations that comprise it. Are the interpretations necessarily *of* something, of a text that is not itself an interpretation? Nietzsche's answer appears to be, "not necessarily." He writes, for instance, of the Frence Revolution that "the text has disappeared under the interpretations."[48] I take this to mean not that the "facts" have disappeared (in which case a historical accident would have no necessary philosophical consequences), but that the different interpretations of the French Revolution no longer enter into "alliances" with one another. The reasons for this are historical and, Nietzsche indicates, have to do with the long and passionate "indignations and enthusiasms" characteristic of later "spectators" of the French Revolution. It is the present impossibility of these alliances that has led to the disappearance of a text.[49]

We remember here that a self that rose up to justice was a self that held together as an alliance of a multiplicity of modes and relations. And yet one of the modes of such a "self" must also be the mode that the "unity" of the self is merely apparent and not given once and for all. This poses the final question about the status of Nietzsche's doctrine of perspectivism — is it not itself a claim to a transcendent position and therefore doomed to self-referential contradiction?

In *Ecce Homo* Nietzsche attempts to bring into an alliance all of his activities, past and future.[50] He proclaims that "I am a one thing (*das Eine*), my books are the other (*das Andre.*)"[51] Here we must realize that the texts that Nietzsche gives us — his writings, his philosophy — are given in such a way that "Nietzsche" cannot be found in them. When Nietzsche asserts in *Ecce Homo*, for instance, that he is both a decadent and its opposite, we are meant to take this claim absolutely literally. The consequence is that the unity of his texts is to be found in the reader and that there is no authorival unity imposed on the text, any more than the subject might impose a unity on the world. Thus, the strictures that Nietzsche applies too his understanding of the subject apply also to Nietzsche's teachings on perspectivism. Perspectivism cannot be a doctrine or a point of view because, properly understood, it makes impossible the epistemological activism that a doctrine requires. The position anticipates the one arrived at in relation to modern texts by Roland Barthes in "The Death of the Author" and extended by Michel Foucault in "What is an Author?"[52] W. D. Williams has summarized his analysis of Nietzsche's style as follows: "Wherever one turns ... one can find the same tendency to disguise himself while letting the reader know that what is being shown is in fact a disguise."[53]

Perspectivism, then, does not consist in asserting, with becoming pluralism, that I "should" have or support a number of different points of view. It asserts, rather, that "I" am a number of different ways of knowing and that there is no such entity as a permanent or privileged self. An order of rank is found in a "grandiose alliance" such as Nietzsche, for instance, claims for himself in *Beyond Good and Evil* and *Ecce Homo*.[54]

If a "subject" is thus a container of multitudes, then it can change both in time and in history. Understanding it is the subject of genealogy. For our purposes, the more important consequence is that whatever actions such a subject engages in must manifest the grandiose alliance that went into making them. Thus, as Williams notes in the passage cited above, Nietzsche's actions (his texts) all by and large constantly call themselves into question even as they prepare the reader for an outrageous, seductive position. "Does not one write books precisely to conceal what one harbors?" Nietzsche writes. "Every philosophy also *conceals* a philosophy; every opinion is also a hideout, every word also a mask."[55] Note that Nietzsche insists on the "also." Philosophy, opinions, words are not only concealments, hiding places, and masks.

What is the importance of the perspectival understanding of the world? Three consequences immediately come to mind. First, it enforces in the writer the necessity for an unrelenting honesty toward self and reader: all pretense must be shown to be pretense. Second, it makes it impossible for the writer to pretend to be the physician of culture — all that one says must also be said about oneself. Finally, no privileged position is available from which to discuss the world as if one were not part of it: philosophy is praxis. As Nietzsche notes in the preface to the second volume of *Human all to human*, "I forced myself, as doctor and patient in the same person, into a diametrically opposite, untried climate of the *soul*, and in particular into a sharpened wandering in foreign parts, in that which is foreign, into a curiosity about every kind of strangeness."[56] *Ecce Homo* is an account of what it took to achieve this:

> Need I say after all this that in matters of *decadence* I am *experienced*? I have spelled them backwards and forwards. Even that filigree art of grasping and comprehending in general, those fingers for *nuances*, that psychology of "seeing around the corner," and whatever else is characteristic of me was learned only then, is the true present of those days in which everything in me became subtler.[57]

As a test of the noble soul the acceptance of perspectivism also provides Nietzsche with an indication of what will have to be done successfully to confront the coming century, with its wars "the like of which have never been seen" and its leveling of all distinctions of value. This, though, is another topic.[58] An indication is gained in this passage from 1888:

> To value anything to be able to live it, I must comprehend it as absolutely necessarily tied in with everything that is — thus for its sake, I must call all existence (*Dasein*) good and know thanks (*Dank wissen*) for the accident in which such priceless things are possible.[59]

In the end, each part of Nietzsche leads the reader to the other parts: perspectivism to horizons to the will to power to eternal return. This may not make him a unified character, but it does describe a grandiose alliance.

NOTES

1   See Tracy B. Strong, *Friedrich Nietzsche and the Politics of Trans-figuration* (Berkeley and Los Angeles: University of California Press, 1975), p. 306. To that discussion, one may add John T. Wilcox, *Truth and Value in Nietzsche: A Study in His Metaethics and Epis-temology* (Ann Arbor: University of Michigan Press, 1974), in which Nietzsche is held to hold both noncognitive ("destructive") elements and cognitive elements("appraising"), which together are "transcog-nitive" (creative). Wilcox correctly says (p. 201) that Nietzsche does not say much about this.

2   See Richard Rorty, *Philosophy and the Mirror of Nature* (Princeton: Princeton University Press, 1979), esp. pp. 380ff.

3   VIII 1, pp. 141–2 (WM 410). All references to Nietzsche, unless otherwise noted, are from the Colli and Montinari edition (Berlin: Gruyter, 1968) using their abbreviations. Translations are my own, informed wherever possible by those of Walter Kaufmann.

4   VIII 2, p. 6 (WM 462).

5   I have developed this general theme in an essay on "Nihilism and Political Theory," in John S.Nelson(ed.), *What Should Political Theory Be Now?* (Albany: State University of New York Press, 1983). See also my *Friedrich Nietzsche and the Politics of Transfiguration*, chap. 3. See the important essay by W. D. Williams, "Nietzsche's Masks," in Malcolm Pasley (ed.), *Nietzsche: Imagery and Thought* (Berkeley and Los Angeles: University of California Press, 1978), pp. 83–103.

6   Alexander Nehamas, "Immanent and Transcendent Perspectivism in Nietzsche," *Nietzsché-studien*, Band 12. 1983 (Berlin: Gruyter, 1983), pp. 473–90. See my "Comment," ibid, immediately following.

7   There is a relative to Nehamas's distinction in Jean Granier, *Le problème de la verité dans la philosophie de Nietzsche* (Paris: Seuil, 1966), p. 322.

8   See Wilfred Sellars, "Empiricism and the Philosophy of Mind." in *Science, Perception and Reality* (London: Routledge and Kegan Paul, 1962).

9   My translation differs from Kaufmann, who does not add "in all." "*Wir wissen nicht wie viele and was fuer Arten es Alles giebt.*"

10 VIII 3, p. 165 (WM 636).

11 VI 2, p. 259 (WM Vorrede I).

12 VIII 3, pp. 22–3 (WM 426).

13 VIII 2, p. 295 (WM 477).

14 VIII 1, p. 323 (WM 481).

15 It is Thoreau's burden in *Walden* to make this point manifest to his readers. In this sense, as Stanley Cavell notes in *The Senses of Walden* (New York: Viking Press, 1972). *Walden* can be said to provide a "transcendental deduction of the category of the thing-it-itself" (p. 140n).

16 VIII 1, p. 104 (WM 518); VIII 3, pp. 165–6 (WM 636); see VIII 1, pp. 102–3 (WM 561 and 486).

17 VIII 1, p. 12 (WM 556).

18 *Die Unschuld des Werdens,* Herausgegben von A. Baeumler (Stuttgart: Kroner Verlag, 1956), vol. 2, p. 24.

19 VII 2, PP. 179–80 (WM 259). Cf. Martin Heidegger, *Nietzsche* (Pfullingen: Neske, 1961), vol. 1, pp. 632ff.

20 VII 3, p. 382 (WM490). Nietzsche is thus willing to "deconstruct" the subject in the manner of Derrida, but not to destroy him as I think Derrida suggests Nietzsche does. See *Eperons/Spurs* (Chicago: University of Chicago Press, 1979).

21 See, for instance, Bruno Snell, *The Discovery of the Mind* (New York: Harper & Row, 1960). See also my discussion in *Friedrich Nietzsche and the Politics of Transfiguration*, chap. 6. For a more sociological discussion, see ibid, chap. 2 and Johannes Goudsblom, *Nihilism and Culture* (Oxford: Basil Blackwell, 1979).

22 VIII 1, p. 196 (not in WM) See also WL.

23 V 2, p. 232 (FW 324).

24 Granier, *Le probléme de la verite*, pp. 357–66.

25 VII 1, p. 695 (WM 667).

26 Michael Holquist, "The Politics of Representation" (unpublished typescript), p. 19.

27 Friedrich Nietzsche, *Gesammt Ausgabe* (Leipzig: Nauman, 1898), vol. 12, p. 13 (No. 22).

28 VI, pp. 52–3 (JGB 39). One thinks here also of Max Weber, who, in response to a question as to why he learned so much, answered, with probably a conscious echo of this aphorism: "I want to see how much I can bear." See Marianne Weber, *Max Weber: Ein Lebensbild* (Tübingen: Mohr, 1976). See also Williams, pp. 96–8: cf. V 2 pp. 19–20 (FW Vorrede 4). Paradoxically, Nietzsche shares something like the old Calvinist epistemology. Calvin had argued that one could/should never pretend to know the world as it is – such was only for God. Human knowledge was necessarily from a point of view – that of the creaturely sinner. In this light. Nietzsche's last letter to Burckhardt, in which he claims identification with "all names in history," makes chilling sense. *Vollendung* is, in fact, madness. For a further discussion, see my "Oedipus as Hero: Family and Family Metaphors in Nietzsche," *boundary 2: a journal of post modern literature* (Spring/Fall, 1981), pp. 311–36.

29 III 1, p. 129 (GT 21); see also A. Kremer-Marietti, *L'homme et les*

labyrinthes (Paris: Seuil, 1972), pp. 77ff.

30   III 1, p. 248 (HL, 1); VI 2, p. 49 (JGB 34).

31   VIII 2, p. 17 (WM 507). Part of the force of Nietzsche's critique of the historicism, which dominated the thought of his time, was that it saw human beings as necessarily prisoners of a past that they had in fact made. To the degree that one cannot free oneself from the mold of the past [VIII 1, p. 545 (not in WM)] – one's own past – one is destined not only to repeat it, but finally to be annihilated in it. The past is always in danger of being taken for truth. Thus, "man must have, and from time to time, use the strength to break up and dissolve a past, in order to be able to live" [III 1, p. 261 (HL 3)].

32   IV 2, p. 14 (MA 1886 preface 6). See Friedrich Nietzsche, *Einleitung zu den Vorlesen ueber Sophocles' Oedipus Rex*, in *Gesammelte Werke* (Munich: Musarion, 1920–1929), vol. 2, p. 257. See also my discussion of the chorus, *Friedrich Nietzsche and the Politics of Transfiguration*, chap. 6.

33   VI 2, p. 99 (JGB 150).

34   V 2, pp. 308–9 (FW 374).

35   Nietzsche suggests various factors as productive of this syndrome. The most general is in VIII 2, p. 277 (WM 708), as the "hypothesis of being" (*Hypothese des Seienden*); at other times he suggests the subject-object distinction.

36   *Friedrich Nietzsche and the Politics of Transfiguration*, chap. 8.

37   VIII 1, p. 159 (WM 254). See also VI 2, pp. 21–2 (JGB 13). See also the comparison between the will to power and Freud's doctrine of eros in F. A. Lea, *The Tragic Philosopher* (London: Methuen, 1957).

38   VI 2, p. 49 (JGB 34).

39   VI 2, p. 51 (JGB 36).

40   This is the source of Heidegger's analysis of the will to power as *physis*. For a discussion and a criticism that now appears too strong see *Friedrich Nietzsche and the Politics of Transfiguration*, pp. 275–6 and the references cited there.

41   VIII 1, p. 192 (not in WM). This seems to me to show the essential fallacy in the claim of R. H. Grimm, *Nietzsche's Theory of Knowledge* (Berlin and New York: Gruyter, 1977) to the effect that if there were to be a theory of knowledge that was more encompassing than the will to power, Nietzsche would welcome it as a confirmation of his theory rather than a disproof. Grimm's position has been extended, unsuccessfully I think, in Philip J. Kain. "Nietzsche, Skepticism and Eternal Recurrence," *Canadian Journal of Political Science* (September, 1983), pp. 365–87.

42   VIII 1, p. 353 (WM 574).

43   VIII 3, p. 165 (WM 636).

44   VIII 1, p. 230 (WM 617).

45   See here the discussion of active and passive return in Gilles Deleuze, *Nietzsche et la philosophie* (Paris: Presses Universitaires de France, 1962) and my argument about eternal return in *Friedrich Nietzsche*

and the Politics of Transfiguration, chap. 9.

46 VIII 1, p. 192 (not in WM).

47 Alexander Nehamas, "How One Becomes What One Is," *The Philosophical Review* (July, 1983). pp. 485–517. Bernd Magnus has suggested that the world for Nietzsche is a kind of pentimento of interpretations. Nehamas's "Immanent and Transcendent: Perspectives in Nietzsche" argues against this on the grounds that, even if a lost Aristotelian text for us has become its transcriptions and interpretations, there was nonetheless an original text. See my argument about this problem below. See Bernd Magnus. *Nietzsche's Existential Imperative* (Bloomington and London: Indiana University Press, 1978) and his "Nietzsche's Mitigated Skepticism," *Nietzsche Studien* (Gruyter: Berlin and New York: 1980), vol. 9, pp. 260–7. I am conscious here of the influence of W. Isel, *The Art of Reading* (Baltimore: Johns Hopkins University Press, 1978).

48 VI 3. p. 263 (EH, Warum Ich so weise bin, 1): see also the earlier version in VIII 3, p. 442.

49 See VIII 3, pp. 165–6 (WM 636). Helene Keyssar has suggested that this should be seen in light of the position advanced in Walter Benjamin's "The Work of Art in an Age of Mechanical Reproduction," in his *Illuminations*. What, one might ask, is the status of the "text" if there can exist a potentially unlimited number of identical copies? Certainly, they are not interpretations.

50 Cf. VI 3, p. 318 (EH, Warum Ich so gute Bücher schreibe – Die Unzeitgemässen, 2); V 2 pp. 224–5 (FW 307); VI 2 pp. 56–8 (JGB 44); see Nehamas, "How One Becomes What One Is," p. 416.

51 VI 3, p. 296 (EH, Warum Ich so gute Bücher schreibe, 1).

52 Roland Barthes, "The Death of the Author," *Image, Music, Text* (New York: Hill and Wang, 1977), pp. 142–8; Michel Foucault, "What Is an Author:" *Language, Counter-Memory, Practice* (Ithaca: Cornell University Press, 1977), pp. 113–38, esp. pp. 131ff.

53 Williams, "Nietzsche's Masks," p. 102.

54 VI 2, pp. 241–2 (JGB 283, 284).

55 VI 2, p. 244 (JGB 289).

56 IV 3, p. 9 (MAM ii, Vorwort 5).

57 VI 3, p. 263 (EH, Warum Ich so weise bin, 1); see also the earlier version in VIII 3, p. 442.

58 As I have come (dangerously) close to anthropology, see here Clifford Geertz, "From the Native's Point of View: On the Nature of Anthropological Understanding," in K. Basso and N. Selby (eds), *Meaning in Anthropology* (Albuquerque: University of New Mexico Press, 1976), pp. 236–7. Peter Winch has advanced a position like that which Nehamas attributes to Nietzsche in "Understanding a Primitive Society," *American Philosophical Quarterly* (October, 1964), pp. 307–24. Winch's position has been criticized in much the same way that I have defended Nietzsche in Hanna F. Pitkin, *Wittgenstein and Justice* (Berkeley and Los Angeles: University of California Press,

1972) and to a lesser extent by Alasdair MacIntyre in "Rationality and the Explanation of Action" in *Against the Self-Images of the Age* (London: Duckworth, 1971), pp. 244–59. For a slightly different point of view, see Robert Eden. *Political Leadership and Nihilism* (Gainesville: University of Florida Press, 1984).

59   VII 2, p. 179 (partly in WM 907). See EH, epigraph.

10

Individual and Mass Behavior in Extreme Situations

BRUNO BETTELHEIM

PURPOSE OF THE INVESTIGATION

The author spent approximately one year in the two biggest German concentration camps for political prisoners, at Dachau and at Buchenwald. During this time he made observations and collected material, part of which will be presented in this paper. It is not the intention of this presentation to recount once more the horror story of the German concentration camp for political prisoners.

It is assumed that the reader is roughly familiar with it, but it should be reiterated that the prisoners were deliberately tortured.[1] They were inadequately clothed, but nevertheless exposed to heat, rain, and freezing temperatures as long as seventeen hours a day, seven days a week. They suffered from extreme malnutrition, but had to perform hard labor.[2] Every single moment of their lives was strictly regulated and supervised. They were never permitted to see any visitors, nor a minister. They were not entitled to any medical care, and when they received it, it was rarely administered by medically trained persons.[3] The prisoners did not know exactly why they were imprisoned, and never knew for how long. This may explain why we shall speak of the prisoners as persons finding themselves in an "extreme" situation.

The acts of terror committed in these camps arouse in the minds of civilized persons justified and strong emotions, and those emotions lead them sometimes to overlook that terror is, as far as the Gestapo is concerned, only a means for attaining certain ends.[4] By using extravagant means which fully absorb the investigator's interest, the Gestapo only too often succeeds in hiding its real purposes. One of the reasons that this happens so frequently

Reprinted by permission of The American Psychological Association, Inc from *Journal of Abnormaland Social P'sychology* 38, 4 (October, 1943), pp. 417–52.

in respect to the concentration camps is that the persons most able to discuss them are former prisoners, who obviously are more interested in what happened to them than in why it happened. If one desires to understand the purposes of the Gestapo, and the ways in which they are attained, emphasis on what happened to particular persons would be erroneous. According to the well-known ideology of the Nazi state the individual as such is either nonexistent or of no importance. An investigation of the purposes of the concentration camps must, therefore, emphasize not individual acts of terror, but their transindividual purposes and results.

Anticipating the results of this discussion and of further investigations, it may be said that the results which the Gestapo tried to obtain by means of the camps are varied; the author thinks that he was able to recognize some of them. In the context of this presentation it may be mentioned that they were the following different, although intimately related, goals: *to break the prisoners as individuals* and to change them into docile masses, from which no individual or group act of resistance could arise; *to spread terror among the rest of the population* by using the prisoners as hostages for good behavior, and by demonstrating what happens to those who oppose the Nazi rulers; *to provide the Gestapo members with a training ground* in which they are so educated as to lose all human emotions and attitude and learn the most effective ways of breaking resistance in a defenseless civilian population; *to provide the Gestapo with an experimental laboratory* in which to study the effective means for breaking civilian resistance, the minimum food, hygienic and medical requirements needed to keep prisoners alive and able to perform hard labor when the threat of punishment takes the place of all other normal incentives, and the influence on performance if no time is allowed for anything but hard labor and if the prisoners are separated from their families.

In this paper, which, considering the complexity of the problem with which it is dealing, is comparatively short, an effort will be made to deal adequately with at least one aspect of it, namely, with the concentration camp as a means of producing changes in the prisoners which will make them more useful subjects of the Nazi state.

These changes are produced by exposing the prisoners to situations particularly suitable for this purpose. Their nature is such as to warrant calling them extreme. By means of their extreme character they force the prisoners to adapt themselves entirely and with the greatest speed. This adaptation produces interesting types of private, individual, and mass behavior. We call "private" behavior that which originates to a large degree in a subject's particular background and personality, rather than in the experiences to which the Gestapo exposed him, although these experiences were instrumental in bringing about the private behavior. We call "individual" behavior that which, although developed by individuals more or less independently of one another, is clearly the result of experiences common to all prisoners. The pattern of these behaviors was similar in nearly all prisoners with only slight deviations from the average, these deviations originating in the prisoners' particular background and personality. We call "mass" behavior those phenomena which could be observed *only* in a group of prisoners when functioning as a more or less unified mass. Although these three types of behaviour were somewhat overlapping and a sharp discrimination between them seems difficult, the subdivision seems advisable for this paper. We shall restrict our discussion mainly to individual and mass behavior, as the title indicates. One example of private behavior will be discussed on the following pages.

If we thus assume that what happens in the camp has, among others, the purpose of changing the prisoners into useful subjects of the Nazi state, and if this purpose is attained by means of exposing them to extreme situations, then a legitimate way to carry on our investigation is by an historical account of what occurred in the prisoners from the moment they had their first experience with the Gestapo up to the time when the process of adaptation to the camp situation was practically concluded. In analyzing this development different stages can be recognized, which will furnish us with appropriate subdivisions. The first of these stages centers around *the initial shock of finding oneself unlawfully imprisoned*. The main event of the second stage is *the transportation into the camp and the first experiences in it*. The next stage is characterized by a slow process of changing the prisoner's life and personality. It occurs step by step, continuously. It is *the adaptation to the camp situation*. During this process it is difficult to recognize the impact of what is going on. One way to make it more obvious is to compare two groups of prisoners, one in whom the process has only started, namely, the "new" prisoners, with another one in whom the process is already far advanced. This other group will consist of the "old" prisoners. The final stage is reached when *the prisoner has adapted himself to the life in the camp*. This last stage seems to be characterized, among other features, by a definitely changed attitude to, and evaluation of, the Gestapo.

WHY THE MATERIAL WAS COLLECTED

Before discussing these different stages of a prisoner's development a few remarks on why and how the material presented in this paper was collected seems advisable. At this moment it seems easy to say why it was collected, because it is of sociological and psychological interest and contains observations which, to the author's knowledge, have rarely been published in scientific fashion. To accept this as an answer for the "why" would constitute a flagrant example of logification post eventum. The former training of the writer and his psychological interests were helpful in collecting the material and in conducing the investigation; but he did not study his behavior, and that of his fellow prisoners, in order to add to pure scientific research. The study of these behaviors was a mechanism developed by him ad hoc in order that he might have at least some intellectual interests and in this way be better equipped to endure life in the camp. His observing and collecting of data should rather be considered as a particular type of detense developed in such an extreme situation. It was individually developed, not enforced by the Gestapo, and based on this particular prisoner's background, training, and interests. It was developed to protect this individual against a disintegration of his personality. It is, therefore, a characteristic example of a private behavior. These private behaviors seem always to follow the path of least resistance; that is, they follow the individual's former life interests closely.

Since it is the only example of a *private behavior* presented in this paper, a few words on why and how it was developed may be of interest. The writer had studied and was familiar with the pathological picture presented by certain types of abnormal behavior. During the first days in prison, and particularly during the first days in the camp, he realized that he behaved differently from the way he used to. At first he rationalized that these changes in behavior were only surface phenomena, the logical result of his peculiar situation. But soon he realized that what happened to him, for instance, the split in his person into one who observes and one to whom things happen, could no longer be called normal, but was a typical psychopathological phenomenon. So he asked himself, "Am I going insane, or am I already insane?" To find an answer to this urgent question was obviously of prime importance. Moreover, he saw his fellow prisoners act in a most peculiar way, although he had every reason to assume that they, too, had been normal persons before being imprisoned. Now they suddenly appeared to be pathological liars, to be unable to restrain themselves, to be unable to make objective evaluations, etc. So another question arose, namely, "How can I protect myself against becoming as they are?" The answer to both questions was comparatively simple: to find out what had happened in them, and to me. If I did not change any more than all other normal persons, then what happened in me and to me was a process of adaptation and not the setting in of insanity. So I set out to find what changes had occurred and were occurring in the prisoners. By doing so I suddenly realized that I had found a solution to my second problem: by occupying myself during my spare time with interesting problems, with interviewing my fellow prisoners, by pondering my findings for the hours without end during which I was forced to perform exhausting labor which did not ask for any mental concentration, I succeeded in killing the time in a way which seemed constructive. To forget for a time that I was in the camp seemed at first the greatest advantage of this occupation. As time went on, the enhancement of my self-respect due to my ability to continue to do meaningful work despite the contrary efforts of the Gestapo became even more important than the pastime...

THE INITIAL SHOCK

In presentation, the initial psychological shock of being deprived of one's civil rights and unlawfully locked into a prison may be separated from the shock of the first deliberate and extravagant acts of torture to which the prisoners were exposed. These two shocks may be analyzed separately because the author, like most of the prisoners, spent several days in prison without being exposed to physical torture before being transported into the camp. This transportation into the camp, and the "initiation" into it, is often the first torture which the prisoner has ever experienced and is, as a rule, physically and psychologically the worst torture to which he will ever be exposed. This initial torture, incidentally, is called by the Gestapo the prisoner's "welcome" to the camp.

The prisoners' reactions on being brought into prison can best be analyzed on the basis of two categories: the socio-economic class to which they belonged and their political education...

The *politically educated prisoners* found support for their self-esteem in the fact that the Gestapo had singled them out as important enough to take revenge on. The members of different parties relied on different types of rationalizations for this building-up of their egos. Former members of radical-leftist groups, for example, found in the fact of their imprisonment a demonstration of how dangerous for the Nazis their former activities had been.

Of the main socio-economic classes, the lower classes were almost wholly represented either by former criminals or by politically educated prisoners. Any estimation of what might have been the reaction of noncriminal and nonpolitical members of the lower classes must remain conjecture and guesswork.

The great majority of the *nonpolitical middle-class prisoners*, who were a small minority among the prisoners of the concentration camps, were least able to withstand the initial shock. They found themselves utterly unable to comprehend what had happened to them. They seemed more than ever to cling to what up to now had given them self-esteem. Again and again they assured the members of the Gestapo that they never opposed Naziism. In their behavior became apparent the dilemma of the politically uneducated German middle classes when confronted with the phenomenon of National socialism. They had no consistent philosophy which would protect their integrity as human beings, which would give them the force to make a stand against the Nazis. They had obeyed the law handed down by the ruling classes, without ever questioning its wisdom. And now this law, or at least the law-enforcing agencies, turned against them, who always had been its staunchest supporters. Even now they did not dare to oppose the ruling group, although such opposition might have provided them with self-respect. They could not question the wisdom of law and of the police, so they accepted the behavior of the Gestapo as just. What was wrong was that *they* were made objects of a persecution which in itself *must* be right, since it was carried out by the authorities. The only way out of this particular dilemma was to be convinced that it must be a "mistake." These prisoners continued to behave in this way despite the fact that the Gestapo, as well as most of their fellow prisoners, derided them for it.

Although the guards used them for their own self-aggrandizement, they were not free from anxieties when doing so. They realized that they, too, belonged to the same socio-economic stratum of society.[5] The insistence on legality of the official German internal policy may find its explanation in an effort to dissolve the anxieties of the middle-class followers who feel that illegal acts destroy the foundation of their existence. The height of this farce of legality was reached when prisoners in the camp had to sign a document stating that they agreed to their imprisonment and that they were well pleased with the way they had been treated. It did not seem farcical to the Gestapo, which put great emphasis on such documents as a demonstration that everything happened according to law and order. Gestapo members were, for instance, permitted to kill prisoners, but not to steal from them; instead they forced prisoners to sell their possessions, and then to make a "gift" of the money they received to some Gestapo formation.

The great desire of the middle-class prisoners was that their status as such should be respected in some way. What they resented most was to be treated "like ordinary criminals." After some time they could not help realizing their actual situation. Then they seemed to disintegrate. The several suicides which happened in prison and during the transportation into camp were practically confined to members of this group. Later on, members of this group were the ones who behaved in the most antisocial way; they cheated their felow prisoners, a few turned spies in the service of the Gestapo. They lost their their middle-class characteristics, their sense of propriety, and their self-respect; they became shiftless and seemed able to disintegrate as autonomous persons. They no longer seemed able to form a life-pattern of their own, but followed the patterns developed by other groups of prisoners.

Members of the *upper classess* segregated themselves as much as possible. They, too, seemed unable to accept as real what was happening to them. They expressed their conviction that they would be released within the shortest time because of their importance. This conviction was absent among the middle-class prisoners, who harbored the identical hope for a near release, not as individuals, but as a group. The upper-class prisoners never formed a group, they remained more or less isolated, each of them with a group of middle-class "clients." Their superior position could be upheld by the amount of money they could distribute,[6] and by a hope on the part of their "clients" that they might help them once they had been released. This hope was steadily kindled by the fact that many of the upper-class prisoners really were released from prison, or camp, within a comparatively short time...

Summary.   It seems that most, if not all, prisoners tried to react against the initial shock by mustering forces which might prove helpful in supporting their badly shaken self-esteem .Those groups which found in their past life some basis for the erection of such a buttress to their endangered egos seemed to succeed. Members of the lower class derived a certain satisfaction from the absence of class differences among the prisoners. Political prisoners found their importance as politicians once more demonstrated by being imprisoned. Members of the upper class could exert at least a certain amount of leadership among the middle-class prisoners. Members of "anointed" families felt in prison as superior to all other human beings as they had felt outside of it. Moreover, the initial shock seemed to relieve guilt-feelings of various kinds, such as guilt-feeling originating in political inactivity, or inefficiency, or in acting badly to one another, and for casting aspersion on friends and relatives in an unjustified way. The reason why it was either relieved or did not develop was the actual punishment the prisoners had to endure.

THE TRANSPORTATION INTO CAMP AND THE FIRST EXPERIENCES IN IT

After having spent several days in prison, the prisoners were brought into the camp. During this transportation they were exposed to constant tortures of various kinds. Many of them depended on the fantasy of the particular Gestapo member in charge of a group of prisoners. Still, a certain pattern soon became apparent. Corporal punishment, consisting of whipping, kicking, slapping, intermingled with shooting and wounding with the bayonet, alternated with tortures the obvious goal of which was extreme exhaustion. For instance, the prisoners were forced to stare for hours into glaring lights, to kneel for hours, and so on. From time to time a prisoner got killed; no prisoner was permitted to take care of his or another's wounds. These tortures alternated with efforts on the part of the guards to force the prisoners to hit one another, and to defile what the guards considered the prisoners' most cherished values. For instance, the prisoners were forced to curse their God, to accuse themselves of vile actions, accuse their wives of adultery and of prostitution. This continued for hours and was repeated at various times. According to reliable reports, this kind of initiation never took less than 12 hours and frequently lasted 24 hours. If the number of prisoners brought into the camp was too large, or if they came from nearly places, the ceremony took place during the first day in camp.

The purpose of the tortures was to break the resistance of the prisoners, and to assure the guards that they were really superior to them. This can be seen from the fact that the longer the tortures lasted, the less violent they became. The guards became slowly less excited, and at the end even talked with the prisoners. As soon as a new guard took over, he started with new acts of terror, although not as violently as in the beginning, and he eased up sooner than his predecessor. Sometimes prisoners who had already spent time in camp were brought back with a group of new prisoners. These old prisoners were not tortured if they could furnish evidence that they had already been in the camp. That these tortures were planned can be seen from the fact that during the author's transportation into the camp after several prisoners had died and many had been wounded in tortures lasting for 12 hours, the command, "Stop mistreating the prisoners," came and from this moment on the prisoners were left in peace till they arrived in the camp when another group of guards took over and started anew to take advantage of them.

It is difficult to ascertain what happened in the minds of the prisoners during the time they were exposed to this treatment. Most of them became so exhausted that they were only partly conscious of what happened. In general, prisoners remembered the details and did not mind talking about them, but they did not like to talk about what they had felt and thought during the time of torture. The few who volunteered information made vague statements which sounded like devious rationalizations, invented for the purpose of justifying that they had endured treatment injurious to their self-respect without trying to fight back. The few who had tried to fight back could not be interviewed; they were dead.

The writer can vividly recall his extreme weariness, resulting from a bayonet wound he had received early in the course of transportation and from a heavy blow on the head. Both injuries led to the loss of a considerable amount of blood, and made him groggy. He recalls vividly, nevertheless, his thoughts and emotions during the transportation. He wondered all the time that man can endure so much without committing suicide or going insane. He wondered that the guards really tortured prisoners in the way it had been described in books on the concentration camps; that the Gestapo was so simple-minded as either to enjoy forcing prisoners to defile themselves or to expect to break their resistance in this way. He wondered that the guards were lacking in fantasy when selecting the means to torture the prisoners; that their sadism was without imagination. He was rather amused by the repeated statement that guards do not shoot the prisoners but kill them by beating them to death because a bullet costs six pfennigs, and the prisoners are not worth even so much. Obviously the idea that these men, most of them formerly influential persons, were not worth such a trifle impressed the guards considerably. On the basis of this introspection it seems that the writer gained emotional strength from the following facts: that things happened according to expectation; that, therefore, his future in the camp was at least partly predictable from what he already was experiencing and from what he had read; and that the Gestapo was more stupid than he had expected, which eventually provided small satisfaction. Moreover, he felt pleased with himself that the tortures did not change his ability to think or his general point of view. In retrospect these considerations seem futile, but they ought to be mentioned because, if the author should be asked to sum up in one sentence what, all during the time he spent in the camp, was his main problem, he would say: *to safeguard his ego in such a way, that, if by any good luck he should regain liberty, he would be approximately the same person he was when deprived of liberty.*

He has no doubt that he was able to endure the transportation, and all that followed, because right from the beginning he became convinced that these horrible and degrading experiences somehow did not happen to "him" as a subject but only to "him" as an object. The importance of this attitude was corroborated by many statements of other prisoners, although none would go so far as to state definitely that an attitude of this type was clearly developed already during the time of the transportation. They couched their feelings usually in more general terms such as, "The main problem is to remain alive and unchanged," without specifying what they meant as unchanged. From additional remarks it became apparent that what should remain unchanged was individually different and roughly covered the person's general attitudes and values.

All the thoughts and emotions which the author had during the transportation were extremely detached. It was as if he watched things happening in which he only vaguely participated. Later he learned that many prisoners had developed this same feeling of detachment, as if what happened really did not matter to oneself. It was strangely mixed with a conviction that "this cannot be true, such things just do not happen." Not only during the transportation but all through the time spent in camp, the prisoners had to convince themselves that this was real, was really happening, and not just a nightmare. They were never wholly successful.[7]

This feeling of detachment which rejected the reality of the situation in which the prisoners found themselves might be considered a mechanism safeguarding the integrity of their personalities. Many prisoners behaved in the camp as if their life there would have no connection with their "real" life; they went so far as to insist that this was the right attitude. Their statements about themselves, and their evaluation of their own and other persons' behavior, differed considerably from what they would have said and thought outside of camp. This separation of behavior patterns and schemes of values inside and outside of camp was so strong that it could hardly be touched in conversation; it was one of the many "taboos" not to be discussed.[8] The prisoners' feelings could be summed up by the following sentence: "What I am doing here, or what is happening to me, does not count at all; here everything is permissible as long and insofar as it contibutes to helping me to survive in the camp."

One more observation made during the transportation ought to be mentioned. No prisoner fainted. To faint meant to get killed. In this particular situation fainting was no device protecting a person against intolerable pain and in this way facilitating his life; it endangered a prisoner's existence because anyone unable to follow orders was killed. Once the prisoners were in the camp the situation changed and a prisoner who fainted sometimes received some attention or was usually no longer tortured. The result of this changed attitude of the guards was that prisoners who did not faint under the more severe strains during the transportation, in the camp usually fainted when exposed to great hardships, although they were not as great as those endured during the transportation.

Summary. During the transportation the prisoners were exposed to physical and mental tortures, the purpose of which seemed to be to break any ability to resist the Gestapo. They seemed, moreover, to serve the purpose of overcoming the Gestapo members' fear of the prisoners who were more intelligent and belonged usually to a higher social group. During the transportation the prisoners developed a state of detachment, feeling as if what happened did not really happen to them as persons.

THE ADAPTATION TO THE CAMP SITUATION

Differences in the Response to Extreme and to Suffering Experiences

It seems that camp experiences which remained within the normal frame of reference of a prisoner's life experience were dealt with by means of the normal psychological mechanisms. Once the experience transcended this frame of reference, the normal mechanisms seemed no longer able to deal adequately with it and new psychological mechanisms were needed. The experience during the transportation was one of those transcending the normal frame of reference and the reaction to it may be described as "unforgettable, but unreal". ...

Attitudes similar to those developed toward the transportation

could be observed in other extreme situations. On a terribly cold
winter night when a snow storm was blowing, all prisoners were
punished by being forced to stand at attention without overcoats
– they never wore any – for hours.[9] This, after having worked
for more than 12 hours in the open, and having received hardly
any food. They were threatened with having to stand all through
the night. After about 20 prisoners had died from exposure the
discipline broke down. The threats of the guards became ineffective.
To be exposed to the weather was a terrible torture; to see one's
friends die without being able to help, and to stand a good chance
of dying, created a situation similar to the transportation, except
that the prisoners had by now more experience with the Gestapo.
Open resistance was impossible, as impossible as it was to do
anything definite to safeguard oneself. A feeling of utter indifference
swept the prisoners. They did not care whether the guards shot
them; they were indifferent to acts of torture committed by the
guards. The guards had no longer any authority, the spell of fear
and death was broken. It was again as if what happened did not
"really" happen to oneself. There was again the split between the
"me" to whom it happened, and the "me" who really did not
care and was just an interested but detached observer. Unfortu-
nate as the situations was, they felt free from fear and therefore
were actually happier than at most other times during their camp
experiences.

Whereas the extremeness of the situation probably produced the
split mentioned above, a number of circumstances concurred to
create the feeling of happiness in the prisoners. Obviously it was
easier to withstand unpleasant experiences when all found themselves in "the same boat." Moreover, since everybody was convinced
that his chances to survive were slim, each felt more heroic and
willing to help others than he would feel at other moments when
helping others might endanger him. This helping and being helped
raised the spirits. Another factor was that they were not only free
of the fear of the Gestapo, but the Gestapo had actually lost its
power, since the guards seemed reluctant to shoot all prisoners.[10]
After more than 80 prisoners had died, and several hundred had
their extremities so badly frozen that they had later to be amputated,
the prisoners were permitted to return to the barracks. They were
completely exhausted, but did not experience that feeling of happiness which some of them had expected. They felt relieved that
the torture was over, but felt at the same time that they no longer
were free from fear and no longer could strongly rely on mutual
help. Each prisoner as an individual was now comparatively safer,

but he had lost the safety originating in being a member of a unified group. This event was again freely discussed, in a detached way, and again the discussion was restricted to facts; the prisoners' emotions and thoughts during this night were hardly ever mentioned. The event itself and its details were not forgotten, but no particular emotions were attached to them; nor did they appear in dreams.

The psychological reactions to events which were somewhat more within the sphere of the normally comprehensible were decidedly different from those to extreme events. It seems that prisoners dealt with less extreme events in the same way as if they had happened outside of the camp. For example, if a prisoner's punishment was not of an unusual kind, he seemed ashamed of it, he tried not to speak about it. A slap in one's face was embarrassing, and not to be discussed. One hated individual guards who had kicked one, or slapped one, or verbally abused one much more than the guard who really had wounded one seriously. In the latter case one eventually hated the Gestapo as such, but not so much the individual inflicting the punishment. Obviously this differentiation was unreasonable, but it seemed to be inescapable. One felt deeper and more violent aggressions against particular Gestapo members who had committed minor vile acts than one felt against those who had acted in a much more terrible fashion.

The following tentative interpretation of this strange phenomenon should be accepted with caution. It seems that all experiences which might have happened during the prisoner's "normal" life history provoked a "normal" reaction. Prisoners seemed, for instance, particularly sensitive to punishments similar to those which a parent might inflict on his child. To punish a child was within their "normal" frame of reference, but that they should become the object of the punishment destroyed their adult frame of reference. So they reacted to it not in an adult, but in a childish way — with embarrassment and shame, with violent, impotent, and unmanageable emotions directed, not against the system, but against the person inflicting the punishment. A contributing factor might have been that the greater the punishment, the more could one expect to receive friendly support which exerted a soothing influence. Moreover, if the suffering was great, one felt more or less like a martyr, suffering for a cause, and the martyr is supposed not to resent his martyrdom.

This, incidentally, raises the question as to which psychological phenomena make it possible to submit to martyrdom and which are those leading others to accept it as such. This problem transcends the frame of this presentation, but some observations pertinent to it may be mentioned. Prisoners who died under tortures *qua* prisoners, although martyrs to their political conviction, were not considered martyrs. Those who suffered due to efforts to protect others were accepted as martyrs. The Gestapo was usually successful in preventing the creation of martyrs, due either to insight into the psychological mechanisms involved or to its anti-individualistic ideology. If a prisoner tried to protect a group, he might have been killed by a guard, but if his action came to the knowledge of the camp administration then the whole group was always more severely punished than it would have been in the first place. In this way the group came to resent the actions of its protector because it suffered under them. *The protector was thus prevented from becoming a leader, or a martyr, around whom group resistance might have been formed.*

Let us return to the initial question of why prisoners resented minor vile acts on the part of the guards more than extreme experiences. It seems that if a prisoner was cursed, slapped, pushed around "like a child" and if he was, like a child, unable to defend himself, this revived in him behavior patterns and psychological mechanisms which he had developed when a child. Like a child he was unable to see his treatment in the general context of the behavior of the Gestapo and hated the individual Gestapo member. He swore that he was going "to get even" with him, well knowing that this was impossible. He could develop neither a detached attitude nor an objective evaluation which would have led him to consider his suffering as minor when compared with other experiences. The prisoners as a group developed the same attitude to minor sufferings; not only did they not offer any help, on the contrary they blamed the prisoner who suffered for having brought about his suffering by his stupidity of not making the right reply, of letting himself get caught, of not being careful enough, in short accused him of having behaved like a child. So the degradation of the prisoner by means of being treated like a child took place not only in his mind, but in the minds of his fellow prisoners, too. This attitude extended to small details. So, for instance, a prisoner did not resent being cursed by the guards when it occurred during an extreme experience, but he hated the guards for similar cursing, and was ashamed of suffering from it, when it occurred during some minor mistreatment. It should be emphasized that as time went on the difference in the reaction to minor and major sufferings slowly seemed to disappear. This change in reaction was only one of many differences between old and new prisoners. A few others ought to be mentioned.

DIFFERENCES IN THE PSYCHOLOGICAL ATTITUDES OF OLD AND NEW PRISONERS

In the following discussion we refer by the term "new prisoners" to those who had not spent more than one year in the camp; "old" prisoners are those who have spent at least three years in the camp. As far as the old prisoners are concerned the author can offer only observations but no finding based on introspection.

It has been mentioned that the main concern of the new prisoners seemed to be to remain intact as a personality and to return to the outer world the same persons who had left it; all their emotional efforts were directed towards this goal. Old prisoners seemed mainly concerned with the problem of how to live as well as possible within the camp. Once they had reached this attitude, everything that happened to them, even the worst atrocity, was "real" to them. No longer was there a split between one to whom things happened and the one who observed them. Once this stage was reached of taking everything that happened in the camp as "real," there was every indication that the prisoners who had reached it were afraid of returning to the outer world. They did not admit it directly, but from their talk it was clear that they hardly believed they would ever return to this outer world because they felt that only a cataclysmic event − a world war and world revolution − could free them; and even then they doubted that they would be able to adapt to this new life. They seemed aware of what had happened to them while growing older in the camp. They realized that they had adapted themselves to the life in the camp and that this process was coexistent with a basic change in their personality.

The most drastic demonstration of this realization was provided by the case of a formerly very prominent radical German politician. He declared that according to his experience nobody could live in the camp longer than five years without changing his attitudes so radically that he no longer could be considered the same person he used to be. He asserted that he did not see any point in continuing to live once his real life consisted in being a prisoner in a concentration camp, that he could not endure developing those attitudes and behaviors he saw developing in all old prisoners. He therefore had decided to commit suicide on the sixth anniversary of his being brought into the camp. His fellow prisoners tried to watch him carefully on this day, but nevertheless he succeeded.

There was, of course, considerable variation among individuals in the time it took them to make their peace with the idea of having to spend the rest of their lives in the camp. Some became part of the camp life rather soon, some probably never. When a new prisoner was brought into the camp, the older ones tried to teach him a few things which might prove helpful in his adjustment. The new prisoners were told that they should try by all means to survive the first days and not to give up the fight for their lives, that it would become easier the longer time they spent in camp. They said, "If you survive the first three months you will survive the next three years." This, despite the fact that the yearly mortality was close to 20 percent.[11] This high death rate was mostly due to the large number of new prisoners who did not survive the first few weeks in the camp, either because they did not care to survive by means of adapting themselves to the life in camp or because they were unable to do so. How long it took a prisoner to cease to consider life outside the camp as real depended to a great extent on the strength of his emotional ties to his family and friends. The change to accepting camp life as real never took place before spending two years in camp. Even then everyone was overtly longing to regain freedom. Some of the indications from which one could learn about the changed attitude were: scheming to find oneself a better place in the camp rather than trying to contact the outer world,[12] avoiding speculation about one's family, or world affairs,[13] concentrating all interest on events taking place inside of the camp. When the author expressed to some of the old prisoners his astonishment that they seemed not to be interested in discussing their future life outside the camp, they frequently admitted that they no longer could visualize themselves living outside the camp, making free decisions, taking care of themselves and their families...

Old prisoners did not like to be reminded of their families and former friends. When they spoke about them, it was in a very detached way. They liked to receive letters, but it was not very important to them, partly because they had lost contact with the events related in them. It has been mentioned that they had some realization of how difficult it might be for them to find their way back, but there was another contributing factor, namely, the prisoners' hatred of all those living outside of the camp, who "enjoyed life as if we were not rotting away."

This outside world which continued to live as if nothing had happened was in the minds of the prisoners represented by those whom they used to know, namely, by their relatives and friends. But even this hatred was very subdued in the old prisoners. It seemed that, as much as they had forgotten to love their kin, they had lost the ability to hate them. *They had learned to direct great amount of aggression against themselves so as not to get into too many conflicts with the Gestapo, while the new prisoners still directed their aggressions against the outer world, and − when not supervised − against the Gestapo.* Since the old prisoners did not show much emotion either way, they were unable to feel strongly about anybody.

Old prisoners did not like to mention their former social status or their former activities, whereas new prisoners were rather boastful about them. New prisoners seemed to try to back their self-esteem by letting others know how important they had been, with the very obvious implication that they still were important. Old prisoners seemed to have accepted their state of dejection, and to compare it with their former splendor − and anything was magnificent when compared with the situation in which they found themselves − was probably too depressing.

HOPES ABOUT LIFE AFTER LIBERATION

Closely connected with the prisoners' beliefs about, and attitudes towards, their families were their beliefs and hopes concerning their life after release from camp. Here the prisoners embarked a great deal on individual and group daydreams. To indulge in them was one of the favorite pastimes if the general emotional climate in the camp was not too depressed. There was a marked difference between the daydreams of the new and the old prisoners. *The longer the time a prisoner had spent in camp, the less true to reality were his daydreams*; so much so that the hopes and expectations of the old prisoners often took the form of eschatological or messianic hopes; this was in line with their expectation that only such an event as the end of the world would liberate them. They would daydream of the coming world war and world revolution. They were convinced that out of this great upheaval they would emerge as the future leaders of Germany at least, if not of the world. This was the least to which their sufferings entitled them. These grandiose expectations were coexistent with great vagueness as to their future private lives. In their daydreams they were certain to emerge as the future secretaries of state, but they were less certain whether they would continue to live with their wives and children. Part of these daydreams may be explained by the fact that they seemed to feel that only a high public position could help them to regain their standing within their families.

The hopes and expectations of the new prisoners about their

future lives were much more true to reality. Despite their open ambivalence about their families, they never doubted that they were going to continue to live with them just where they had left off. They hoped to continue their public and professional lives in the same way as they used to live them.

Most of the adaptations to the camp situation mentioned so far were more or less individual behaviors, according to our definition. The changes discussed in the next section, namely, the regression to infantile behavior, was according to our definition a mass phenomenon. The writer is of the opinion – partly based on introspection, and partly on discussions with the few other prisoners who realized what was happening – that this regression would not have taken place if it had not happened in all prisoners. Moreover, whereas the prisoners did not interfere with another's daydreams or with his attitudes to his family, they asserted their power as a group over those prisoners who objected to deviations from normal adult behavior. They accused those who would not develop a childlike dependency on the guards as threatening the security of the group, an accusation which was not without foundation, since the Gestapo always punished the group for the misbehavior of individual members. This regression into childlike behavior was, therefore, even more inescapable than other types of behavior imposed on the individual by the impact of the conditions in the camp.

REGRESSION INTO INFANTILE BEHAVIOR

The prisoners developed types of behavior which are characteristic of infancy or early youth. Some of these behaviors developed slowly, others were immediately imposed on the prisoners and developed only in intensity as time went on. Some of these more or less infantile behaviors have already been discussed, such as ambivalence to one's family, despondency, finding satisfaction in daydreaming rather than in action.

Whether some of these behavior patterns were deliberately produced by the Gestapo is hard to ascertain. Others were definitely produced by it, but again we do not know whether it was consciously done. It has been mentioned that even during the transportation the prisoners were tortured in a way in which a cruel and domineering father might torture a helpless child; here it should be added that the prisoners were also debased by techniques which went much further into childhood situations. They were forced to soil themselves. In the camp the defecation was strictly regulated; it was one of the most important daily events, discussed in great detail. During the day the prisoners who wanted to defecate had to obtain the permission of the guard. It seemed as if the education to cleanliness would be once more repeated. It seemed to give pleasure to the guards to hold the power of granting or withholding the permission to visit the latrines. (Toilets were mostly not available.) This pleasure of the guards found its counterpart in the pleasure the prisoners derived from visiting the latrines, because there they usually could rest for a moment, secure from the whips of the overseers and guards. They were not always so secure, because sometimes enterprising young guards enjoyed interfering with the prisoners even at these moments.

The prisoners were forced to say "thou" to one another, which in Germany is indiscriminately used only among small children. They were not permitted to address one another with the many titles to which middle- and upper-class Germans are accustomed. On the other hand, they had to address the guards in the most deferential manner, giving them all their titles.

The prisoners lived, like children, only in the immediate present; they lost the feeling for the sequence of time, they became unable to plan for the future or to give up immediate pleasure satisfactions to gain greater ones in the near future. They were unable to establish durable object-relations. Friendships developed as quickly as they broke up. Prisoners would, like early adolescents, fight one another tooth and nail, declare that they would never even look at one another or speak to one another, only to become close friends within a few minutes. They were boastful, telling tales about what they had accomplished in their former lives, or how they succeeded in cheating foremen or guards, and how they sabotaged the work. Like children they felt not at all set back or ashamed when it became known that they had lied about their prowess.

Another factor contributing to the regression into childhood behavior was the work the prisoners were forced to perform. New prisoners particularly were forced to perform nonsensical tasks, such as carrying heavy rocks from one place to another, and after a while back to the place where they had picked them up. On other days they were forced to dig holes in the ground with their bare hands, although tools were available. They resented such nonsensical work, although it ought to have been immaterial to them whether their work was useful. They felt debased when forced to perform "childish" and stupid labor, and preferred even harder work when it produced something that might be considered useful. There seems to be no doubt that the tasks they performed, as well as the mistreatment by the Gestapo which they had to endure, contributed to their disintegration as adult persons.

The author had a chance to interview several prisoners who before being brought into the camp had spent a few years in prison, some of them in solitary confinement. Although their number was too small to permit valid generalizations, it seems that to spend time in prison does not produce the character changes described in this paper. As far as the regression into childhood behaviors is concerned, the only feature prison and camp seem to have in common is that in both the prisoners are prevented from satisfying their sexual desires in a normal way, which eventually leads them to the fear of losing their virility. In the camp this fear added strength to the other factors detrimental to adult types of behavior and promoted childlike types of behavior.

Summary. Significant differences could be observed when comparing old and new prisoners. They seemed to originate in personality changes which were brought about by the impact of the camp experiences on the prisoners. One of the differences was a changed frame of reference, indicated by the difference in evaluating extreme experiences as "real" or unreal. Old prisoners had more or less lost contact with their families and the world outside the camp. Their evaluation of their own importance had become fantastic, as could be seen from their hopes about their lives after liberation. These exaggerated hopes were partly due to the feeling that they were atoning for others and were, therefore, entitled to reward. All changes produced by living in the camp seemed to force the prisoners back into childhood attitudes and behaviors and they became in this way more or less willing tools of the Gestapo.

THE FINAL ADJUSTMENT TO THE LIFE IN THE CAMP

A prisoner had reached the final stage of adjustment to the camp situation when he had changed his personality so as to accept as his own the values of the Gestapo. A few examples may illustrate how this acceptance expressed itself.

The Gestapo considered, or pretended to consider, the prisoners the scum of the earth. They insisted that none of them was any better than the others. One of the reasons for this attitude was probably to impress the young guards who received their training in the camp that they were superior to even the most outstanding prisoner and to demonstrate to them that the former foes of the Nazis were now subdued and not worthy of any special attention. If a formerly prominent prisoner had been treated better, the simple guard would have thought that he is still influential; if he had been treated worse, they might have thought that he is still dangerous. This was in line with the desire to impress the guards that even a slight degree of opposition against the Nazi system led to the entire destruction of the person who dared to oppose, and that the degree of opposition made no difference in this respect. Occasional talks with these guards revealed that they really believed in a Jewish-capitalistic world conspiracy against the German people, and whoever opposed the Nazis participated in it and was therefore to be destroyed, independent of his role in the conspiracy. So it can be understood why their behavior to the prisoners was that normally reserved for dealing with one's vilest enemy.

The prisoners found themselves in an impossible situation due to the steady interference with their privacy on the part of the guards and other prisoners. So a great amount of aggression accumulated. In the new prisoners it vented itself in the way it might have done in the world outside the camp. But slowly prisoners accepted, as expression of their verbal aggressions, terms which definitely did not originate in their previous vocabularies, but were taken over from the very different vocabulary of the Gestapo. From copying the verbal aggressions of the Gestapo to copying their form of bodily aggressions was one more step, but it took several years to make this step. It was not unusual to find old prisoners, when in charge of others, behaving worse than the Gestapo, in some cases because they were trying to win favor with the Gestapo in this way but more often because they considered this the best way to behave toward prisoners in the camp.

Practically all prisoners who had spent a long time in the camp took over the Gestapo's attitude toward the so-called unfit prisoners. Newcomers presented the old prisoners with difficult problems. Their complaints about the unbearable life in camp added new strain to the life in the barracks, so did their inability to adjust to it. Bad behavior in the labor gang endangered the whole group. So a newcomer who did not stand up well under the strain tended to become a liability for the other prisoners. Moreover, weaklings were those most apt eventually to turn traitors. Weaklings usually died during the first weeks in the camp anyway, so it seemed as well to get rid of them sooner. So old prisoners were sometimes instrumental in getting rid of the unfit, in this way making a feature of Gestapo ideology a feature of their own behavior. This was one of the many situations in which old prisoners demonstrated toughness and molded their way of treating other prisoners according to the example set by the Gestapo. That this was really a taking-over of Gestapo attitudes can be seen from the treatment of traitors. Self-protection asked for their elimination, but the way in which they were tortured for days and slowly killed was taken over from the Gestapo.

Old prisoners who seemed to have a tendency to identify themselves with the Gestapo did so not only in respect to aggressive behavior. They would try to arrogate to themselves old pieces of Gestapo uniforms. If that was not possible, they tried to sew and mend their uniforms so that they would resemble those of the guards. The length to which prisoners would go in these efforts seemed unbelievable, particularly since the Gestapo punished them for their efforts to copy Gestapo uniforms. When asked why they did it they admitted that they loved to look like one of the guards.

The identification with the Gestapo did not stop with the copying of their outer appearance and behavior. Old prisoners accepted their goals and values, too, even when they seemed opposed to their own interests. It was appalling to see how far formerly even politically well-educated prisoners would go in this identification. At one time American and English newspapers were full of stories about the cruelties committed in the camps. The Gestapo punished the prisoners for the appearance of these stories true to their policy of punishing the group for whatever a member or a former member did, and the stories must have originated in reports of former prisoners. In discussions of this event old prisoners would insist that it is not the business of foreign correspondents or newspapers to bother with German institutions and expressed their hatred of the journalists who tried to help them. The writer asked more than one hundred old political prisoners the following question: "If I am lucky and reach foreign soil, should I tell the story of the camp and arouse the interest of the cultured world?" He found only two who made the unqualified statement that everyone escaping Germany ought to fight the Nazis to the best of his abilities. *All others were hoping for a German revolution, but did not like the idea of interference on the part of a foreign power.*

When old prisoners accepted Nazi values as their own they usually did not admit it, but explained their behavior by means of rationalizations. For instance, prisoners collected scrap in the camp because Germany was low on raw materials. When it was pointed out that they were thus helping the Nazis, they rationalized that through the saving of scrap Germany's working classes, too, became richer. When erecting buildings for the Gestapo, controversies started whether one should build well. New prisoners were for sabotaging, a majority of the old prisoners for building well. They rationalized that the new Germany will have use for these buildings. When it was pointed out that a revolution will have to destroy the fortresses of the Gestapo, they retired to the general statement that one ought to do well any job one has to do. It seems that the majority of the old prisoners had realized that they could not continue to work for the Gestapo unless they could convince themselves that their work made some sense, so they had to convince themselves of this sense.

The satisfaction with which some old prisoners enjoyed the fact that, during the twice daily counting of the prisoners, they really had stood well at attention can be explained only by the fact that they had entirely accepted the values of the Gestapo as their own. Prisoners prided themselves of being as tough as the Gestapo members. This identification with their torturers went so far as copying their leisure-time activities. One of the games played by the guards was to find out who could stand to be hit longest without uttering a complaint. This game was copied by the old prisoners, as though they had not been hit often and long enough without needing to repeat this experience as a game.

Often the Gestapo would enforce nonsensical rules, originating in the whims of one of the guards. They were usually forgotten as soon as formulated, but there were always some old prisoners who would continue to follow these rules and try to enforce them on others long after the Gestapo had forgotten about them. Once, for instance, a guard on inspecting the prisoners' apparel found that the shoes of some of them were dirty on the inside. He ordered all prisoners to wash their shoes inside and out with water and soap. The heavy shoes treated this way became hard as stone. The order was never repeated, and many prisoners did not even execute it when given. Nevertheless there were some old prisoners who not only continued to wash the inside of their shoes every day but cursed all others who did not do so as negligent and dirty. These prisoners firmly believed that the rules set down by the Gestapo were desirable standards of human behavior, at least in the camp situation.

Other problems in which most old prisoners made their peace with the values of the Gestapo included the race problem, although race discrimination had been alien to their scheme of values before they were brought into the camp. They accepted as true the claim that Germany needed more space ("Lebensraum"), but added "as long as there does not exist a world federation," they believed in the superiority of the German race. It should be emphasized that this was not the result of propaganda on the side of the Gestapo. The Gestapo made no such efforts and insisted in its statements that it was not interested in how the prisoners felt as long as they were full of fear of the Gestapo. Moreover, the Gestapo insisted that it would prevent them from expressing their feelings anyway. The Gestapo seemed to think it impossible to win the prisoners for its values, after having made them subject to their tortures.

Among the old prisoners one could observe other developments which indicated their desire to accept the Gestapo along lines which definitely could not originate in propaganda. It seems that, since they returned to a childlike attitude toward the Gestapo, they had a desire that at least some of those whom they accepted as all-powerful father-images should be just and kind. They divided their positive and negative feelings — strange as it may be that they should have positive feelings, they had them — toward the Gestapo in such way that all positive emotions were concentrated on a few officers who were rather high up in the hierarchy of camp administrators, but hardly ever on the governor of the camp. They insisted that these officers hide behind their rough surfaces a feeling of justice and propriety; he, or they, were supposed to be genuinely interested in the prisoners and even trying, in a small way, to help them. Since nothing of these supposed feelings and efforts ever became apparent, it was explained that he hid them so effectively because otherwise he would not be able to help the prisoners. The eagerness of these prisoners to find reasons for their claims was pitiful. A whole legend was woven around the fact that of two officers inspecting a barrack one had cleaned his shoes from mud before entering. He probably did it automatically, but it was interpreted as a rebuff to the other officer and a clear demonstration of how he felt about the concentration camp.

After so much has been said about the old prisoners' tendency to conform and to identify with the Gestapo, it ought to be stressed that this was only part of the picture, because the author tried to concentrate on interesting psychological mechanisms in group behavior rather than on reporting types of behavior which are either well known or could reasonably be expected. These same old prisoners who identified with the Gestapo at other moments defied it, demonstrating extraordinary courage in doing so.

Summary. In conclusion it should be emphasized again that this essay is a preliminary report and does not pretend to be exhaustive. The author feels that the concentration camp has an importance reaching far beyond its being a place where the Gestapo takes revenge on its enemies. It is the main training ground for young Gestapo soldiers who are planning to rule and police Germany and all conquered nations; it is the Gestapo's laboratory where it develops methods for changing free and upright citizens not only into grumbling slaves, but into serfs who in many respects accept their masters' values. They still think that they are following their own life goals and values, whereas in reality they have accepted the Nazis' values as their own.

It seems that what happens in an extreme fashion to the prisoners who spend several years in the concentration camp happens in less exaggerated form to the inhabitants of the big concentration camp called greater Germany. It might happen to the inhabitants of occupied countries if they are not able to form organized groups of resistance. The system seems too strong for an individual to break its hold over his emotional life, particularly if he finds himself within a group which has more or less accepted the Nazi system. It seems easier to resist the pressure of the Gestapo and the Nazis if one functions as an individual; the Gestapo seems to know that and therefore insists on forcing all individuals into groups which they supervise. Some of the methods used for this purpose are the hostage system and the punishment of the whole group for whatever a member of it does; not permitting anybody to deviate in his behavior from the group norm, whatever this norm may be; discouraging solitary activities of any kind, etc. The main goal of the efforts seems to be to produce in the subjects childlike attitudes and childlike dependency on the will of the leaders. The most effective way to break this influence seems to be the formation of democratic groups of resistence of independent, mature, and self-reliant persons, in which every member backs up, in all other members, the ability to resist. If such groups are not formed it seems very difficult not to become subject to the slow process of personality disintegration produced by the unrelenting pressure of the Gestapo and the Nazi system.

Inasmuch as the concentration camp is the laboratory of the Gestapo for subjecting not only free men, but even the most ardent foes of the Nazi system, to the process of disintegration from their position as autonomous individuals, it ought to be studied by all persons interested in understanding what happens to a population subject to the methods of the Nazi system. It is hoped that by understanding what happens to the unhappy persons under Nazi domination it will be possible to devise methods by means of which they will be helped to resurrect within a short time as authomonomous and self-reliant persons.

NOTES

1 For an official report on life in these camps see *Papers concerning the treatment of German nationals in Germany* (London: His Majesty's Stationery Office, 1939).

2 The daily food the prisoners received yielded approximately 1800 calories, whereas for the labor they were forced to perform the average caloric requirement is from 3,000 to 3,300 calories.

3 Surgical operations, for instance, were performed by a former printer. There were many M.D.s in the camp, but no prisoner was permitted to work in the camp in his civilian capacity because that would not have implied a punishment.

4 The concentration camps for political prisoners are administered by the "Elite" formations of the "SS" groups, called "Deathhead" regiments. Every member of these regiments has to spend at least three months of his training as a guard in these camps. If he does not perform satisfactorily in this capacity, he is transferred back to the non-elite formations of the "SS."

There are many types of concentration camps in Germany. If the author speaks of concentration camps, the meaning is always camps for political prisoners. Up to the time of the war there were three big camps of this type and a few smaller ones, all for men, and one small camp for women. Up to that time the total of prisoners in these camps never exceeded 60,000. Contrary to widespread opinion, only a small minority were Jews. The many other German concentration camps, such as those for forced labor, were not administered by the Gestapo, and the conditions in them were very different.

5 Most soldiers and noncommissioned officers of the "SS" were very young, between 17 and 20 years old, and the sons of farmers, of small shopkeepers, or of the lower class of the civil servants.

6 Money was very important to the prisoners because at certain times they were permitted to buy cigarettes and some extra food. To be able to buy food meant to avoid starvation. Since most political prisoners, most criminals and many middle-class prisoners had no money, they were willing to make easier the lies of those wealthy prisoners who were willing to pay for it.

7 There were good indications that most guards embraced a similar attitude, although for different reasons. They tortured the prisoners partly because they enjoyed demonstrating their superiority, partly

because their superiors expected it of them. But, having been educated in a world which rejected brutality, they felt uneasy about what they were doing. It seems that they, too, had an emotional attitude towards their acts of brutality which might be described as a feeling or unreality. After having been guards in the camp for some time, they got accustomed to inhuman behavior, they became "conditioned" to it; it then became part of their "real" life.

8 Some aspects of this behavior seem similar to those described in literature as "depersonalization," still there seem to be so many differences between the phenomena discussed in this paper and the phenomenon of depersonalization that it seemed not advisable to use this term.

9 The reason for this punishment was that two prisoners had tried to escape. On such occasions all prisoners were always punished very severely, so that in the future they would give away secrets they had learned, because otherwise they would have to suffer. The idea was that every prisoner ought to feel responsible for any act committed by any other prisoner. This was in line with the principle of the Gestapo to force the prisoners to feel and act as a group, and not as individuals.

10 This was one of the occasions in which the antisocial attitudes of certain middle-class prisoners became apparent. Some of them did not participate in the spirit of mutual help, some even tried to take advantage of others for their own benefit.

11 The prisoners in charge of a barrack kept track of what happened to the inhabitants of their barrack. In this way it was comparatively easy to ascertain how many died and now many were released. The former were always in the majority.

12 New prisoners would spend all their money on efforts to smuggle letters out of the camp or to receive communications without having them censored. Old prisoners did not use their money for such purposes. They used it for securing for themselves "soft" jobs, such as clerical work in the offices of the camp or work in the shops where they were at least protected against the weather while at work.

13 It so happened that on the same day news arrived of a speech by President Roosevelt, denouncing Hitler and Germany, and rumors spread that one officer of the Gestapo would be replaced by another. The *new* prisoners discussed the speech excitedly, and paid no attention to the rumors, the *old* prisoners paid no attention to the speech, but devoted all their conversations to the changes in camp officers.

11

Walt Whitman and the Culture of Democracy

GEORGE KATEB

I think that Walt Whitman is a great philosopher of democracy. Indeed, he may be the greatest. As Thoreau said: Whitman "is apparently the greatest democrat the world has ever seen."[1] To put it more academically, he is perhaps the greatest philosopher of the culture of democracy. He writes the best phrases and sentences about democracy. By democratic culture, I mean these things especially. First, democratic culture is (or can be) the soil for the creation of new works of high art — great poems and moral writings, in particular. Second, democratic culture is (or is becoming) a particularist stylization of life — that is, a distinctive set of appearances, habits, rituals, dress, ceremonies, folk traditions, and historical memories. Third, democratic culture is (or can be) the soil for the emergence of great souls whose greatness consists in themselves being like works of art in the spirit of a new aristocracy. All these meanings are interconnected, and appear in Whitman's writings throughout his life. Perhaps they receive their most powerful expression in *Democratic Vistas*. But in my judgement the central meaning when we study Whitman is democratic culture as the setting in which what I have elsewhere called "democratic individuality" (a phrase close to Whitman's usage), is slowly being disclosed. I believe that the setting for democratic individuality is a greatly more powerful and original idea than any of the other ideas of democratic culture that I have just mentioned.

In other places, I have tried to suggest that working together with Emerson and Thoreau, Whitman tries to draw out the fuller moral and existential significance of rights. These are the rights that individuals have as persons, and that the political system of democracy exists in order to protect, and also to embody in its workings. Democratic individuality is what rights-based individualism in a democracy could eventually become, once the political

Reprinted by permission of SAGE publications from *Political Theory* 18, 4 (November, 1990).

separation from the Old World was complete; and had already become, to some degree, in their time. I see the Emersonians as trying to encourage the tendency to democratic individuality; to urge it forward so that it may express itself ever more confidently and therefore more splendidly. In their conception of democratic individuality I find three components: self-expression, resistance on behalf of others, and receptivity or responsiveness (being "hospitable") to others. My judgement is that for the Emersonians the most important component of democratic individuality, by far, is receptivity or responsiveness. An individual's insistence on first being oneself expressively is valuable mostly as a preparation for receptivity or responsiveness: behavioral non-conformity loosens the hold of narrow or conventional methods of seeing and feeling (as well as preparing a person to take a principled stand in favor of those denied their rights).

This responsiveness or receptivity can also be described as a way — a profoundly democratic way — of being connected to others and to nature. As Whitman says in "Song of the Open Road": "Here the profound lesson of reception, nor preference nor denial."[2] It is a way that deepens the sort of connectedness already present in rights-based individualism, but that only time and a steady commitment to rights can call forth. Time is needed because rights-based individualism is such a strange idea, and so untypical of past human experience, that those who live it and live by it — even though imperfectly — have to keep remembering, or keep learning as if they never knew, both the basic meaning and the farther implications of what they profess and enact. And the steady commitment therefore turns out to be not so steady after all, but only as steady as the strangeness permits.

I would like to explore the connectedness that emanates from democratic individuality, as Whitman perceives and perfects it. He knows, let it be said immediately, the extent of the strangeness, and the steadiness for what it is, in democratic society. He says in the *Preface* to *Leaves of Grass* (1876):

> For though perhaps the main points of all ages and nations are points of resemblance, and, even while granting evolution, are substantially the same, there are some vital things in which this Republic, as to its individualities, and as a compacted Nation, is to specially stand forth, and culminate modern humanity. And these are the very things it least morally and mentally knows — (though curiously enough, it is at the same time faithfully acting upon them.)

In the *Preface*, 1872, he looks back on what he has been doing since he began writing *Leaves of Grass*. He says:

> "Leaves of Grass," already published, is, in its intentions, the song of a great composite *democratic individual*, male or female. And following on and amplifying the same purpose, I suppose I have in my mind to run through the chants of this volume (if ever completed) the thread-voice, more or less audible, of an aggregated, inseparable, unprecedented, vast, composite, electric *democratic nationality*.

For me, Whitman's greatness does not lie in his pursuit of an image of a democratic American nationality; an image — in my phrase — of a particularist stylization of life. Such a notion strikes me as being of secondary importance at best. How important to the world is one more stylization? Even more, I do not think that the notion is consistent with the project of proposing "a great composite democratic individual." A "compacted Nation" (Preface, 1876) is antithetical to a composite individual. Nationhood is too close to a conception of group identity: a shared pride in tribal attributes rather than in adherence to a distinctive and principled human self-conceptualization that may one day be available to persons everywhere in the world. As national poetry, "Drum-Taps" is full of a hateful belligerence: Whitman sees and exults in the indissociable bond between nationhood and war. No, Whitman's greatness lies in his effort, the greatest effort so far made, to say — to sing — the democratic individual, especially as such an individual lives in receptivity or responsiveness, in a connectedness different from any other. Such connectedness is not the same as nationhood or group identity. (A later point in this paper is that it is not the same as "adhesiveness".)

I would like to suggest that his individualist effort attains its greatest height in the poem "Song of Myself." This is not to deny that everywhere in Whitman's work we will find resources for enriching or refining the poem's teaching. It is also true that he is sometimes less literal in this poem than he is elsewhere and later. But "Song of Myself" is of supreme value; it can organize one's reading of Whitman's body of writing. In thinking about this poem as the central work, one can make discoveries about the culture of democracy.

The poem is full of complexities. This democratic poem, like all of Whitman's best work, is immensely difficult; it is only barely accessible. His characterization of his own poems (in "As

Consequent, etc.") perfectly suits "Song of Myself": "O little shells, so curious-convolute, so limpid-cold and voiceless. / Your tidings old, yet ever new and untranslatable." And if "Song of Myself" said − like any great work − unexpected things in its time, it remains − like any great work − altogether unexpected. So let us try to see what "Song of Myself" teaches. I mean to treat this poem as a work in political theory, which is what Whitman himself encourages (to say the least). Now and then, it is wise, however, to recall a line from "Myself and Mine:" ". . . reject those who would expound me, for I cannot expound myself."

Whitman makes major additions from version to version and omits a few lines here and there. We should be content, I think, with the last version, that of 1891−2, even though it is interesting to study Whitman's changes. One change, however, should be noticed. Whitman did not call the poem "Song of Myself" until 1881. In the first version of 1855, the poem, like all the poems in the first edition of *Leaves of Grass*, had no title. Thereafter, the poem is successively called, "Poem of Walt Whitman," "Walt Whitman," and at last "Song of Myself."

All its various titles are odd − as, indeed, the title of the collection (*Leaves of Grass*) is odd. The poem's titles are odd because when we read it we do not find the poem autobiographical, except in a few unimportant details. The egotistical titles are not the titles of an egotistical work. Nor is the work self-referring or self-revelatory in any usual sense. There is scarcely anything intimate in it. It tells no story about the writer. Perhaps it would be all the more odd if the poem were self-revealing: until rather late in life, Whitman had little fame. Why should anyone have cared to hear an account of his life in 1855?

In the very first section of the poem Whitman says: ". . . what I assume you shall assume, / For every atom belonging to me as good belongs to you." Notice the extreme rapidity of movement in mood in these two lines. "What I assume you shall assume" seems to indicate that the poet is demanding that his readers obey him in their thought: a sentiment worse than egotistical. But then, in the next line, he is telling us that the reason we are to assume what he assumes is that "every atom belonging to me as good belongs to you." It is not that we must obey him as we read him. Rather, if we understand the poem we will see that the poet and his readers are alike, and therefore we will come to assume what the poet does. In telling of himself the poet is telling us about ourselves: that is what is to be assumed. His words about himself are words about us. As he proclaims in the climax of one of his long and observant catalogues of expressive human roles and functions: "... of these one and all I weave the song of myself." In a Notebook entry (1855–6), Whitman says: "I have all lives, all effects, all hidden invisibly in myself ... they proceed from me."[3] In fact, if luck had made any of his readers democratic poets (and contingency is the thing that makes the greatest difference), we would have said or sung poems with the same purport as "Song of Myself:" "(It is you talking just as much as myself, I act as the tongue of you, / Tied in your mouth, in mine it begins to be loosen'd.)" (Sect. 47)

We are alike in a certain way: living in a rights-based democracy enables and encourages a certain recognition of likeness. What is the nature of this likeness? Whitman says, "... every atom belonging to me as good belongs to you." Let us emphasize the word "atom." What does it mean in this poem? An atom is a potentiality, I think. Every individual is composed of potentialities. Therefore, when I perceive or take in other human beings as they lead their lives or play their parts, I am only encountering external actualizations of some of the countless number of potentialities in me, in my soul. These atoms are in everyone; hence "every atom belonging to me as good belongs to you." The difficult and important complication is that in one's experience of others, one encounters their personalities, not their souls. The world contains an amazing diversity of personalities. Contingency has a great share in realizing any potentiality. Souls, however, are the same: infinite potentialities.

At this point, I should try to say something about the categories Whitman uses or suggests in speaking of the different (so to speak, structural) aspects of the individual. I am guided to some degree by Roy Harvey Pearce and Harold Bloom.[4]

The key term is soul; it frequently occurs in "Song of Myself" and in all Whitman's work. It has both a secular meaning and a religious one, while the boundaries of the two meanings are not always distinct. Whitman intends, I think, some fluidity of definition. In its secular meaning, the soul is what is given in the person, and in all persons the given is the same: the same desires, inclinations, and passions as well as aptitudes and incipient talents. The secular soul is made up of the unwilled, the unbidden, the dreamt, the inchoate and unshaped. It is the reservoir of potentialities. Its roots are wordless. It exists to be observed and worked on; to be realized. In its religious meaning, soul is unique and unalterable individual identity; one's genius or "eidolon;" the "real Me" (from "As I Ebb'd With the Ocean of Life"); the "actual me" (from "Passage to India"). It seems to be untouched by experience; and it survives death to find numberless incarnations. For me, the Whitman that matters is the one who believes in the secular soul, not the one who fancies he believes in the religious soul (towards which he does sometimes turn a skeptical glance).

The sharply contrasting term to soul is, of course, body. Whitman sometimes speaks dualistically of the soul and the body. He means to proclaim that the rights of body are as sacred as those of the soul. He celebrates not only sex but the senses, which take their turn in being praised in "Song of Myself." When he does this, he is defying those whose religious conception of the soul is more conventional than Whitman's own, and who associate the body with sin and damnation. On the other hand, Whitman's secular soul is unthinkable without the body; and conversely. There is little point to the contrast.

What then is the self, insofar as it is not a synonym for the whole individual?

In "Pioneers! O Pioneers!" he says: "I too with my soul and body, / We, a curious trio." From this verse and others I would infer that the self (the I, the ego) is active self-consciousness and disciplined creative energy. It is a purely secular category that Whitman does not want us to confuse with soul, especially in its religious sense. The self does its great work when it observes its soul and body as from a distance; and exploits the faculty of speech to tell as much of the truth as possible about them. The self is power that draws on its given resources of soul and body to become a poet: everybody is at least a part-way poet. It is with the poet's virtues of receptivity (in whatever way or degree possible) that each self democratically connects to the world of persons, creatures, and things. "You be my poem" (from "To You") helps to define connectedness.

The other work the self does is to put together a social persona, a personality, and thus enable the individual to lead a life. The creative energy of the self realizes one or another potentiality of the soul (and body). The personality is what is immediately recognizable by others: one's characteristics as they flow to and from one's work and social relations. Personality has surface and depths.

"Song of Myself" begins with "I celebrate myself." What the poem celebrates is soul, body, and self; but especially the inexhaustibility of the soul, and the power of the self to observe the soul and make democratic poetical understanding. The poem does not really celebrate personality or social persona; it merely admires and praises it. Whitman depends on it to keep things going: he does not love society as society. He is not a novelist and is not a sponsor of novelists whose ultimate reality is well-rounded characters that appeal to our sense that each person is what he or she is, just like that.

One last point: the crucial meaning of "composite" is not the structural condition of having aspects (soul, body, self, and personality), but rather the indefinite multiplicity of the soul.

I have made Whitman's teaching cumbersome. Some less clumsy effort must nevertheless be faithful to its complexity. Whitman is not saying anything simple, and I think that despite occasional vagueness or inconsistency, he sustains his distinctions concerning the aspects of the individual throughout his work. William James's great and intricate writing on "The Consciousness of Self" in *The Principles of Psychology*, vol. I, bears some important resemblances to Whitman's understanding of aspects. The views of both stem from a will to democratize human self-conception.

In any case, Whitman is suggesting two main things. All the personalities that I encounter, I already am: that is to say, I could become or could have become something like what others are; and that necessarily means, in turn, that all of us are always indefinitely more than we actually are. I am potentially all personalities and we equally are infinite potentialities. Whitman's poetic aim is to talk or sing his readers into accepting this highest truth about human beings. Democracy covers it over less than all other cultures. If people take thought, they will have to acknowledge that, first, they have all the impulses or inclinations or desires (for good and for bad) that they see realized around them, even if they act on other ones; and consequently, second, that each of us is, in Emerson's word, an "infinitude," or in another formulation of Emerson's, "an inner ocean." The deepest moral and existential meaning of equal rights is this kind of equal recognition granted by every individual to every individual. Democratic connectedness is mutual acceptance. Rejection of any other human being, for one reason or another, for apparently good reasons as well as for bad ones, is self-rejection. A principal burden of Whitman's teaching, therefore, is that the differences between individuals do not go as deep as the commonalities. Personality is not the (secular) soul. He explicitly says in "To You" that every endowment (talent) and virtue is latent in every individual, not merely every impulse or desire.

If I am right in the suggestions that I am making concerning the poetic aim of "Song of Myself," the result is rather strange (to use

that word again). The great poem of individualism in a democracy
is not individualist in any conventional sense. After all, to be
individual originally meant to be indivisible. Clearly, "Song of
Myself" is not asking us to pretend that we are indivisible. It is
more than a matter of having aspects: soul, body, self, personality.
The (secular) soul itself is a crowded house. (Later on, in "One's-
Self I Sing" (1867), he can refer to each of us as "a simple separate
person." If he is still consistent with his earlier teachings, "Simple"
would have to connote unpretentious yet precious; not indivisible.)
I read the odd and funny line, "It is time to explain myself — let us
stand up" as a pleased reference to inner multiplicity (Sect. 44).
More famously, he says towards the end of the poem:

> Do I contradict myself?
> Very well then I contradict myself,
> (I am large, I contain multitudes.) (Sect. 51)

Our potentialities are not only numberless but — and for that
reason — conflicting. We are inhabited by tumultuous atoms.
We are composite, not even composed. In "Crossing Brooklyn
Ferry" he goes so far as to posit "myself disintegrated, everyone disintegrated." I think that Whitman would have admired
Nietzsche's convolutedly Platonic saying that the body is "but a
social structure composed of many souls."[5] Whitman's radicalism
shows in his distance from Plato's dream of harmony between
the aspects of the individual, and of stillness in the house of
the potentialities.

Yet, in abandoning in "Song of Myself" the idea that the individual is indivisible, he is not creating an altogether new sense of
individualism. He sees that more than a few American individuals
are aware of their own composite nature and of their own unde-
finability. The telling point is not so much that the United States is
a pluralist society, made up of all psychological and sociological
types, as it is that democratic individuals see (if only unsteadily)
that each of them contains the raw material of all types, and yet is
more than any type or all types, and is even more than its special
personality. (Of course, it counts for a good deal that the democracy
is as expressively diverse as it is, and is so on a plane of equality
rather than hierarchically.)

Let me now summarize provisionally what Whitman is doing in
"Song of Myself." He is presenting a portrait of himself, but it is
not a portrait of his social or everyday personality. It is not a
story, either, of the things he has done or the particular experiences

that have shaped his personality or even shaped the course of his life. To tell these things is not to tell of what is most important about himself. "Song of Myself" is not like a photo or realistic drawing; but it is, nevertheless, the best and fullest account of himself — and, also, of course, of everyone else.

The question persists: why does Whitman not give a conventionally realistic account of himself, on the assumption that somehow he could have interested the world in his personality? The answer must be that the portrait he gives is more truly himself than any realistic account could ever hope to be. How, then, to describe this portrait: Whitman's phrase is best: it is a portrait of "a great composite *democratic individual*." Everyone is composite, and in a democracy each one can and should see himself or herself as a "great composite *democratic individual*." If the (secular) soul is potentiality, an honest portrait of oneself will register one's ability to perceive, and to identify or sympathize or empathize with, all the actualized potentialities that one tries to take in; and will also impart the sense that no actualization is definitive of anyone. The net impression left by "Song of Myself" is oneself as it were simultaneously but vicariously actualized in all directions. Oneself democratically perfected is truly a collage; one is "stucco'd" all over with personalities (Sect. 31). A person is also a Picasso-like concurrence or many perspectives within one frame. Whitman cannot talk about himself just by talking about himself; nor can anyone. If I talk honestly — that is to say, poetically — about myself I must talk about others. Perhaps I must talk much more about them than about myself, as Whitman does. "Song of Myself" is — to use the title of one of Gertrude Stein's books — *Everybody's Autobiography*. As he put in a draft, "I celebrate myself to celebrate you."[6]

Thus the poem seeks to teach that so far from being indivisible or even coherently multiple, one is, and should be glad to be, at any given moment, a composite — that is, ambiguous and ambivalent; and that in a timeless but mortal sense, one is an immense and largely untapped reservoir of potentiality. D. H. Lawrence has referred to Whitman's attempt to articulate an "accumulative identity."[7] One lifetime is not enough to realize more than a few potentialities, so that one lives many lievs (on earth) only through the ability to perceive and identify with others, and thus in an unarrogant sense, to become them, if only for a minute now and then. Whitman's emphasis on absorbing others is precisely, for him, the best way of letting them be, of not possessing them. In "A Song For Occupations," he provides a succinct account of what it means to connect to others by identifying with them:

> Neither a servant nor a master I,
> . . . .
> If you stand at work in a shop I stand as nigh as the
> nighest in the same shop,
> If you bestow gifts on your brother or
> dearest friend I demand as good as your
> brother or dearest friend,
> If your lover, husband, wife, is welcome
> by day or night, I must be personally as
> welcome,
> If you become degraded, criminal, ill, then I become so
> for your sake.

The individual demands to share the goods, the suffering, the fate of the stranger, and does so by imagining the stranger's life as a life he or she could lead and never feel out of place. As Whitman says in his earliest Notebook: "a man only is interested in anything when he identifies himself with it."[8] Whitman wants to coax us into thinking that we can identify with anything if we try, and that if we try we show not presumption but democratic honesty.

"Song of Myself" teaches its lessons about the individual not only in what it says directly. Part of Whitman's poetic subtlety consists in saying much about himself and every person through the compositional and structural traits of the poem. The poet is talking about the nature of himself and of every individual in the formal qualities he has chosen. I do not refer to the absence of rhyme, the uneven lines, or the variety of rhythms in "Song of Myself" (and almost all of his poetry). Free verse does, to be sure, make a cultural point. There can be beauty when the inherited forms are abandoned, and new forms are created. New forms express a new sense of artistic beauty: the artistic beauty appropriate for a new world, for a democracy. On the other hand, it is undeniably relevant for understanding the meaning of self-disclosure that Whitman creates a poem that is made up of genres. "Song of Myself," for example, contains anecdotes, not all of which lend themselves easily to emblematic uses; philosophical reflections on the nature of the person, but also on a full range of other questions that are made existential; descriptions of particulars that are observed with an eerie closeness; epic lists of localities and of human types; and lyrical passages of adoration and despair. This assortment of genres is a way of saying that adequate speech about oneself cannot be confined to any one genre.

My main interest, however, is rather that the *sequence* of passages and the poem's *texture* reflect the nature of the individual. These are the formal qualities that especially matter because they conduce to the feeling that our nature is strange (to use that word yet again); that oneself is a strange place. I believe that Whitman means to teach the lesson that if we are poetically persuaded of this strangeness, we will grow more in mutual recognition, in democratic acceptance. Feelings of superiority and other discriminations will exist, even exist intensely, but their validity will be challenged by a poetically enhanced awareness of the vastness of every individual equally.

By sequence (not plot or progression) and texture I mean such qualities as the poem's discontinuities, abrupt transitions, and sudden eruptions into different tones; its overall indifference to the demand that a story about oneself be a story; the seeming disproportion of attention accorded in it to small matters; its startling conjunctions and almost arbitrarily associated matters; the blank spaces in it caused by the many things left unsaid but that a reader could have expected; its occasional hallucinatory quality; the dream-like suddenness of emergences and vanishings in it; and the poet's dream-like mobility of identity which consists in mobilities of foci (both grand and microscopic) and of tense and perspective.

These compositional and structural traits are needed to provide an accurate portrait of the whole person. If the direct teaching of the poem is that one is multiple, that one will find, if one looks honestly, others inside oneself; the formal qualities of the poem teach a related lesson: namely, that one is (or should be) mysterious to oneself, as others are (or should be) to themselves. Exploring or examining oneself makes one less familiar to oneself. Knowing oneself is therefore knowing that there is no single, transparent entity to know. Hence knowing oneself is coming to know that one cannot really know oneself – at least not fully and not definitely. "As if I were not puzzled at myself!" he says (in an untitled poem excluded from the final edition.)[9] The Socratic paradox of knowledge as ignorance is transferred by "Song of Myself" to self-knowledge. What mistily emerges from democratized self-examination is not so much inhibition as surprise. Montaigne's identification of self-contempt as the fruit of self-knowledge suffers a partial rebuke. The limits of self-knowldege are the limits of poetical speech, and Whitman says that though speech is the twin of his vision, speech "is unequal to measure itself." At any given moment there is always more to know about oneself than one can say. He addresses these unpoetical words to the faculty of poetical speech:

> My final merit I refuse you, I refuse putting from me
> what I really am,
> Encompass worlds, but never try to encompass me, ...
> Writing and talk do not prove me, ... (Sect. 25)

If honest, one becomes almost another to oneself. By far the most important result would be that the passion to judge, condemn, and punish others, is reduced and replaced to a major degree by the desire to accept or empathize or sympathize with them. If an individual is composite, it should become greatly more difficult to equate a person with any of his or her deeds, no matter how awful; perhaps, also, no matter how good. As he programatically says in "Great are the Myths," (a poem he dropped from the final edition):

> What the best and worst did, we could do,
> What they felt, do we not feel it in ourselves?
> What they wished, do we not wish the same?[10]

I believe that the direct and the indirect lessons of the poem are great democratic lessons in connectedness. The ideas of the individual as composite, and of the individual as honestly unfamiliar to itself, are ways of awakening all of us to human equality on the highest moral and existential plane. To admit one's compositeness and ultimate unknowability is to open oneself to a kinship to others that is defined by receptivity or responsiveness to them. It intensifies the mutuality between strangers that is intrinsic to the idea of rights-based individualism in a democracy.

Whitman's work is to encourage us to become ever more consistent in living the life of equal rights. He admits everyone and everything into his poem. His mode is intensification. "I am a look," he says in a fragment.[11] He poetizes everyone and everything. He invests them with beauty so that we may look at them, look as if for the first time, or look again, and not look away; and then to feel instead of freezing. He freshens the beauty of beautiful persons (and beautiful natural and man-made things). He goes far — as far as Emerson and Thoreau — in trying to connect us to the world through a sense of beauty that dares to limit the ravenous appetite of the sense of moral virtue, because it easily turns (and for good reasons) world-despairing or even world-hating. But he is not content with doing only that. Whitman poetizes what is not conventionally thought beautiful: he tries to make wondrous the common, the commonplace, the everyday, "the plain landscape" (as he puts it in a Notebook).[12] Even more, he tries to have us think it possible that what is cheap or coarse or ugly or artless has its own beauty also — the beauty that any person or thing has, just by being there: or has, just by force of wanting to be looked at rather than turned away from. Even when he calls ugliness ugly, as in "Faces," and parades it, the depiction is so vivid that ugliness becomes humanly indispensable. As he says in an excluded poem, "Thoughts — 1: Visages:" "Of ugliness — To me there is just as much in it as there is in beauty."[13]

Similarly, in order to encourage what he calls sympathy, or what we can also call empathy, he enhances the humanity of human beings, the creatureliness of animals, the quiddity of things. He shows poetically, and invites us to share, his sympathy with what is already quite sympathetic, but what, in our hurry, we do not sympathize with enough. But, more importantly, he poetically conveys the need to sympathize with what is unattractive or even repellent. He makes poetic room for the homely, the unimportant, the obscure, the overlooked, the despised, the wicked, and the diseased. He gives the best interpretation of the democratic idea that unequals must be treated equally, and saves it from demotic perversion.

And all the while, of course, his constant appeal is for us to exercise recognition: to recognize that when one learns to perceive more beauty and feel more sympathy, one is only doing justice to *oneself*, to one's composite nature. Just as I am more than others can take in, so are they more. It is especially important to feel that the unbeautiful are not only unbeautiful and that the wicked are not only wicked, and to do this, as Whitman does enough of the time, without depending on any religious conception of the soul.

To live democratically, to live receptively and responsively, is risky and therefore the invitation to it is easily resisted. Whitman knows that. This is why he understands life in a democratic culture as heroic. Intensified democratic connectedness is heroic. What makes it so is the extraordinary amount of self-overcoming that is required. Many things in oneself must be overcome. One is the disposition to think that one is one's personality, and that therefore it is all right to live one's life solely dedicated to the prohibitions and allowances of one's role or function, or solely devoted to cultivating one's peculiarities and differences — what

Mill favorably calls "eccentricity." Another thing that must be overcome is the inevitable desire to close oneself to experience by finding others, or aspects of nature, condemnable or horrible. The failure of recognition and hence of acceptance is a perpetual possibility and a frequent occurrence. Self-overcoming as the over-coming of fear and disgust is the poet's constant message.

Unblinking attention to surfaces and depths is facilitated by the conviction that what one perceives or intuits or interprets is not exhaustively constitutive of the individuals one encounters or imagines. One can endure the surfaces and depths all the better when one knows that people could exceed in all directions the given, particular aspect we encounter. Or, one can exult in the surfaces or depths all the more when one knows that they are mere temporary manifestations of a residual and inexhaustible potentiality, that they are only promises. Whitman thus aims to attach us more tightly to others as they are, whatever they are, while, and because, he points to the undefinable soul each is, to which we cannot attach ourselves, and which we can only revere.

In a very late poem, "Grand is the Seen," he says lines that can be read, in spite of Whitman, in a strictly this-worldly and mortal way, and given a general relevance:

> Grand is the seen, the light, to me − grand are
> the sky and stars,
> Grand is the earth, and grand are lasting time and
> space,
> And grand their laws, so multiform, puzzling, evolutionary
> But grander far the unseen soul of me...
> ....
> More evolutionary vast, puzzling, O my soul!
> More multiform far − more lasting thou than they.

The visible is inferior to the invisible, but Whitman manages to raise the inferior (mere personalities) yet make the superior (souls) appear real.

For example, the life of work elicits from Whitman, in "A Song For Occupations," the emblematic judgement that in it there is "far more than you estimated, (and far less also)." His poetizing has thus a two-way motion. Life is poetically richer than is com-monly assumed, but also less real than the souls from which it emanates. Part of Whitman's mission is to awaken admiration of the surfaces and depths of social beings and their relations. But he wants admiration to be honestly aware of the contingent nature of actuality and the real nature of potentiality. This awareness can lead to a more poignant admiration of what is there, and thus avoid the bad faith that makes the world falsely solid and falsely necessary. (I hope that I am not making Whitman too Sartrean.)

Of course, my reading of Whitman runs the risk of ending up in a paradox; namely, that of suggesting that no single manifestation is good in itself, but that an indefinite number of potential manifestations has infinite worth. In answer, I would say that Whitman builds the feeling that what gives indefinite potentiality its worth is precisely the reverence towards anyone that it may arouse, and hence the acceptance of everyone that it should lead to. To doer is more than the sum of deeds...

Another lesson that Whitman teaches is that the composite individual will live for itself in a manner greatly different from the self-absorption of non-democratic cultures. First, all that Whitman says about the individual is an instigation to act out more and more of one's potentiality. "Once more I enforce you to give play to yourself," he says in "So Long!" (in a line dropped from the final edition).[14] That means to lead a more experimental life. It may also mean to seek a heterogeneous accumulation of experiences, as if only in that way can numerous yearnings of one's soul be accommodated. Whitman's hope is that with so much to gain, there cannot be very much to lose. He says in "A Song of the Rolling Earth" that "undeniable growth" establishes the reality of soul. Second, and relatedly, in any given activity, the idea that one is always capable of more than what one is now doing should affect the quality of how one does what one is doing. Whitman's greatest formulation appears in the fourth section of "Song of Myself:"

Apart from the pulling and hauling stands what I am,
Stands amused, complacent, compassionating, idle, unitary,
Looks down, is erect, or bends an arm on an impalpable certain rest.
Looking with side-curved head curious what will come next,
Both in and out of the game and watching and wondering at it.

There is a whole ethic of action compressed in these five lines, and it is an ethic that peculiarly suits a democracy because of the consecration that democracy gives to the will to transform action into contentious play; to replace military combat by "saner wars, sweet wars, life-giving wars." ("The Return of the Heroes") "In and out of the game" is democratic seriousness: nothing is for keeps is a truth that should be embraced rather than resented.

Democracy has sometimes been associated with grossness, a pleb ian, underbred grossness. Edmund Burke said in *Reflections on the Revolution in France* that under the system of aristocratic manners, "vice itself lost half its evil by losing all its grossness." Well, Whitman is trying to suggest that democracy has its own grace, the grace of being "both in and out;" hence the grace of unsolemnity, of looseness; and that this grace is enabled finally by the understanding that those towards whom one acts are one's equals, are oneself in the most important respects. This is no mere stylization. It is easier to be graceful if we never feel that we are in the presence of aliens. Democratic grace is caught in Whitman's almost rhetorical questions about the democratic individual: "The friendly and flowing savage, who is he? / Is he waiting for civilization, or past it and mastering it?" (Sect. 39)

The ethic of "in and out of the game" Whitman dares to apply even to suffering, whether one's own or that of someone else. He is suggesting that if I stop my own momentum in order to observe others, their hurts can register more painfully on me. If I am not quite completely in my own game, I can have a chance to notice what is happening to others who may be caught up in my game or in some other. On the other hand, if I am not quite completely in my own game, I am able, perhaps, to observe my own hurts rather than merely suffering them; and they may, therefore, register less painfully on me.

It is at this point, perhaps, that even an appreciative reader of Whitman may think that his idealization of the composite individual asks too much and may, in addition, ask for the wrong thing. His poetic identification with all who suffer may seem forced. I would like to take up sketchily some of the difficulties that the overall aspiration to an intensified connectedness may encounter.

To begin with, one can ask, are there not inevitable and desirable limits on the ability to perceive beauty? How far can one go in seeing beauty when, by conventional standards of both taste and decency, what presents itself is trivial or shameless or hideous? Why not rather encourage a greater effort at esthetic improvement? Whitman himself is eager to see a more esthetically accomplished and vibrant culture.

There is good sense in this complaint, as Whitman's own more conventional estheticism, as found especially in *Democratic Vistas*, demonstrates. In response, I suppose one can say that what comes to characterize American art more and more in the twentieth century is the uncanny and persistent appetite to make art out of junk, and thus to get us both to re-define what art is and to look again at what we are disposed to overlook or disdain or throw away as junk. This characteristic is faithful to the spirit of Whitman's work. It is a democratic characteristic; it is radical; it is heroic in a new way. And, for these reasons, it is best not to establish too quickly the limits on generous perception, and, instead, to anticipate that American art will frequently manage to redeem esthetically the apparently unredeemable. What artists do professionally, others can do without planning. (This phenomenon exists apart from the insidiously attractive qualities of mass or popular art: attractive precisely to the well-educated because they detect in some of this art a seriousness that repays generous perception.)

Greater difficulties are encountered in the matter of sympathy or empathy. Are there not both proper moral and inevitable mental limits to the ability to identify with human beings? Let us leave aside the admirable wish to establish kinship with animals and indeed with inanimate nature, as Whitman tries to do. Let us even grant Whitman the amazing mobility of identity that he poetically claims when for example he says: "I turn the bridegroom out of bed and stay with the bride myself, / I tighten her all night to my thighs and lips." (Sect. 33) and then immediately goes on to say: "My voice is the wife's voice, the screech by the rail of the / stairs, / They fetch my man's body up dripping and drown'd." (Sect. 33) He moves from identity with the bridegroom to identity with the established married woman; from consummation to loss. He is both sexes and many conditions. Let us allow that an individual, democratically prepared, can perform such feats of empathy, and should want to.

What does one say, however, when Whitman writes:

I am the man, I suffered, I was there.
. . . .
I am the hounded slave, I wince at the bite of dogs,
Hell and despair are upon me...
Agonies are one of my changes of garments,
I do not ask the wounded person how he feels, I myself
  become the
wounded person,
My hurts turn livid upon me as I lean on a cane and observe.
                                        (Sect. 33)

When encountering or imagining a hounded slave, what does it mean to become the hounded slave? Whitman amazingly says, "My hurts," not "His hurts." But is he encouraging us to feign transfers of identity? At the same time, one leans on a cane and observes. The extreme of empathy is claimed, and at the same time the extreme of detachment is being admitted, and not only admitted but insisted on. The question arises as to whether there are sufferings so terrible that the lucky unsuffering individual, no matter how intensely democratic in reception, cannot share them in imagination. Similarly, are there not acts of criminality so atrocious that one should not be encouraged to try to understand the person who is responsible for them? Can one find the Hitler and the Stalin in oneself, if one only tried? Whitman insists a number of times that he is as evil as the worst person. It is not possible to believe him. Do not even the greatest tragedians and novelists take short cuts in their impersonations of madness and criminality, and have to?

Furthermore, is it not the case that when we encounter people performing their deeds they are often simply acting according to rules? There is no personality to understand. All that needs to be understood is the rules that people are following. Such understanding may be hard to come by, but empathy or sympathy may have no place in the attempt to achieve it. More generally, may it not be the case that people, even in one's own culture, are just too different from each other? Is not what is most important about all of us not our potentiality, but our divergent personalities, the sum of what, in each case, our particular culture has made us? Or, put more generously, what is perhaps best about us is the way we take one potentiality and realize or embody it fully, and therefore achieve something definite and formed. What could be better than shaping a life by means of a voluntary and resourceful submission to a discipline or project? Sartre, the great theorist of bad faith, was also the great theorist of project. Is not reality found there and only there? Yet another question may arise. If Whitman means that one must try to see individuals from even the most dissimilar cultures as actualizations of one's own potentialities, is he not presuming to understand what he really cannot? Is not even the most democratically determined observer confined in his or her perspective?

To all these questions concerning moral and mental limits to sympathy or empathy (and there are more), one may be able to give only hesitant answers. I will not pretend to give any answers here. Is Whitman conscious of these problems? Does it matter whether we say that he is or is not? He certainly appears reckless. In "Song of the Answerer," he says, "Every existence has its idiom," but immediately insists that the poet "resolves all tongues into his own," without loss. Yet, in that remarkable poem, "The Sleepers," Whitman raises the possibility that he understands that his radical empathy is only a dream, that mobile identity is only a dream (and that only in sleep or death are people alike and equal).

> I dream in my dream all the dreams of
> the other dreamers,
> And I become the other dreamers.
> I am a dance —
> . . . .
> I am the actor, the actress, the voter, the politician,
> . . . .
> I am she who adorn'd herself and folded her hair
> expectantly.

Does it help to enlist so austere a philosopher as Collingwood in defense of Whitman's effort at empathy? In his *Autobiography*, he characterizes the historian:

> If he is able to understand, by rethinking them, the thoughts of a great many different kinds of people, it follows that he must be a great many kinds of man. He must be, in fact, a microcosm of all the history he can know. Thus his own self-knowledge is at the same time his knowledge of the world of human affairs.[15]

Could it be that unless a claimed kinship is the basis of observation, all appreciation of "otherness" tends to turn into a mere patronizing esthetic of the picturesque or into a paternalist anthropological solicitude? Human beings will be denatured, in either case, by being seen or imagined only as surfaces. More likely, otherness will arouse fear and disgust.

Finally I would only say again that, at the least, it is democratic not to draw the limits too narrowly, and not to give up too quickly or complacently in epistemological defeat. Whitman is straining to extend the limits of knowing, and it is democratically better to err on the side of presumptuousness than on the side of bafflement. Implied in Whitman's idea of the burden of perception and sympathy that the spirit of democracy means to impose is the will to activate the feeling of contingency: it is a matter of chance that any person has been born and then been raised in one way rather than another. Further, every life is interwoven with chance, with good and bad luck. Things could easily have turned out differently. The proper way of acknowledging contingency is to realize that the same biological being that I am could have been culturally situated in an indefinitely great number of places and acquired a different personality and outward life in each case. And all the time, if I look inward, I can see the beginning of other possibilities I do not act on or act out, and that make me indefinitely more than my socially shaped personality.

Now, Nietzsche, the great theorist of helpless and bounded perspective-seeing and of the pathos of distance, can nevertheless say:

> ... to *want* to see differently, is no small discipline and preparation of the intellect for its future "objectivity" — the latter understood not as "contemplation without interest" (which is a nonsensical absurdity), but as the ability *to control* one's Pro and Con and to dispose of them, so that one knows how to employ a *variety* of perspectives and affective interpretations in the service of knowledge.[16]

Or, as Wallace Stevens — great heir of both Whitman and Nietzsche — says about the aim of poetical perception and feeling: "it is a visibility of thought, / In which hundreds of eyes, in one mind, see at once."[17]

Whitman has his own perspectivism, and it corresponds to a person's inner multiplicity in a double sense. On the one hand, the composite individual has many eyes to see diversity appropriately. On the other hand, he or she, like anything else, needs to be seen by many eyes — not only by the many sets of eyes of many individuals, but also by any one individual's many eyes. But Whitman's final lesson is solitude, not the adventures of human connectedness. He would not be a defender of individuality if he taught otherwise. His work urges each of us back to a solitary relation with something unconceptualizable — perhaps the sheer fact of existence, of one's being and the being of anything else, even and especially when "cheaper, easier, nearer" ("A Song of the Rolling Earth"). What makes this solitude democratic — a democratic transcendence of democratic culture — is the as it were philosophical self-respect (what de Tocqueville saw as natural Cartesianism) that democracy encourages in each person, and that Whitman's work tries so profoundly and so desperately to make convincing. Democratic culture therefore opens the possibility for each to take himself or herself seriously as directly connected to whatever is irreducible, to that around which the mind can never close. In "Song of Myself," he gives a perfectly secular indication, (induced by musical passion): "... to feel the puzzle of puzzles, / And that we call Being. / To be in any form, what is that? (Sects. 26–27) One's culmination is impersonal contemplation of the puzzle. For the sake of this, one must be one and only one. One's end is found alone.

As he puts it matchlessly, though still too religiously, in *Democratic Vistas*:

> ... Alone, and identity, and the mood – and the soul emerges, and all statements, churches, sermons, melt away like vapors. Alone, And silent thought and awe, and aspiration – and then the interior consciousness, like a hitherto unseen inscription, in magic ink, beams out its wonderous lines to the sense ... it is exclusively for then noiseless operation of one's isolated Self, to enter the pure ether of veneration, reach the divine levels, and commune with the unutterable.[18]

NOTES

1 Quoted in F. O. Matthiessen, *American Renaissance: Art and Expression in the Age of Emerson and Whitman* (New York: Oxford University Press, 1941), p. 649.
2 I have used throughout Walt Whitman *Leaves of Grass*, ed. Sculley Bradley and Harold W. Blodgett (New York: Norton Critical Editions, 1973). Section numbers of "Song of Myself" are given in the text
3 Bradley and Blodgett, p. 707.
4 Roy Harvey Pearce's *Introduction* to the Facsimile Edition of the 1860 Text of *Leaves of Grass* (Ithaca: Cornell University Press, 1961), pp. vii–li; and Pearce, *The Continuity of American Poetry* (1961) (Princeton: Princeton University Press paperback, 1977), pp. 69–83. Harold Bloom, *Poetics of Influence*, ed. John Hollander (Schwab: New Haven, 1988), pp. 297–307.
5 Friedrich Nietzsche, *Beyond Good and Evil*, trans. Walter Kaufmann (New York: Vintage, 1966), sect. 19, p. 26.
6 Quoted in Matthiessen, *American Renaissance*, p. 555.
7 D. H. Lawrence, "Whitman" (1921) in Bradley and Blodgett, pp. 842–50, at p. 845.
8 Quoted in Matthiessen, *American Renaissance*, p. 518.
9 Bradley and Blodgett, p. 595.

10   Bradley and Blodgett, p. 585.
11   Bradley and Blodgett, p. 694.
12   Bradley and Blodgett, p. 672.
13   Bradley and Blodgett, p. 597.
14   Bradley and Blodgett, p. 638.
15   R. G. Collingwood, *An Autobiography* (London: Oxford University Press, 1939), p. 115.
16   Friedrich Nietzsche, *On the Genealogy of Morals*, trans. Walter Kaufmann, (New York: Vintage, 1969), Third Essay, Sect. 12, p. 119.
17   Wallace Stevens, "An Ordinary Evening in New Haven," Sect. XXX, in *The Collected Poems* (New York: Vintage, 1982), p. 488.
18   John Kowenhoven (ed.), *Leaves of Grass and Selected Prose* (New York: Modern Library, 1950), p. 491.

12

A Manifesto for Cyborgs: Science, Technology, and Socialist Feminism in the 1980s

DONNA HARAWAY

AN IRONIC DREAM OF COMMON LANGUAGE
FOR WOMEN IN THE INTEGRATED CIRCUIT

This essay is an effort to build an ironic political myth faithful to feminism, socialism, and materialism. Perhaps more faithful as blasphemy is faithful, than as reverent worship and identification. Blasphemy has always seemed to require taking things very seriously. I know no better stance to adopt from within the secular-religious, evangelical traditions of US politics, including the politics of socialist feminism. Blasphemy protects one from the Moral Majority within, while still insisting on the need for community. Blasphemy is not apostasy. Irony is about contradictions that do not resolve into larger wholes, even dialectically, about the tension of holding incompatible things together because both or all are necessary and true. Irony is about humor and serious play. It is also a rhetorical strategy and a political method, one I would like to see more honored within socialist feminism. At the center of my ironic faith, my blasphemy, is the image of the cyborg.

A cyborg is a cybernetic organism, a hybrid of machine and organism, a creature of social reality as well as a creature of fiction. Social reality is lived social relations, our most important political construction, a world-changing fiction. The international women's movements have constructed "women's experience," as well as uncovered or discovered this crucial collective object. This experience is a fiction and fact of the most crucial, political kind. Liberation rests on the construction of the consciousness, the imaginative apprehension, of oppression, and so of possibility. The cyborg is a matter of fiction and lived experience that changes

Reprinted by permission of *Socialist Review* from *Socialist Review* 80 (1985), pp. 65–107.

what counts as women's experience in the late twentieth century. This is a struggle over life and death, but the boundary between science fiction and social reality is an optical illusion.

Contemporary science fiction is full of cyborgs – creatures simultaneously animal and machine, who populate worlds ambiguously natural and crafted. Modern medicine is also full of cyborgs, of couplings between organism and machine, each conceived as coded devices, in an intimacy and with a power that was not generated in the history of sexuality. Cyborg "sex" restores some of the lovely replicative baroque of ferns and invertebrates (such nice organic prophylactics against heterosexism). Cyborg replication is uncoupled from organic reproduction. Modern production seems like a dream of cyborg colonization of work, a dream that makes the nightmare of Taylorism seem idyllic. Modern war is a cyborg orgy, coded by C^3I, command-control-communication-intelligence, an $84 billion item in 1984's US defense budget. I am making an argument for the cyborg as a fiction mapping our social and bodily reality and as an imaginative resource suggesting some very fruitful couplings. Foucault's biopolitics is a flaccid premonition of cyborg politics, a very open field.

By the late twentieth century, our time, a mythic time, we are all chimeras, theorized and fabricated hybrids of machine and organism; in short, we are cyborgs. The cyborg is our ontology; it gives us our politics. The cyborg is a condensed image of both imagination and material reality, the two joined centers structuring any possibility of historical transformation. In the traditions of Western science and politics – the tradition of racist, male-dominant capitalism; the tradition of progress; the tradition of the appropriation of nature as resource for the productions of culture; the tradition of reproduction of the self from the reflections of the other – the relation between organism and machine has been a border war. The stakes in the border war have been the territories of production, reproduction, and imagination. This essay is an argument for pleasure in the confusion of boundaries and for responsibility in their construction. It is also an effort to contribute to socialist-feminist culture and theory in a postmodernist, non-naturalist mode and in the utopian tradition of imagining a world without gender, which is perhaps a world without genesis, but maybe also a world without end. The cyborg incarnation is outside salvation history. Nor does it mark time on an Oedipal calendar, attempting to heal the terrible cleavages of gender in oral symbiotic utopia or post-Oedipal apocalypse. As Zoe Sofoulis argues in her unpublished manuscript on Lacan, Klein and nuclear culture,

Lacklein, the most terrible and perhaps the most promising monsters in cyborg worlds are embodied in non-Oedipal narratives with a different logic of repression, which we need to understand for our survival.

The cyborg is a creature in a postgender world; it has no truck with bisexuality, pre-Oedipal symbiosis, unalienated labor, or other seductions to organic wholeness through a final appropriation of all the powers of the parts into a higher unity. In a sense, the cyborg has no origin story in the Western sense; a "final" irony since the cyborg is also the awful apocalyptic telos of the West's escalating dominations of abstract individuation, an ultimate self untied at last from all dependency, a man in space. An origin story in the Western humanist sense depends on the myth of original unity, fullness, bliss, and terror, represented by the phallic mother from whom all humans must separate, the task of individual development and of history, the twin potent myths inscribed most powerfully for us in psychoanalysis and Marxism. Hilary Klein has argued that both Marxism and psychoanalysis, in their concepts of labor and of individuation and gender formation, depend on the plot of original unity out of which difference must be produced and enlisted in a drama of escalating domination of woman/ nature. The cyborg skips the step of original unity, of identification with nature in the Western sense. This is its illegitimate promise that might lead to subversion of its teleology as Star Wars.

The cyborg is resolutely committed to partiality, irony, intimacy, and perversity. It is oppositional, utopian, and completely without innocence. No longer structured by the polarity of public and private, the cyborg defines a technological *polis* based partly on a revolution of social relations in the *oikos*, the household. Nature and culture are reworked; the one can no longer be the resource for appropriation or incorporation by the other. The relationships for forming wholes from parts, including those of polarity and hierarchical domination, are at issue in the cyborg world. Unlike the hopes of Frankenstein's monster, the cyborg does not expect its father to save it through a restoration of the garden, that is, through the fabrication of a heterosexual mate, through its completion in a finished whole, a city and cosmos. The cyborg does not dream of community on the model of the organic family, this time without the Oedipal project. The cyborg would not recognize the Garden of Eden; it is not made of mud and cannot dream of returning to dust. Perhaps that is why I want to see if cyborgs can subvert the apocalypse of returning to nuclear dust in the manic compulsion to name the Enemy. Cyborgs are not reverent; they do not remember the cosmos. They are wary of holism, but needy for connection — they seem to have a natural feel for united front politics, but without the vanguard party. The main trouble with cyborgs, of course, is that they are the illegitimate offspring of militarism and patriarchal capitalism, not to mention state socialism. But illegitimate offspring are often exceedingly unfaithful to their origins. Their fathers, after all, are inessential.

I will return to the science fiction of cyborgs at the end of the essay, but now I want to signal three crucial boundary breaddowns that make the following political fictional (political scientific) analysis possible. By the late twentieth century in United States, scientific culture, the boundary between human and animal, thoroughly breached. The last beachheads of uniqueness have been polluted, if not turned into amusement parks — language, tool use, social behavior, mental events. Nothing really convincingly settles the separation of human and animal. Many people no longer feel the need of such a separation; indeed, many branches of feminist culture affirm the pleasure of connection with human and other living creatures. Movements for animal rights are not irrational denials of human uniqueness; they are clear-sighted recognition of connection across the discredited breach of nature and culture. Biology and evolutionary theory over the last two centuries have simultaneously produced modern organisms as objects of knowledge and reduced the line between humans and animals to a faint trace re-etched in ideological struggle or professional disputes between life and social sciences. Within this framework, teaching modern Christian creationism should be fought as a form of child abuse.

Biological-determinist ideology is only one position opened up in scientific culture for arguing the meanings of human animality. There is much room for radical political people to contest for the meanings of the breached boundary. The cyborg appears in myth precisely where the boundary between human and animal is transgressed. Far from signaling a walling off of people from other living things, cyborgs signal disturbingly and pleasurably tight coupling. Bestiality has a new status in this cycle of marriage exchange.

The second leaky distinction is between animal-human (organism) and machine. Pre-cybernetic machines could be haunted; there was always the specter of the ghost in the machine. This dualism structured the dialogue between materialism and idealism that was settled by a dialectical progeny called spirit or history, according to taste. But basically machines were not self-moving, self-designing, autonomous. They could not not achieve man's dream, only mock it. They were not man, an author of himself, but only a caricature of that masculinist reproductive dream. To think they were otherwise was paranoid. Now we are not so sure. Late twentieth-century machines have made thoroughly ambiguous the difference between natural and artificial, mind and body, self-developing and externally designed, and many other distinctions that used to apply to organisms and machines. Our machines are disturbingly lively, and we ourselves frighteningly inert.

Technological determinism is only one ideological space opened up by the reconceptions of machine and organism as coded texts through which we engage in the play of writing and reading the world. "Textualization" of everything in post-structuralist, postmodernist theory has been damned by Marxists and socialist feminists for its utopian disregard for lived relations of domination that ground the "play" of arbitrary reading.[1] It is certainly true that postmodernist strategies, like my cyborg myth, subvert myriad organic wholes (e.g., the poem, the primitive culture, the biological organism). In short, the certainty of what counts as nature — a source of insight and a promise of innocence — is undermined, probably fatally. The transcendent authorization of interpretation is lost and with it the ontology grounding Western epistemology. But the alternative is not cynicism or faithlessness, that is, some version of abstract existence, like the accounts of technological determinism destroying "man" by the "machine" or "meaningful political action" by the "text." Who cyborgs will be is a radical question; the answers are a matter of survival. Both chimpanzees and artifacts have politics, so why shouldn't we?[2]

The third distinction is a subset of the second: The boundary between physical and nonphysical is very imprecise for us. Pop physics books on the consequences of quantum theory and the indeterminacy principle are a kind of popular scientific equivalent to the Harlequin romances as a marker of radical change in American white heterosexuality: they get it wrong, but they are on the right subject. Modern machines are quintessentially microelectronic devices: they are everywhere and they are invisible. Modern machinery is an irreverent upstart god, mocking the Father's ubiquity and spirituality. The silicon chip is a surface for writing; it is etched in molecular scales disturbed only by atomic noise, the ultimate interference for nuclear scores. Writing, power, and technology are old partners in Western stories of the origin of civilization, but miniaturization has changed our experience of mechanism. Miniaturization has turned out to be about power;

small is not so much beautiful as pre-eminently dangerous, as in Cruise missiles. Contrast the TV sets of the 1950s or the news cameras of the 1970s with the TV wristbands or hand-sized video cameras now advertised. Our best machines are made of sunshine; they are all light and clean because they are nothing but signals, electromagnetic waves, a section of a spectrum. These machines are eminently protable, mobile — a matter of immense human pain in Detroit and Singapore. People are nowhere near so fluid, being both material and opaque. Cyborgs are ether, quintessence.

The ubiquity and invisibility of cyborgs is precisely why these Sunshine Belt machines are so deadly. They are as hard to see politically as materially. They are about consciousness — or its simulation.[3] They are floating signifiers moving in pickup trucks across Europe, blocked more effectively by the witch-weavings of the displaced and so unnatural Greenham women, who read the cyborg webs of power very well, than by the militant labor of older masculinist politics, whose natural constituency needs defense jobs. Ultimately, the "hardest" science is about the realm of greatest boundary confusion, the realm of pure number, pure spirit, C^3I, cryptography, and the preservation of potent secrets. The new machines are so clean and light. Their engineers are sun worshippers mediating a new scientific revolution associated with the night dream of post-industrial society. The diseases evoked by these clean machines are "no more" than the minuscule coding changes of an antigen in the immune system, "no more" than the experience of stress. The "nimble" fingers of "Oriental" women, the old fascination of little Anglo-Saxon Victorian girls with dollhouses, and women's enforced attention to the small take on quite new dimensions in this world. There might be a cyborg Alice taking account of these new dimensions. Ironically, it might be the unnatural cybrog women making chips in Asia and spiral dancing in Santa Rita jail after an antinuclear action whose constructed unities will guide effective oppositional strategies.

So my cyborg myth is about transgressed boundaries, potent fusions, and dangerous possibilities which progressive people might explore as one part of needed political work. One of my premises is that most American socialists and feminists see deepened dualisms of mind and body, animal and machine, idealism and materialism in the social practices, symbolic formulations, and physical artifacts associated with high technology and scientific culture. From *One-Dimensional Man* to *The Death of Nature*,[4] the analytic resources developed by progressives have insisted on the necessary domination of technics and recalled us to an imagined organic body to integrate our resistance. Another of my premises is that the need for unity of people trying to resist worldwide intensification of domination has never been more acute. But a slightly perverse shift of perspective might better enable us to contest for meanings, as well as for other forms of power and pleasure in technologically mediated societies.

From one perspective, a cyborg world is about the final imposition of a grid of control on the planet, about the final abstraction embodied in a Star Wars apocalypse waged in the name of defense, about the final appropriation of women's bodies in a masculinist orgy of war.[5] From another perspective, a cyborg world might be about lived social and bodily realities in which people are not afraid of their joint kinship with animals and machines, not afraid of permanently partial identities and contradictory standpoints. The political struggle is to see from both perspectives at once because each reveals both dominations and possibilities unimaginable from the other vantage point. Single vision produces worse illusions than double vision or many-headed monsters. Cyborg unities are monstrous and illegitimate; in our present political circumstances, we could hardly hope for more potent myths for resistance and recoupling. I like to imagine the Livermore Action Group, LAG, as a kind of cyborg society, dedicated to realistically converting the laboratories that most fiercely embody and spew out the tools of technological apocalypse, and committed to building a political form that actually manages to hold together witches, engineers, elders, perverts, Christians, mothers, and Leninists long enough to disarm the state. Fission Impossible is the name of the affinity group in my town. (Affinity: related not by blood but by choice, the appeal of one chemical nuclear group for another, avidity.)

FRACTURED IDENTITIES

It has become difficult to name one's feminism by a single adjective — or even to insist in every circumstance upon the noun. Consciousness of exclusion through naming is acute. Identities seen contradictory, partial, and strategic. With the hard-won recognition of their social and historical constitution, gender, race, and class cannot provide the basis for belief in "essential" unity. There is nothing about being "female" that naturally binds women. There is not even such a state as "being" female, itself a highly complex category constructed in contested sexual scientific discourses and other social practices. Gender, race, or class consciousness is an achievement forced on us by the terrible historical experience of the contradictory social realities of patriarchy, colonialism, racism and capitalism. Who counts as "us" in my own rhetoric? Which identities are available to ground such a potent political myth called "us." and what could motivate enlistment in this collectivity? Painful fragmentation among feminists (not to mention among women) along every possible fault line has made the concept of woman elusive, an excuse for the matrix of women's dominations of each other. For me — and for many who share a similar historical location in white, professional, middle-class, female, radical, North American, mid-adult bodies — the sources of a crisis in political identity are legion. The recent history for much of the US Left and the US feminism has been a response to this kind of crisis by endless splitting and searches for a new essential unity. But there has also been a growing recognition of another response through coalition — affinity, not identity.

Chela Sandoval, from a consideration of specific historical moments in the formation of the new political voice called women of color, has theorized a hopeful model of political identity called "oppositional consciousness," born of the skills for reading webs of power by those refused stable membership in the social categories of race, sex, or class.[6] "Women of color," a name contested at its origins by those whom it would incorporate, as well as a historical consciousness marking systematic breakdown of all the signs of Man in Western traditions, constructs a kind of post-modernist identity out of otherness, difference, and specificity. This post-modernist identity is fully political, whatever might be said about other possible post-modernisms. Sandoval's oppositional consciousness is about contradictory locations and heterochronic calendars, not about relativisms and pluralisms.

Sandoval emphasizes the lack of any essential criterion for identifying who is a woman of color. She notes that the definition of the group has been by conscious appropriation of negation. For example, a chicana or a US black woman has not been able to speak as a woman or as a black person or as a chicano. Thus, she was at the bottom of a cascade of negative identities, left out of even the "privileged" oppressed authorial categories called "women and blacks," who claimed to make the important revolutions. The category "woman" negated all nonwhite women; "black" negated all nonblack people, as well as all black women. But there was also no "she," no singularity, but a sea of differences among US women who have affirmed their historical identity as US women of color. This identity marks out a self-consciously constructed space that cannot affirm the capacity to act on the basis of natural identification, but only on the basis of conscious coalition, of affinity, of political kinship. Unlike the "woman" of some streams of the white women's movement in the United States, there is no naturalization of the matrix, or at least this is what Sandoval argues is uniquely available through the power of oppositional consciousness.

Sandoval's argument has to be seen as one potent formulation for feminists out of the worldwide development of anti-colonialist discourse, that is, discourse dissolving the West and its highest product – the one who is not animal, barbarian, or woman: that is, man, the author of a cosmos called history. As Orientalism is deconstructed politically and semiotically, the identities of the Occident destabilize, including those of its feminists. Sandoval argues that "women of color" have a chance to build an effective unity that does not replicate the imperializing, totalizing revolutionary subjects of previous Marxisms and feminisms which had not faced the consequences of the disorderly polyphony emerging from decolonization.

Katie King has emphasized the limits of identification and the political/poetic mechanics of identification built into reading "the poem," that generative core of cultural feminism. King criticizes the persistent tendency among contemporary feminists from different "moments" or "conversations" in feminist practice to taxonomize the women's movement to make one's own political tendencies appear to be the telos of the whole. These taxonomies tend to remake feminist history to appear to be an ideological struggle among coherent types persisting over time, especially those typical units called radical, liberal, and socialist feminism. Literally, all other feminisms are either incorporated or marginalized, usually by building an explicit ontology and epistemology.[7] Taxonomies of feminism produce epistemologies to police deviation from official women's experience. Of course, "women's culture," like women of color, is consciously created by mechanisms inducing affinity. The rituals of poetry, music, and certain forms of academic practice have been pre-eminent. The politics of race and culture in the US women's movements are intimately interwoven. The common achievement of King and Sandoval is learning how to craft a poetic/political unity without relying on a logic of appropriation, incorporation, and taxonomic identification.

The theoretical and practical struggle against unity-through-domination or unity-through-incorporation ironically not only undermines the justifications for patriarchy, colonialism, humanism, positivism, essentialism, scientism, and other unlamented-isms, but all claims for an organic or natural standpoint. I think that radical and socialist/Marxist feminisms have also undermined their/our own epistemological strategies and that this is a crucially valuable step in imagining possible unities. It remains to be seen whether all epistemologies as Western political people have known them fail us in the task to build effective affinities.

It is important to note that the effort to construct revolutionary standpoints, epistemologies as achievements of people committed to changing the world, has been part of the process showing the limits of identification. The acid tools of post-modernist theory and the constructive tools of ontological discourse about revolutionary subjects might be seen as ironic allies in dissolving Western selves in the interests of survival. We are excruciatingly conscious of what it means to have a historically constituted body. But with the loss of innocence in our origin, there is no expulsion from the Garden either. Our politics lose the indulgence of guilt with the *naïveté* of innocence. But what would another political myth for socialist feminism look like? What kind of politics could embrace partial, contradictory, permanently unclosed constructions of personal and collective selves and still be faithful, effective — and, ironically, socialist feminist?

I do not know of any other time in history when there was greater need for political unity to confront effectively the dominations of race, gender, sexuality, and class. I also do not know of any other time when the kind of unity we might help build could have been possible. None of "us" have any longer the symbolic or material capability of dictating the shape of reality to any of "them." Or at least "we" cannot claim innocence from practicing such dominations. White women, including Euroamerican socialist feminists, discovered (i.e., were forced kicking and screaming to notice) the noninnocence of the category "woman." That consciousness changes the configuration of all previous categories; it denatures them as heat denatures a fragile protein. Cyborg feminists have to argue that "we" do not want any more natural matrix of unity and that no construction is whole. Innocence, and the corollary insistence on victimhood as the only ground for insight, has done enough damage. But the constructed revolutionary subject must give late twentieth-century people pause as well. In the fraying of identities and in the reflexive strategies for constructing them, the possibility opens up for weaving something other than a shroud for the day after the apocalypse that so prophetically ends salvation history.

But Marxist/socialist feminisms and radical feminisms have simultaneously naturalized and denatured the category "woman" and consciousness of the social lives of "women." Perhaps a schematic caricature can highlight both kinds of moves. Marxian socialism is rooted in an analysis of wage labor which reveals class structure. The consequence of the wage relationship is systematic alienation, as the worker is dissociated from his [sic] product. Abstraction and illusion rule in knowledge; domination rules in practice. Labor is the pre-eminently privileged category enabling the Marxist to overcome illusion and find that point of view which is necessary for changing the world. Labour is the humanizing activity that makes man; labor is an ontological category permitting the knowledge of a subject, and so the knowledge of subjugation and alienation.

In faithful filiation, socialist feminism advanced by allying itself with the basic analytic strategies of this Marxism. The main achievement of both Marxist feminists and socialist feminists was to expand the category of labor to accommodate what (some) women did, even when the wage relation was subordinated to a more comprehensive view of labor under capitalist patriarchy. In particular, women's labor in the household and women's activity as mothers generally, that is, reproduction in the socialist feminist sense, entered theory on the authority of analogy to the Marxian concept of labor. The unity of women here rests on an epistemology based on the ontological structure of "labor." Marxist/socialist feminism does not "naturalize" unity; it is a possible achievement based on a possible standpoint rooted in social relations. The essentializing move is in the ontological structure of labor or of its analogue, women's activity. The inheritance of Marxian humanism, with its pre-eminently Western self, is the difficulty for me. The contribution from these formulations has been the emphasis on the daily responsibility of real women to *build* unities, rather than to naturalize them.

Catherine MacKinnon's version of radical feminism is itself a caricature of the appropriating, incorporating, totalizing tendencies of Western theories of identity grounding action.[8] It is factually and politically wrong to assimilate all of the diverse "moments" or "conversations" in recent women's politics named radical feminism to MacKinnon's version. But the teleological logic of her theory shows how an epistemology and ontology — including their negations — erase or police difference. Only one of the effects of MacKinnon's theory is the rewriting of the history of the polymorphous field called radical feminism. The major effect is the production of a theory of experience, of women's identity, that is a kind of apocalypse for all revolutionary standpoints. That is, the totalization built into this tale of radical feminism achieves its end – the unity of women – by enforcing the experience of and testimony to radical nonbeing. As for the Marxist/socialist feminist, consciousness is an achievement, not a natural fact. MacKinnon's theory eliminates some of the difficulties built into humanist revolutionary subjects, but at the cost of radical reductionism.

MacKinnon argues that feminism necessarily adopted a different analytical strategy from Marxism, looking first not at the structure of class, but at the structure of sex/gender and its generative relationship, men's constitution and appropriation of women sexually. Ironically, MacKinnon's "ontology" constructs a non-subject, a nonbeing. Another's desire, not the self's labor, is the origin of "woman." She therefore develops a theory of consciousness that enforces what can count as "women's" experience – anything that names sexual violation, indeed, sex itself as far as "women" can be concerned. Feminist practice is the construction of this form of consciousness; that is, the self-knowledge of a self-who-is-not.

Perversely, sexual appropriation in this feminism still has the epistemological status of labor, that is, the point from which analysis able to contribute to changing the world must flow. But sexual objectification, not alienation, is the consequence of the structure of sex/gender. In the realm of knowledge, the result of sexual objectification is illusion and abstraction. However, a woman is not simply alienated from her product, but in a deep sense she does not exist as a subject, or even potential subject, since she owes her existence as a woman to sexual appropriation. To be constitued by another's desire is not the same thing as to be alienated in the violent separation of the laborer from his product.

MacKinnon's radical theory of experience is totalizing in the extreme; it does not so much marginalize as obliterate the authority of any other women's political speech and action. It is a totalization producing what Western patriarchy itself never succeeded in doing – feminists' consciousness of the nonexistence of women, except as products of men's desire. I think MacKinnon correctly argues that no Marxian version of identity can firmly ground women's unity. But in solving the problem of the contradictions of any Western revolutionary subject for feminist purposes, she develops an even more authoritarian doctrine of experience. If my complaint about socialist/Marxian standpoints is their unintended erasure of polyvocal, unassimilable, radical difference made visible in anticolonial discourse and practice, MacKinnon's intentional erasure of all difference through the device of the "essential" nonexistence of women is not reassuring.

In my taxonomy, which like any other taxonomy is a reinscription of history, radical feminism can accommodate all the activities of women named by socialist feminists as forms of labor only if the activity can somehow be sexualized. Reproduction had different tones of meanings for the two tendencies, one rooted in labor, one in sex, both calling the consequences of domination and ignorance of social and personal reality "false consciousness."

Beyond either the difficulties or the contributions in the argument of any one author, neither Marxist nor radical-feminist points of view have tended to embrace the status of a partial explanation; both were regularly constituted as totalities. Western explanation has demanded as much; how else could the Western author incorporate its others? Each tried to annex other forms of domination by expanding its basic categories through analogy, simple listing, or addition. Embarrassed silence about race among white radical and socialist feminists was one major, devastating political consequence. History and polyvocality disappear into political taxonomies that try to establish genealogies. There was no structural room for race (or for much else) in theory claiming to reveal the construction of the category "woman" and social group "women" as a unified or totalizable whole. The structure of my caricature looks like this:

Socialist Feminism –
    structure of class//wage labor//alienation
    labor, by analogy reproduction, by extension sex, by
        addition race
Radical Feminism –
    structure of gender//sexual appropriation//objectification
    sex, by analogy labor, by extension reproduction, by
        addition race

In another context, the French theorist Julia Kristeva claimed women appeared as a historical group after World War II, along with groups like youth. Her dates are doubtful, but we are now accustomed to remembering that as objects of knowledge and as historical actors, "race" did not always exist, "class" has a historical genesis, and "homosexuals" are quite junior. It is no accident that the symbolic system of the family of man – and so the essence of woman – breaks up at the same moment that networks of connection among people on the planet are unprecedentedly multiple, pregnant, and complex. "Advanced capitalism" is inadequate to convey the structure of this historical moment. In the Western sense, the end of man is at stake. It is no accident that woman disintegrates into women in our time. Perhaps socialist feminists were not substantially guilty of producing essentialist theory that suppressed women's particularity and contradictory interests. I think we have been, at least through unreflective participation in the logics, languages, and practices of white humanism and through searching for a single ground of domination to secure our revolutionary voice. Now we have less excuse. But in the consciousness of our failures, we risk lapsing into boundless difference and giving up on the confusing task of making partial, real connection. Some differences are playful: some are poles of world historical systems of domination. Epistemology is about knowing the difference.

THE INFORMATICS OF DOMINATION

In this attempt at an epistemological and political position. I would like to sketch a picture of possible unity, a picture indebted to socialist and feminsit principles of design. The frame for my sketch is set by the extent and importance of rearrangements in worldwide social relations tied to science and technology. I argue for a politics rooted in claims about fundamental changes in the nature of class, race, and gender in an emerging system of world order analogous in its novelty and scope to that created by industrial capitalism; we are living through a movement from an organic, industrial society to a polymorphous, information system – from all work to all play, a deadly game. Simultaneously material and ideological, the dichotomies may be expressed in the following chart of transitions from the comfortable old hierarchical dominations to the scary new networks I have called the informatics of domination:

Representation	Simulation
Bourgeois novel, realism	Science fiction, postmodernism
Organism	Biotic component
Depth, integrity	Surface, boundary
Heat	Noise
Biology as clinical practice	Biology as inscription
Physiology	Communications engineering

Small group	Subsystem
Perfection	Optimization
Eugenics	Population Control
Decadence, *Magic Mountain*	Obsolescence, *Future Shock*
Hygiene	Stress management
Microbiology, tuberculosis	Immunology, AIDS
Organic division of labor	Ergonomics/cybernetics of labor
Functional specialization	Modular construction
Reproduction	Replication
Organic sex role specialization	Optimal genetic strategies
Biological determinism	Evolutionary inertia, constraints
Community ecology	Ecosystem
Racial chain of being	Neo-imperialism. United Nations humanism
Scientific management in home/factory	Global factory/electronic cottage
Family/market/factory	Women in the integrated circuit
Family wage	Comparable worth
Public/private	Cyborg citizenship
Nature/culture	Fields of difference
Cooperation	Communications enhancement
Freud	Lacan
Sex	Genetic engineering
Labor	Robotics
Mind	Artificial intelligence
World War II	Star Wars
White capitalist patriarchy	Informatics of domination

This list suggests several interesting things. First, the objects on the right-hand side cannot be coded as "natural," a realization that subverts naturalistic coding for the left-hand side as well. We cannot go back ideologically or materially. It's not just that "god" is dead; so is the "goddess." Or both are revivified in the worlds charged with microelectronic and biotechnological politics. In relation to objects like biotic components, one must think not in terms of essential properties, but in terms of design, boundary constraints, rates of flows, systems logics, costs of lowering constraints. Sexual reproduction is one kind of reproductive strategy among many, with costs and benefits as a function of the system environment. Ideologies of sexual reproduction can no longer reasonably call on notions of sex and sex role as organic aspects in natural objects like organisms and families. Such reasoning will be unmasked as irrational, and ironically corporate executives reading *Playboy* and anti-porn radical feminists will make strange bedfellows in jointly unmasking the irrationalism.

Likewise for race, racist and anti-racist ideologies about human diversity have to be formulated in terms of frequencies of parameters. It is "irrational" to invoke concepts like primitive and civilized. For liberals and radicals, the search for integrated social systems gives way to a new practice called "experimental ethnography" in which an organic object dissipates in attention to the play of writing. At the level of ideology, we see translations of racism and colonialism into languages of development and underdevelopment, rates and constraints of modernization. Any objects or persons can be "resonably" thought of in terms of disassembly and reassembly; no "natural" architectures constrain system design. The financial districts in all the world's cities, as well as the export-processing and free-trade-zones, proclaim this elementary fact of "late capitalism." The entire universe of objects that can be known scientifically must be formulated as problems in communications engineering (for the managers) or theories of the text (for those who would resist). Both are cyborg semiologies.

One should expect control strategies to concentrate on boundary conditions and interfaces, on rates of flow across boundaries — and not on the integrity of natural objects. "Integrity" or "sincerity" of the Western self gives way to decision procedures and expert systems. For example, control strategies applied to women's capacities to give birth to new human beings will be developed in the languages of population control and maximization of goal achievement for individual decisionmakers. Control strategies will be formulated in terms of rates, costs of constraints, degrees of freedom. Human beings, like any other component or subsystem, must be localized in a system architecture whose basic modes of operation are probabilistic, statistical. No objects, spaces, or bodies are sacred in themselves; any component can be interfaced with any other if the proper standard, the proper code, can be constructed for processing signals in a common language. Exchange in this world transcends the universal translation effected by capitalist markets that Marx analyzed so well. The privileged pathology affecting all kinds of components in this universe is stress — communications breakdown. The cyborg is not subject to Foucault's biopolitics; the cyborg simulates politics, a much more potent field of operations. Discursive constructions are no joke.

This kind of analysis of scientific and cultural objects of knowledge which have appeared historically since World War II prepares us to notice some important inadequacies in feminist analysis which has proceeded as if the organic, hierarchical dualism ordering discourse in the West since Aristotle still ruled. They have been cannibalized, or as Zoe Sofia (Sofoulis) might put it, they have been "techno-digested." The dichotomies between mind and body, animal and human, organism and machine, public and private, nature and culture, men and women, primitive and civilized are all in question ideologically. The actual situation of women is their integration/exploitation into a world system of production/ reproduction and communication called the informatics of domination. The home, work place, market, public arena, the body itself – all can be dispersed and interfaced in nearly infinite, polymorphous ways, with large consequences for women and others – consequences that themselves are very different for different people and which make potent oppositional international movements difficult to imagine and essential for survival. One important route for reconstructing socialist-feminist politics is through theory and practice addressed to the social relations of science and technology, including crucially the systems of myth and meanings structuring our imaginations. The cyborg is a kind of disassembled and reassembled, postmodern collective and personal self. This is the self feminists must code.

Communications technologies and biotechnologies are the crucial tools recrafting our bodies. These tools embody and enforce new social relations for women worldwide. Technologies and scientific discourses can be partially understood as formalizations, that is, as frozen moments, of the fluid social interactions constituting them, but they should also be viewed as instruments for enforcing meanings. The boundary is permeable between tool and myth, instrument and concept, historical systems of social relations and historical anatomies of possible bodies, including objects of knowledge. Indeed, myth and tool mutually constitute each other.

Furthermore, communications sciences and modern biologies are constructed by a common move – the translation of the world into a problem of coding, a search for a common language in which all resistance to instrumental control disappears and all heterogeneity can be submitted to disassembly, reassembly, investment, and exchange.

In communications sciences, the translation of the world into a problem in coding can be illustrated by looking at cybernetic (feedback controlled) systems theories applied to telephone technology, computer design, weapons deployment, or data-base construction and maintenance. In each case, solution to the key questions rests on a theory of language and control; the key operation is determining the rates, directions, and probabilities of flow of a quantity called information. The world is subdivided by boundaries differentially permeable to information. Information is just that kind of quantifiable element (unit, basis of unity) which allows universal translation and so unhindered instrumental power (called effective communication). The biggest threat to such power is interruption of communication. Any system breakdown is a function of stress. The fundamentals of this technology can be condensed into the metaphor C^3I, command-control-communication-intelligence, the military's symbol for its operations theory.

In modern biologies, the translation of the world into a problem in coding can be illustrated by molecular genetics, ecology, sociobiological evolutionary theory, and immunobiology. The organism has been translated into problems of genetic coding and read-out. Biotechnology, a writing technology, informs research broadly.[9] In a sense, organisms have ceased to exist as objects of knowledge, giving way to biotic components, that is, special kinds of information-processing devices. The analogous moves in ecology could be examined by probing the history and utility of the concept of the ecosystem. Immunobiology and associated medical practices are rich exemplars of the privilege of coding and recognition systems as objects of knowledge, as constructions of bodily reality for us. Biology here is a king of cryptography. Research is necessarily a kind of intelligence activity. Ironies abound. A stressed system goes awry; its communication processes break down; it fails to recognize the difference between self and other. Human babies with baboon hearts evoke national ethical perplexity — for animalrights activists at least as much as for the guardians of human purity. In the United States gay men and intravenous drug users are the most "privileged" victims of an awful immune-system disease that marks (inscribes on the body) confusion of boundaries and moral pollution.

But these excursions into communications sciences and biology have been at a rarefied level; there is a mundane, largely economic reality to support my claim that these sciences and technologies indicate fundamental transformations in the structure of the world for us. Communications technologies depend on electronics. Modern states, multinational corporations, military power, welfare-state apparatuses, satellite systems, political processes, fabrication of our imaginations, labor-control systems, medical constructions of our bodies, commercial pornography, the international division of labor, and religious evangelism depend intimately upon electronics. Microelectronics is the technical basis of simulacra, that is, of copies without originals.

Microelectronics mediates the translations of labor into robotics and word processing, sex into genetic engineering and reproductive technologies, and mind into artificial intelligence and decision procedures. The new biotechnologies concern more than human reproduction. Biology as a powerful engineering science for re-designing materials and processes has revolutionary implications for industry, perhaps most obvious today in areas of fermentation, agriculture, and energy. Communications sciences and biology are constructions of natural-technical objects of knowledge in which the difference between machine and organism is thoroughly blurred; mind, body, and tool are on very intimate terms. The "multinational" material organization of the production and re-production of daily life and the symbolic organization of the production and reproduction of culture and imagination seem equally implicated. The boundary-maintaining images of base and superstructure, public and private, or material and ideal never seemed more feeble.

I have used Rachel Grossman's image of women in the integrated circuit to name the situation of women in a world so intimately restructured through the social relations of science and technology.[10] I use the odd circumlocution, "the social relations of science and technology," to indicate that we are not dealing with a tech-nological determinism, but with a historical system depending upon structured relations among people. But the phrased should also indicate that science and technology provide fresh sources of power, that we need fresh sources of analysis and political action.[11] Some of the rearrangements of race, sex, and class rooted in high-tech-facilitated social relations can make socialist feminism more relevant to effective progressive politics...

WOMEN IN THE INTEGRATED CIRCUIT

Let me summarize the picture of women's historical locations in advanced industrial societies, as these positions have been re-structured partly through the social relations of science and tech-nology. If it was ever possible ideologically to characterize women's lives by the distinction of public and private domains — suggested by images of the division of working-class life into factory and home, of bourgeois life into market and home, and of gender existence into personal and political realms — it is now a totally misleading ideology, even to show how both terms of these dichotomies construct each other in practice and in theory. I prefer a network ideological image, suggesting the profusion of spaces and identities and the permeability of boundaries in the personal body and in the body politic. "Networking" is both a feminist practice and a multinational corporate strategy weaving is for oppositional cyborgs...

CYBORGS A MYTH OF POLITICAL IDENTITY

I want to conclude with a myth about identity and boundaries which might inform late twentieth-century political imaginations...

[After considering transformations wrought by the work and writings of women of color, Haraway continues:]

Certain dualisms have been persistent in Western traditions; they have all been systemic to the logics and practices of domination of women, people of color, nature, workers, animals − in short, domination of all constituted as others, whose task is to mirror the self. Chief among these troubling dualisms are self/other, mind/body, culture/nature, male/female, civilized/primitive, reality/ appearance, whole/part, agent/resource, maker/made, active/ passive, right/wrong, truth/illusion, total/partial, God/man. The self is the One who is not dominated, who knows that by the service of the other; the other is the one who holds the future, who knows that by the experience of domination, which gives the lie to the autonomy of the self. To be One is to be autonomous, to be powerful, to be God; but to be One is to be an illusion and so to be involved in a dialectic of apocalypse with the other. Yet, to be other is to be multiple, without clear boundaries, frayed, insubstantial. One is too few, but two are too many.

High-tech culture challenges these dualisms in intriguing ways. It is not clear who makes and who is made in the relation between human and machine. It is not clear what is mind and what is body in machines that resolve into coding practices. Insofar as we know ourselves in both formal discourse (e.g., biology) and in daily practice, (e.g., the homework economy in the integrated circuit), we find ourselves to be cyborgs, hybrids, mosaics, chimeras. Biological organisms have become biotic systems, communications devices like others. There is no fundamental, ontological separation in our formal knowledge of machine and organism, of technical and organic. The replicant Rachel in the film *Blade Runner* stands as the image of a cyborg culture's fear, love, and confusion.

One consequence is that our sense of connection to our tools is heightened. The trance state experienced by many computer users has become a staple of science-fiction film and cultural jokes. Perhaps paraplegics and other severely handicapped people can (and sometimes do) have the most intense experiences of complex hybridization with other communication devices. Anne McCaffrey's prefeminist *The Ship Who Sang* explored the consciousness of a cyborg, hybrid of girl's brain and complex machinery, formed after the birth of a severely handicapped child. Gender, sexuality, embodiment, skill all were reconstituted in the story. Why should our bodies end at the skin or include at best other beings encapsulated by skin? From the seventeenth century till now, machines could be animated — given ghostly souls to make them speak or move or to account for their orderly development and mental capacities. Or organisms could be mechanized — reduced to body understood as resource of mind. These machine/organism relationships are obsolete, unnecessary. For us, in imagination and in other practice, machines can be prosthetic devices, intimate components, friendly selves. We don't need organic holism to give impermeable wholeness, the total woman and her feminist variants (mutants?). Let me conclude this point by a very partial reading of the logic of the cyborg monsters of my second group of texts, feminist science fiction.

The cyborgs populating feminist science fiction make very problematic the statuses of man or woman, human, artifact, member of a race, individual identity, or body. Katie King clarifies how pleasure in reading these fictions is not largely based on identification. Students facing Joanna Russ for the first time, students who have learned to take modernist writers like James Joyce or Virginia Woolf without flinching, do not know what to make of *The Adventures of Alyx* or *The Female Man*, where characters refuse the reader's search for innocent wholeness while granting the wish for heroic quests, exuberant eroticism, and serious politics. *The Female Man* is the story of four versions of one genotype, all of whom meet, but even taken together do not make a whole, resolve the dilemmas of violent moral action, nor remove the growing scandal of gender. The feminist science fiction of Samuel Delany, especially *Tales of Neveryon*, mocks stories of origin by redoing the neolithic revolution, replaying the founding moves of Western civilization to subvert their plausibility. James Tiptree, Jr., an author whose fiction was regarded as particularly manly until her "true" gender was revealed, tells tales of reproduction based on nonmammalian technologies like alternation of generations or male brood pouches and male nurturing. John Varley constructs a supreme cyborg in his arch-feminist exploration of Gaea, a mad goddess-planet-trickster-old-woman-technological device on whose surface an extraordinary array of post cyborg symbioses are spawned. Octavia Butler writes of an African sorceress pitting her powers of transformation against the genetic manipulations of her rival (*Wild Seed*), of time warps that bring a modern US black woman into slavery where her actions in relation to her white master-ancestor determine the possibility of her own birth (*Kindred*), and of the illegitimate insights into identity and community of an adopted cross-species child who came to know the enemy as self (*Survivor*). In her recent novel, *Dawn* (1987), the first installment of a series called (*Xenogenesis*), Butler tells the story of Lilith Iyapo, whose personal name recalls Adam's first and repudiated wife and whose family name marks her status as the widow of the son of Nigerian immigrants to the United States. A black woman and a mother whose child is dead, Lilith mediates the transformation of humanity through genetic exchange with extraterrestrial lovers/rescuers/estroyers/genetic engineers, who reform earth's habitats after the nuclear holocaust and coerce surviving humans into intimate fusion with them. It is a novel that interrogates reproductive, linguistic, and nuclear politics in a mythic field structured by late twentieth-century race and gender.

Because it is particularly rich in boundary transgressions, Vonda McIntyre's *Superluminal* can close this truncated catalogue of promising and dangerous monsters who help redefine the pleasures and politics of embodiment and feminist writing. In a fiction where no character is "simply" human, human status is highly problematic. Orca, a genetically altered diver, can speak with killer whales and survive deep ocean conditions, but she longs to explore space as a pilot, necessitating bionic implants jeopardizing her kinship with the divers and cetaceans. Transformations are effected by virus vectors carrying a new developmental code, by transplant surgery, by implants of microelectronic devices, by analogue doubles, and by other means. Laenea becomes a pilot by accepting a heart implant and a host of other alterations allowing survival in transit at speeds exceeding that of light. Radu Dracul sruvives a virus-caused plague on his outerworld planet to find himself with a time sense that changes the boundaries of spatial perception for the whole species. All the characters explore the limits of language, the dream of communicating experience, and the necessity of limitation, partiality, and intimacy even in this world of protean transformation and connection. *Superluminal* stands also for the defining contradictions of a cyborg world in another sense; it embodies textually the intersection of feminist theory and colonial discourse in the science fiction I have alluded to in this essay. This is a conjunction with a long history that many first world feminists have tried to repress, including myself in may readings of *Superluminal* before being called to account by Zoe Soufoulis, whose different location in the world system's informatics of domination made her acutely alert to the imperialist moment of all science-fiction cultures, including women's science fiction. From an Australian feminist sensitivity. Sofoulis remembered more readily McIntyre's role as writer of the adventures of Captain Kirk and Spock in "Star Trek" than her rewriting the romance in *Superluminal*.

Monsters have always defined the limits of community in Western imaginations. The centaurs and Amazons of ancient Greece established the limits of the centered polis of the Greek male human by their disruption of marriage and boundary pollutions of the warrior with animality and woman. Unseparated twins and hermaphrodites were the confused human material in early modern France who grounded discourse on the natural and supernatural, medical and legal, portents and diseases – all crucial to establishing modern identity.[12] The evolutionary and behavioral sciences of monkeys and apes have marked the multiple boundaries of late twentieth-century industrial identities. Cyborg monsters in feminist science fiction define quite different political possibilities and limits from those proposed by the mundane fiction of Man and Woman.

There are several consequences to taking seriously the imagery of cyborgs as other than our enemies. Our bodies, ourselves – bodies are maps of power and identity. Cyborgs are no exceptions. A cyborg body is not innocent; it was not born in a garden; it does not seek unitary identity and so generates antagonistic dualisms without end (or until the world ends); it takes irony for granted. One is too few, and two is only one possibility. Intense pleasure in skill, machine skill, ceases to be a sin, but an aspect of embodiment. The machine is not an it to be animated, worshipped, and dominated. The machine is us, our processes, an aspect of our embodiment. We can be responsible for machines; they do not dominate or threaten us. We are responsible for boundaries; we are they. Up till now (once upon a time), female embodiment seemed to be given, organic, necessary; female embodiment seemed to mean skill in mothering and its metaphoric extensions. Only by being out of place could we take intense pleasure in machines and then with excuses that this was organic activity after all, appropriate to females. Cyborgs might consider more seriously the partial, fluid, sometimes aspect of sex and sexual embodiment. Gender might not be global identity after all, even if it has profound historical breadth and depth.

The ideologically charged question of what counts as daily activity, as experience, can be approached by exploiting the cyborg image. Feminists have recently claimed that women are given to dailiness, that women more than men somehow sustain daily life, and so have a privileged epistemological position potentially. There is a compelling aspect to this claim, one that makes visible unvalued female activity and names it as the ground of life. But the ground of life? What about all the ignorance of women, all the exclusions and failures of knowledge and skill? What about men's access to daily competence, to knowing how to build things, to take them apart, to play? What about other embodiments? Cyborg gender is a local possibility taking a global vengeance. Race, gender, and capital require a cyborg theory of wholes and parts. There is no drive in cyborgs to produce total theory, but there is an intimate experience of boundaries, their construction and deconstruction. There is a myth system waiting to become a political language to ground one way of looking at science and technology and challenging the informatics of domination − in order to act potently.

One last image: organisms and organismic, holistic politics depend on metaphors of rebirth and invariably call on the resources of reproductive sex. I would suggest that cyborgs have more to do with regeneration and are suspicious of the reproductive matrix and of most birthing. For salamanders, regeneration after injury, such as the loss of a limb, involves regrowth of structure and restoration of function with the constant possiility of twinning or other odd topographical productions at the site of former injury. The regrown limb can be monstrous, duplicated, potent. We have all been injured, profoundly. We require regeneration, not rebirth, and the possibilities for our reconstitution include the utopian dream of the hope for a monstrous world without gender.

Cyborg imagery can help express two crucial arguments in this essay: (1) the production of universal, totalizing theory is a major mistake that misses most of reality, probably always, but certainly now; (2) taking responsibility for the social relations of science and technology means refusing an anti-science metaphysics, a demonology of technology, and so means embracing the skillful task of reconstructing the boundaries of daily life, in partial connection with others, in communication with all of our parts. It is not just that science and technology are possible means of great human satisfaction, as well as a matrix of complex dominations. Cyborg imagery can suggest a way out of the maze of dualisms in which we have explained our bodies and our tools to ourselves. This is a dream not of a common language, but of a powerful infidel heteroglossia. It is an imagination of a feminist speaking in tongues to strike fear into the circuits of the super savers of the New Right. It means both building and destroying machines, identities, categories, relationships, spaces, stories. Although both are bound in the spiral dance, I would rather be a cyborg than a goddess.

NOTES

1 Fredric Jameson, "Post Modernism, or the Cultural Logic of Late Capitalism," *New Left Review*, July/August 1984, pp. 53–94. See Marjorie Perloff, "'Dirty' Language and Scramble Systems," *Sulfur* vol. 2, 1984, pp. 178–83; Kathleen Fraser, *Something (Even Human Voices) in the Foreground, a Lake* (Berkeley, CA: Kelsey St. Press, 1984). For feminist modernist/postmodernist cyborg writing, see *How(ever)*, 871 Corbett Ave., San Francisco, CA 94131.
2 Frans de Waal, *Chimpanzee Politics: Power and Sex among the Apes* (New York: Harper & Row, 1982); Langdon Winner, "Do artifacts have politics?" *Daedalus* (Winter 1980): 121–36.
3 Jean Baudrillard, *Simulations*, trans. P. Foss, P. Patton, P. Beitchman (New York: Semiotext(e), 1983). Jameson ("Postmodernism," p. 66) points out that Plato's definition of the simulacrum is the copy for which there is no original, i.e., the world of advanced capitalism, of pure exchange. See *Discourse 9*, Spring/Summer 1987, for a special issue on technology (Cybernetics, Ecology, and the Postmodern Imagination).
4 Herbert Marcuse, *One-Dimensional Man* (Boston: Beacon Press, 1964); Carolyn Merchant, *Death of Nature* (San Francisco: Harper & Row, 1980).
5 Zoe Sofia, "Exterminating Fetuses." *Diacritics*, vol. 14, no. 2, Summer 1984, pp. 47–59, and "Jupiter Space" (Pomona, CA: American Studies Association, 1984).
6 Chela Sandoval, "Dis-Illusionment and the Poetry of the Future: The Making of Oppositional Consciousness," Ph.D. qualifying essay, University of California, Santa Cruz, 1984.
7 Katie King has developed a theoretically sensitive treatment of the workings of feminist taxonomies as genealogies of power in feminist ideology and polemic: Katie King, "Canons without Innocence," Ph.D. thesis, University of California, Santa Cruz, 1987, and "The

Situation of Lesbianism as Feminism's Magical Sign: Contests for Meaning in the US Women's Movement, 1968—72," *Communication* vol. 9, no. 1, 1985, pp. 65—91. King examines an intelligent, problematic example of taxonomizing feminisms to make a little machine producing the desired final position; Alison Jaggar, *Feminist Politics and Human Nature* (Totowa, NJ: Rowman & Allanheld, 1983). My caricature here of socialist and radical feminism is also an example.

8   Catherine MacKinnon, "Feminism, Marxism, Method, and the State: An Agenda for Theory," *Signs*, vol. 7, no. 3, Spring 1982, pp. 515—44. See also MacKinnon, *Feminism Unmodified* (Cambridge, MA: Harvard University Press, 1987).

9   A left entry to the biotechnology debate: *Genewatch*, a Bulletin of the Committee for Responsible Genetics, 5 Doane St, 4th floor, Boston, MA 02109; Susan Wright, "Recombinant DNA Technology and Its Social Transformation, 1972—82," *Osiris*, 2nd series, vol. 2, 1986, pp. 303—60 and "Recombinant DNA: The Status of Hazards and Controls," *Environment*, July/August 1982; Edward Yoxen, *The Gene Business* (New York: Harper & Row, 1983).

10 Rachael Grossman, "Women's Place in the Integrated Circuit," *Radical America*, vol. 14, no. I, 1980, pp. 29—50;

11 The best example is Bruno Latour, *Les Microbes: Guerre et Paix. suivi de lrréductions* (Paris: Métailié, 1984).

12 Page DuBois, *Centaurs and Amazons* (Ann Arbor, MI: University of Michigan Press, 1982); Lorraine Daston and Katharine Park, "Hermaphrodites in Renaissance France," ms., n.d.; Katharine Park and Lorraine Daston, "Unnatural Conceptions: The Study of Monsters in 16th and 17th Century France and England," *Past and Present*, no. 92, August 1981, pp. 20—54. The word *monster* shares its root with the verb *to demonstrate*.

Index